ULTIMATE
HARLEY-DAVIDSON

ULTIMATE
HARLEY-DAVIDSON

HUGO WILSON

DK

LONDON, NEW YORK, MUNICH,
MELBOURNE, DELHI

THIS EDITION

PROJECT EDITOR Alison Sturgeon
PROJECT ART EDITOR Tannishtha Chakraborty
MANAGING EDITOR Laura Buller
MANAGING ART EDITOR Karen Self
ART DIRECTOR Phil Ormerod
ASSOCIATE PUBLISHER Liz Wheeler
REFERENCE PUBLISHER Jonathan Metcalf
PRE-PRODUCTION CONTROLLER Ben Marcus
JACKET DESIGNER Mark Cavanagh
JACKET EDITOR Manisha Majithia

PREVIOUS EDITIONS

SENIOR EDITORS Peter Jones, Neil Lockley
SENIOR ART EDITOR Heather McCarry
MANAGING EDITORS Anna Kruger, Adele Hayward
MANAGING ART EDITORS Karen Self,
Steve Knowlden
DEPUTY ART DIRECTOR Tina Vaughan
DTP DESIGNERS Rob Campbell, Rajen Shah
PICTURE RESEARCHER Jamie Robinson
CATEGORY PUBLISHER Stephanie Jackson
PRODUCTION CONTROLLERS Louise Daly,
Sarah Sherlock
PHOTOGRAPHY BY Dave King

PREVIOUS EDITIONS PACKAGED FOR
DORLING KINDERSLEY BY

ART EDITORS Mark Johnson Davies, Tracy Miles
EDITOR Phil Hunt

First Published in Great Britain in 2000
This Revised Edition Published in 2013
by Dorling Kindersley Limited,
80 Strand, London WC2R 0RL

Copyright © 2000, 2013 Dorling Kindersley Limited
A Penguin Company
Text Copyright © 2000, 2013 Hugo Wilson

2 4 6 8 10 9 7 5 3 1
001–192759 – 01/13

A CIP Catalogue Record for this Book is Available
from the British Library

ISBN 978-1-4093-287-42

Harley-Davidson is a Trademark Owned by H-D USA,
LLC. The Harley-Davidson Name and Model Names
Featured in this Book are used for Descriptive Purposes
Only and Remain the Property of H-D USA, LLC.

Reproduced by Colourscan, Singapore
Printed in China by South China

See our complete catalogue at
www.dk.com

PAGE 2:
1915 BOARD-TRACK RACERS
PAGE 3:
1999 TWIN CAM ENGINE

CONTENTS

JOE WALTER ON A 1915 KT BOARD RACER

MODEL S RACER

THE PANHEAD ENGINE

VRSCA V-ROD

Foreword

Harley-Davidson for many people is synonymous with the motorcycle. This honour is not without merit. Harley has done a great deal for the motorcycle industry as well as motorcycle racing and every Harley-Davidson has a story. Whether it was ridden to Sturgis, raced at Daytona, or used for milk delivery, these motorcycles served their purpose well and with a flare that is Harley-Davidson. The roar of a Harley is pure motorcycle.

The Harleys of the Barber Vintage Motorsports Museum range from board-track racers to a Captain America replica. There are military Harleys, Italian Harleys, touring Harleys, a Harley-powered midget racer, a Knucklehead, and even Roger Reiman's KR that raced on the beach at Daytona and then went on to win the inaugural 200 at the speedway.

Within our research library at the museum of over 2,500 books we have more than 190 just devoted to Harley-Davidson. This one will be a welcome addition and shining star. We are proud to have been a part of it.

George Barber J.

GEORGE W. BARBER

THE BARBER VINTAGE MOTORSPORTS MUSEUM,
BIRMINGHAM, ALABAMA.
www.BarberMuseum.org

Author's Preface

People remember their first Harley-Davidson. The first time they see one, the first time they hear one, the first time they ride one. They get to you like that. Harleys look different, sound different, and certainly ride different to other motorcycles. Their extraordinary appeal makes small boys dream and grown men save. Harley-Davidson has been making motorcycles for over 100 years. The company that started as four young men hand-building simple machines in a wooden shed is now one of the world's most famous brands. You will find some of their most memorable bikes on the pages that follow.

Hugo Wilson

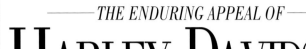

THE ENDURING APPEAL OF

HARLEY-DAVIDSON

1903–2013

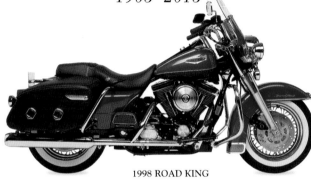

1998 ROAD KING

THE STORY OF Harley-Davidson is enthralling.
It began in an era from which only the
most determined and far-sighted have
survived and in many ways the story reflects
the culture in which the company has
flourished – unparalleled growth punctuated
by periods of decline, but always operating
with a strong spirit of survival.

AN AMERICAN DREAM
*Harley's interpretation of the American Dream
is one of the most coveted symbols of freedom and
independence for bikers around the world.*

THE ENDURING APPEAL OF

HARLEY-DAVIDSON

HARLEY-DAVIDSON HAS BEEN AROUND almost as long as the motorcycle, and longer than the motorcycle has been a half sensible form of transport. In 1903 Harley-Davidson was just four friends in their twenties, all motorcycle fanatics at a time when the only people who owned motorcycles were the seriously rich or those who actually made them. They could not have foreseen the legacy they would leave.

1903 TO 1919

At the turn of the century, America was a place for adventure and challenge. William S. Harley and brothers Arthur, William, and Walter Davidson embarked on their own adventure of becoming motorcycle manufacturers. While some pioneer manufacturers bolted an existing engine into a bicycle frame, the four young men from Milwaukee did it the difficult way. In 1903 they constructed an engine from scratch and redesigned the frame to make it stronger and more suitable for its new role. The first bikes were put together in a 3m x 4.5m (10ft x 15ft) shed on the premises of the Davidsons' family home, though a new "factory" was built in 1906 that measured 8.5m x 24.5m (28ft x 80ft). William Harley interrupted his work at Harley-Davidson to study automotive engineering at the University of Wisconsin where, rumour has it, he developed the sprung fork as a college project. He raised financial support for his studies by waiting at tables and for all four of them the motorcycle project was only a part-time interest until they moved to the larger premises in 1906.

Conditions were rough on the roads of the USA in the early 20th century, and the distances between towns were considerable. If a motorcycle was to be a viable machine rather than an amusement, it had to be reliable, tough, practical, and powerful. The fledgling Harley-Davidson company understood this from the start and even its earliest machines were more robust than most other bikes on the market. While its competitors came and went, Harley continued to develop its machines and enhance its reputation. Production numbers leapt from three machines in 1903 to 50 in 1906, just over 1,100 in 1909, and double that the following year. By 1919 the company was producing over 23,000 bikes a year and was the second biggest manufacturer in the USA behind the mighty Indian operation. Impressive figures considering that the Harley-Davidson Motor Company was only established in 1907.

Threat from the car
The biggest competition to Harley-Davidson, and to the other American motorcycle manufacturers, came from Henry Ford and his Model T car. Following its introduction in 1908, the car gradually became cheaper as mass production developed and it soon became less expensive than all but the most rudimentary of motorcycles. Those who were prepared

THE FIRST HARLEY-DAVIDSON FACTORY IN MILWAUKEE

1900	1901	1902	1903	1904	1905	1906	1907	1908	190
William S. Harley and Arthur Davidson begin early experiments in their basement workshop		Harley-Davidson goes into production, with an output of three motorcycles	Harley-Davidson annual production rises to eight motorcycles		THE SINGLE		The Harley-Davidson Motor Company is formed; a prototype V-twin is built	The first production V-twin, the Model 5-D; 1,149 bikes are built this year	

THE FOUNDING FATHERS ARTHUR DAVIDSON, WALTER DAVIDSON, WILLIAM A. DAVIDSON, AND WILLIAM S. HARLEY

HARLEY-DAVIDSON SIDECAR IN ACTION DURING WORLD WAR I

to spend cash on a motorcycle were either enthusiasts or police departments, who soon recognized that high-performance motorcycles were rather useful for catching misbehaving motorists in low-performance automobiles. For motorcycle manufacturers, it was a case of either developing new technologies of their own to take the motorcycle forward, or simply going out of business. And most of Harley-Davidson's competitors did.

Fortunately, Harley made significant technological advances in its first few years. The sprung fork appeared in 1907, magneto ignition in 1909, mechanical inlet valves in 1911, and chain drive in 1912. Mechanical oil pumps appeared in 1915, along with electric lighting and a three-speed gearbox, by which time one could argue that the motorcycle had achieved a practical form and all further developments were improvements rather than breakthroughs.

Birth of the V-twin

But the most important development for Harley-Davidson occurred between 1907 and 1911. In 1907 the company built its first experimental V-twin-engined machine. Two years later a V-twin was listed as part of the model range, but disappeared the following year, suggesting that it had not been perfected. The V-twin returned in 1911, and is still in

EARLY HARLEY-DAVIDSON HILL-CLIMBER

production nine decades later. Though Harley's bar and shield trademark first appeared in 1910, it is the 45° V-twin that remains a more potent symbol of the company. With hindsight, it's easy to be smart. So when Harley introduced a new lightweight flat-twin in 1919, we can see that it could never have been a success. But in 1919 the company couldn't have realized that its future prospects would be so entwined with the V-twin engine.

The years leading up to the end of the decade were a period of extraordinary growth. By 1914, the tiny workspace of 1903 had grown to an area covering 225,234m^2 (2,424,479ft^2) and the number of employees had risen from four to over 1,500. Harley's bikes had quickly gained a name for being fast and dependable and the company set up a factory race team in 1915 which had immediate success. In addition, Harley was given an official seal of approval by supplying over 20,000 bikes to Allied forces during World War I.

A combination of innovative engineering and shrewd business practice meant that in less than 15-years Harley-Davidson had established itself as one of the world's leading motorcycle manufacturers.

'10 1911 •1912 1913• 1914 •1915 1916 1917• 1918 1919•

Harley-Davidson workforce now up to 149 employees

SILENT GRAY FELLOW

Over 200 Harley-Davidson dealers established across the US

BOARD-TRACK RACER

Harley-Davidson begins military bike production as US enters World War I

MODEL W

1920 TO 1939

The period between the wars saw production slip back in terms of volume as the domestic market shrank. Consequently Harley went on a successful search for export markets – as well as Europe and the British Empire, machines were also exported to Japan. At home, dealers were given increased support, advertising budgets soared, and credit schemes were developed. Everything possible was done to persuade the waverer that they could and should buy a new Harley-Davidson. Though the factory in Milwaukee wasn't running at anything like the capacity that it had been, it was still doing far better than any other manufacturer. In the mid-1920s Harley-Davidson overtook Indian as the biggest motorcycle manufacturer in the United States and for a time it was the biggest in the world.

In motorcycle racing, the board tracks that had provided the main spectacle in the early years of the century – and that had given Harley a number of notable victories – were falling from favour, partly as a result of some appalling accidents. By the mid-1920s, dirt-track racing had become the next big thing and was growing in popularity.

For the bike-buying public, the range of Harleys on offer was changing all the time. The W-series flat-twins, introduced in 1919, were dropped in 1923, having failed on the American market. Small-capacity, single-cylinder machines such as the A and B were brought in to fill a similar market niche. Sales were steady until the models were dropped in the early 1930s.

Far more significant were the new 45cu. in. side-valve V-twins which were launched in 1929. These were built to compete with Indian and Excelsior in what was an expanding area of the market. In 1932, a three-wheeled version of the side-valve V-twin was built – the Servi-Car became popular with the police and production

F.A. LONGMAN ON A WINNING HARLEY-DAVIDSON

continued until the 1970s. When new 74cu. in. side-valve V-twins were introduced in 1930, it signalled the end for Harley's long association with the inlet-over-exhaust engine which had been used on Harleys since its first machines.

The depression bites

The Wall Street Crash of 1929 changed the American economy overnight and the depression that followed had a severe impact on Harley-Davidson and its competitors. The Excelsior-Henderson company stopped motorcycle production in 1931, and in 1933 Harley production slumped to less than 4,000 machines, its lowest figure since 1910. The company survived the Great Depression intact partly because of the family ownership of the firm; quite

1920	1921	1922	1923	1924	1925	1926	1927	1928	192
EIGHT-VALVE RACER		74cu. in. FD and JD V-twins introduced (model year)	Harley withdraws its factory race team	Harley workforce cut from 2,500 to 1,000 employees		AA PEASHOOTER	Ricardo cylinder heads on AA and BA models	JD28	

Though the general economic climate had improved by the mid-1930s, Harley's situation was still uncertain, so the decision to release what is arguably the most significant model in Harley's history was a risky one. The technologically advanced "Knucklehead" had a recirculating lubrication system, a four-speed gearbox, and overhead-valves with hemispherical combustion chambers. This bike is the direct grand-daddy of today's big-twins, but its influence was more than just mechanical. The 1930s was the decade of streamlining, when aerodynamics wasn't a science but a statement. It was about optimism in future technology.

THE VICTORIOUS 1920 HARLEY-DAVIDSON FACTORY RACE TEAM

simply, Harley-Davidson didn't have to humour its shareholders. The families who owned the company had to roll up their sleeves, get on with the job, and wait for the economic climate to improve.

The depression was giving motorcycle racing a hard time too. In 1934 a new racing class was introduced that encouraged production-based machines and amateur racers back onto the tracks. Class C was a big hit, and it soon became the most important racing category in America.

A classic is unveiled

There was a bright side to the era. The 1930s Art Deco movement, with its fresh use of colour and styling, inspired Harley-Davidson to move away from the green colour schemes it had been using as its paint finishes since 1917. And one major new model introduced in 1936 embodied the movement's style and boldness – the 61E "Knucklehead".

THE SIDECAR WAS A GREAT SUCCESS IN THE 1920s, WITH BOTH LEISURE AND RACING MODELS FINDING POPULARITY

And the 61E epitomized the streamlined look, an integrated style that set the tone for the modern motorcycle.

In the run up to World War II, Harley-Davidson was in a comfortable position. It had a solid model range, a good reputation, a wide dealer network, and a secure financial base. It had grown from strength to strength and, most importantly, had survived the worst economic collapse on record.

30	1931	1932	1933	1934	1935	1936	1937	1938	1939

HILL CLIMBER

Series G Servi-Car introduced; Joe Petrali wins US Hill-Climb title on a Harley

RL

61EL

First rally to be held at Sturgis, attracting many bikers

"Boat-tail" tail lights and "cats-eye" consoles introduced

1940 to 1959

By the time the United States entered World War II after the Japanese attack on Pearl Harbour in December 1941, the economy had already adjusted itself to the effects of the conflict. Harley-Davidson's civilian motorcycle production had been put on hold earlier in 1941 as the company geared up for the war effort, and during the following four years over 90,000 military machines were supplied to the Allies. The vast majority of these were side-valve WLAs, their widespread use on the battlefields of Europe helping to advertise the Harley-Davidson name worldwide.

Harley emerged from World War II in good shape, though production and supply of civilian machines did not reach full capacity again until 1947. The war had other consequences for Harley-Davidson and the American motorcycle scene in general. The availability of cheap ex-military motorcycles, and the fact that there were large numbers of demobbed military personnel looking for excitement, gave rise to the trend for customizing motorcycles. Standard bikes were stripped of all extraneous parts to improve handling and increase performance. These bikes became known as "Bobbers", and were the forerunners of the later choppers.

One incident that occurred just after the war damaged the reputation of motorcycling. In July 1947, a large group of bikers known as "The Booze Fighters" met up at the town of Hollister in

A WLA OFFERS SHELTER TO ITS TOMMY-GUN-ARMED DESPATCH RIDER

California and indulged in some exuberant behaviour. This was subsequently reported as a full-scale riot that put the lives and property of the townsfolk in danger. Motorcyclists were now seen as hell-raisers in black leather, a label that took some time to shift. The events at Hollister became the basis of the film *The Wild One*, which starred Marlon Brando (though he actually rode a Triumph in the film).

A changing scene

Another side-effect of the war was that Harley acquired the design for a 125cc two-stroke machine from the German company DKW as part of war reparations. Production of the small bike began in 1948 and, though it was Harley's first two-stroke and a radical departure from its traditional machines, its later derivatives such as the Hummer sold well in prosperous 1950s America. The other major new model for 1948 was an updated version of the "Knucklehead" big-twin, dubbed the "Panhead" because of the appearance of its rocker covers. The following year the arrival of Harley's first hydraulically damped telescopic forks heralded the appearance of the "Hydra-Glide".

1940	1941	1942	1943	1944	1945	1946	1947	1948	1
WLD	Walter Davidson dies; first year of military-only production			U Navy	World War II ends; military bikes sold off to the public	Harley given rights to produce German DKW 125cc machine		WR DIRT TRACK	

Away from Harley's big-twin development, things were moving apace in the motorcycle market. The arrival of British motorcycles in the United States from the late 1940s saw the first real overseas threat to Harley-Davidson's dominant market position. These models were lighter, quicker, and handled better than the traditional Harleys, with an emphasis on performance and looks rather than

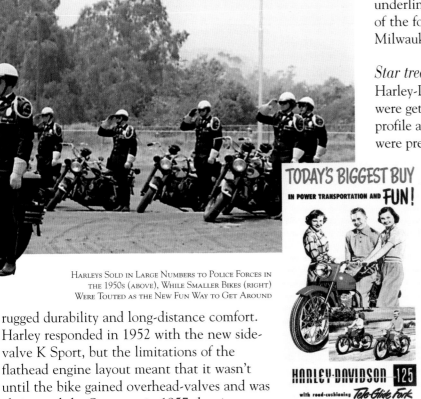

HARLEYS SOLD IN LARGE NUMBERS TO POLICE FORCES IN THE 1950s (ABOVE), WHILE SMALLER BIKES (RIGHT) WERE TOUTED AS THE NEW FUN WAY TO GET AROUND

rugged durability and long-distance comfort. Harley responded in 1952 with the new side-valve K Sport, but the limitations of the flathead engine layout meant that it wasn't until the bike gained overhead-valves and was christened the Sportster in 1957 that it became a real success. It is now the longest surviving motorcycle model in the world.

In a further development, the Indian company, which had been building motorcycles in America since 1901, ended production in 1953. This was the year that Harley-Davidson

was celebrating its 50th anniversary, and Indian's closure left Harley as the only significant manufacturer still operating in the United States. Indian had once been the biggest manufacturer in the world, with an enviable reputation for quality and innovation. The rival company's collapse, with Harley in rude health, underlined the strength of the foundations at the Milwaukee company.

A VERY YOUNG WILLIE G. DAVIDSON

Star treatment

Harley-Davidson bikes were getting more high-profile and Elvis Presley was one of a number of film stars who were prepared to declare themselves Harley owners (though it didn't stop him riding a Honda in the 1964 film *Roustabout*). In 1956 he even appeared on the cover of Harley's magazine, *The Enthusiast*, aboard his KH Sport twin. Others who were used to sell the Harley name included Clark Gable, Tyrone Power, and Roy Rogers. The association between the Harley brand and contemporary "stars" has continued through to the present day.

The late 1950s saw a couple of significant new models being unveiled. In 1957 the unit-construction Sportster appeared, and at last Harley had a model that could match the performance and looks of the British imports. Then in 1958 the big-twin got rear suspension and was renamed the "Duo-Glide", a model that established the blueprint for the big Harley tourer; comparing the profile of a "Duo-Glide" with a modern Harley, it is hard to tell them apart. Given that the Sportster has remained essentially the same since its introduction, it can be argued that Harley's unique styling was established in the 1950s.

1960 TO 1979

In 1960, America was booming and motorcycle sales were strong, but Harley-Davidson wasn't getting as much of the action as it would have liked. Part of the reason was that the scooter market had taken off in the affluent 1950s. Period sales brochures showed scooters being piloted by well-scrubbed college kids in checked shirts. This market was fed by domestic producers and also by imported machines from Italy and Germany. It was unfortunate that when Harley-Davidson chose to enter the market in 1960 with its Topper scooter, the market had started to shrink.

Meanwhile, British-built 500 and 650cc twins continued to sell well and the arrival of Honda (in 1959) and other Japanese manufacturers changed the market again. Their marketing campaigns, targeting people who hadn't previously thought of buying a motorbike, expanded the market for small motorcycles. In addition, they knew that some of the people who started on a small bike would soon be looking for bigger machines.

Harley was able to offer a couple of small bikes of its own for, as well as the Topper, the company had developed a 165cc lightweight two-stroke based on the 125 which first appeared in 1948. Ultimately, however, it was not enough and Harley must have figured that it didn't have the expertise or inclination to compete for small-bike sales without outside help. In 1960 it bought a 50 per cent stake in the Italian company Aermacchi and instantly acquired a selection of small-capacity machines. Aermacchi's bikes were re-badged as Harley-Davidsons to immediately increase the Harley range. Unfortunately, Harley dealers were even more suspicious of the Italian-built machines than they had been of the scooter and sales were disappointing.

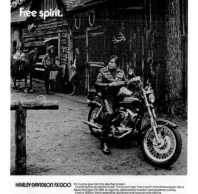

HARLEY'S MERGER WITH AMF
BOOSTED THE COMPANY'S
FINANCIAL POSITION

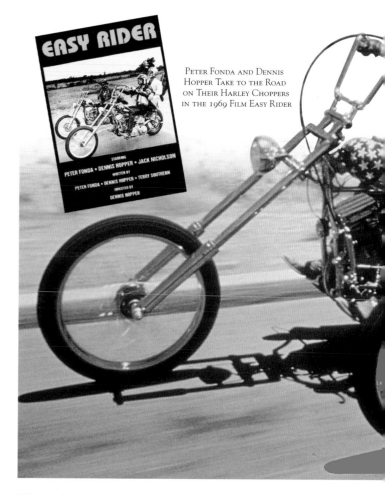

PETER FONDA AND DENNIS
HOPPER TAKE TO THE ROAD
ON THEIR HARLEY CHOPPERS
IN THE 1969 FILM EASY RIDER

The stakes are raised

The arrival of high-spec Japanese imports had another consequence. People wondered why, if a Japanese 125cc machine could have an electric starter, an American 1200cc machine could not. Harley's response was to fit an electric starter to its FL models from 1965 to create the Electra Glide, possibly the most famous motorcycle model ever built. It even had a film named after it, Electra Glide in Blue (1973).

From 1967, all Harley's lightweights were Italian-built, leaving the Milwaukee factory to turn out Sportsters, Electra Glides, and the Servi-Car. But foreign competition was taking significant chunks out of Harley's market share and production figures were in decline. Despite having floated on the stock market in 1965, extra cash was still needed and it was decided

1960 | 1961 | 1962 | 1963 | 1964 | 1965 | 1966 | 1967 | 1968 | 196

FLH DUO-GLIDE

Harley buys stake in Tomahawk fibreglass company; "tombstone" speedometer on twins

ELECTRA GLIDE

74cu. in. "Shovelhead" engine introduced

CRTT

Cal Rayborn wins two Daytona 200-mile races on a Harley

twin engine and frame with the front end of a Sportster to create a new style of factory-built custom bike that is the basis of Harley's success today. And since the FX, Harley-Davidson has realized the benefits of putting out a range of models all based on similar engines, but with different styles.

Harley's lowest point

The 1970s was not a good decade for the motor industry in general and Harley in particular. The oil crisis and tooling problems resulting from the merger with AMF hit sales hard. This was despite the introduction of the XR750, which would go on to become the most successful dirt-track bike in the history of the sport. Harley bowed to the inevitable in 1978 and sold off its interest in Aermacchi, thereby ending its brief

EVEL KNIEVEL PREPARES FOR ANOTHER DEATH-DEFYING STUNT ON A HARLEY-DAVIDSON XR750

THE ALL-CONQUERING HARLEY-DAVIDSON XR750

that Harley-Davidson needed a heavyweight partner. In January 1969, AMF (American Metal Foundries) bought a controlling stake in the company.

By this time, the customizing trend had switched from "Bobbers" to "Choppers". Bikes were given raked frames and improbably long forks, wild paint jobs, and decorative chrome. These additions looked amazing, but often affected performance and handling. Harley-Davidson officially frowned on this trend, but the director of styling, William G. Davidson – the grandson of founder William A. Davidson – was watching it with interest. In 1971 he paid homage to the chopper craze – and to the look popularized by the film *Easy Rider* (1969) – with the FX1200 Super Glide. This new model combined the big-

flirtation with lightweights. By 1979 Harley sales made up just four-per cent of the US market and its bikes were seen as unreliable and idiosyncratic. As the company moved into the next decade it was in desperate need of better quality control and a broader range of products. Things had to improve before the bikes appealed to a wider range of buyers.

70   •1971   1972   1973•   1974   •1975   1976•   1977   •1978   1979•

FX SUPER GLIDE

Rear disc brakes on Servi-Car, but last year in service

250SS

Jay Springsteen wins AMA National title on a Harley

XLCR CAFE RACER

Harley's share of US bike market is just four per cent

1980 to 2003

In 1980 Harley-Davidson was in big trouble. Its market share was small, reliability troubles meant its reputation was in tatters, and its machines were hopelessly outdated compared to the Japanese opposition. People who learnt to ride on trouble-free Japanese machines might have liked the idea of buying a Harley, but found the reality unacceptable.

Noise and emission restrictions were also hitting Harley's old-fashioned engines hard; they got less powerful and more emasculated with each new law that was passed. Even US police departments, which had first bought bikes from Harley-Davidson in 1907 and had continued ever since, were now deserting the company and switching to foreign bikes. What Harley-Davidson needed was to introduce new machines that maintained the essence of the American V-twin, but came with vastly improved performance and reliability.

THE STURGIS RALLY HAS ATTRACTED A WIDE RANGE OF ENTHUSIASTS SINCE 1938

The FLT Tour Glide of 1980 was a good start. A new frame, which isolated the engine and reduced vibration, made riding comfort superior, and the revised design and geometry also improved handling. As did the frame-mounted fairing and Harley's first five-speed transmission. But no matter how good the model was, introducing new bikes was only dealing with the problem at a purely superficial level – Harley's troubles ran much deeper than that. A year later thirteen Harley-Davidson executives, including Willie G. Davidson, bought the company back from AMF. Operating as an independent company again, it was the start of a new era.

Big changes followed almost immediately, and they had to, considering that in 1981 the US market was being flooded with more cheap Japanese imports than at any time in its history. An efficiency drive resulted in the introduction of materials-as-needed production techniques, whereby components were delivered just prior to machine assembly. Though more than one third of the workforce was laid off as a result, the new procedure put an end to the inefficient practice of maintaining stagnant stock. Quality control was also improved and the new model development programme was shifted up two gears. Harley-Davidson petitioned the International Trade Commission (ITC) for tariff restrictions on Japanese motorcycles to give it time to turn the company around and in 1982 President Ronald Reagan duly obliged by slapping tariffs on all Japanese machines over 700cc. As the new management team sought to establish a positive new direction for the company, Harley-Davidson also began an aggressive campaign to protect its trademarks and copyright.

The self-belief returns

A couple of contributory factors around about this time helped Harley's recovery. The Reagan years marked a return of America's patriotism and self-belief, and the Harley-Davidson motorcycle was the ideal representation of that belief. In addition, buyers had started to doubt the value of continually searching for increased performance. They were now looking to buy bikes that made them feel good, rather

•1980	1981	•1982	1983	•1984	•1985	1986	•1987	1988	•1989	1990•

80cu. in. FLT Tour Glide introduced as first of Harley's heavyweight tourers

Special-edition 25th anniversary Sportster model released

XR1000

Only year for FXEF and FXSB models, based on new Evo unit

XLH883

Ultra Classic Electra Glide released with CB and cruise control

The FLSTF Boy introdu with front a rear disc wh

HARLEY-DAVIDSON ON FILM: ARNOLD SCHWARZENEGGER IN *TERMINATOR II* (1991)

For Harley-Davidson, it was an astonishing recovery. In technological terms, the introduction of the Evolution big-twin engine in 1984 was the start of the new beginning. An engine which looked very similar to the Shovelhead, but which was cheaper to make, more reliable, quieter, and more powerful turned out to be the key to success. Even police departments now started buying Harleys again. And Harley-Davidson's innovative product development through the end of the 1980s and into the '90s assured the bike-buying public that it was well and truly back on track. Harley has acquired a unique understanding of what its customers want and the appearance of the radical new V-Rod in the new millennium suggests that the company is now entering a new phase in its long history.

A SAMPLE OF HARLEY-DAVIDSON'S EXTENSIVE MERCHANDISE

The Harley family

One of the things that customers want is to feel like they belong. Look at the formation of HOG (Harley Owners' Group) in 1983, a factory sponsored club which made new riders feel at home. It was a pastiche of the traditional bike club, with leathers and sew-on patches, but without the oily fingernails or the bad-ass attitude. No other enthusiast group sponsored by a manufacturer can boast over 400,000 members worldwide. Rallies such as Daytona and Sturgis attract Harley riders in their tens of thousands each year, but you don't have to own a Harley to feel this sense of belonging. Such has been the success of the company that you can now use your Harley-Davidson credit card to buy Harley after-shave, beer, or a Barbie™ doll. The Harley-Davidson Motor Company has come a long way in its first 100 years.

than ones that out-performed the opposition. Harley-Davidson, the only large-scale American motorcycle manufacturer, with 75 years of heritage, and products that looked like they were history in the 1950s, was perfectly poised to take advantage of the situation. And it did.

Japanese manufacturers realized the way this section of the market was going and, by the end of the 1980s, each of the four big companies had responded by offering variations on Harley's V-twin theme. But it was too late. By 1986 Harley had leapfrogged Honda to become the best-selling superheavyweight bike manufacturer in the United States, aided by one vital ingredient – heritage.

A 1920s 10 CENT STAMP FEATURING HARLEY-DAVIDSON'S POSTAL SERVICE MOTORCYCLE

1990s BELT BUCKLE COMMEMORATING 1920s STAMP

Belt drive is now standard on all Harley models

VR1000

Harley reveals it plans to produce 200,000 bikes a year from 2003

FLSTF Softail introduced with 1940s styling

FAT BOY

VRSCA V-ROD

| 1993 | 1994 | 1995 | 1996 | 1997 | 1998 | 1999 | 2000 | 2001 | 2002 | 2003 |

HILL-CLIMBER SCULPTURE, HARLEY-
DAVIDSON MUSEUM, MILWAUKEE

—————— 2004 TO 2013 ——————

Harley Davidson appeared to start their second century confidently, though they were struggling with a falling share price and were soon to suffer badly in the global recession. They strived to make their bikes more efficient with better dynamics, improving performance and handling while also meeting ever more stringent emissions controls. They expanded their accessories and clothing ranges and pushed the Harley brand and products into new markets around the globe.

As well as factories at Milwaukee, the company had a substantial plant at York, Pennsylvania, assembling the big-twins, and at Kansas City, Missouri, building Sportster and V-Rod models.

Bespoke bikes

Recognizing a growing trend for bespoke custom bikes, for which well-heeled buyers would pay a premium, Harley-Davidson began offering a factory customizing service, and also a limited number of premium-price CVO (Custom Vehicle Operations) built machines with special finishes and factory-fitted accessories. From 2009 they started offering a trike too.

The importance of the brand's heritage was underscored in 2008 with the opening of a 20-acre museum in Milwaukee which contains over 450 motorcycles, and attracts hundreds of thousands of visitors every year.

Harley understood that their loyal customers were wary of them diluting the

brand by producing more conventional sporting motorcycles, and, equally, customers wanting a mainstream motorcycle were suspicious of Harley-Davidsons. Harley went on to invest in Buell (with an all-new engine in 2007) and in 2008 Harley bought the famous Italian MV Agusta marque.

There was an irony here: the factory in which MVs were made had been owned by Harley-Davidson before. It was the same one in which the Harley-Davidson two-strokes had been made until 1978.

Unfortunately the global recession affected the company badly. Suddenly their market shrank rapidly and dramatic restructuring and cost-cutting were required. The Buell division was closed (just as they won their first AMA Pro Racing championship) and, less than two years after it was acquired, MV Agusta was sold at a substantial loss. Production of the company's traditional bikes was reduced and so was the workforce.

In adversity the company focused on making its existing machines better with incremental improvements in quality and innovation. They sought out new buyers, working to attract women and younger riders at home, and moved into growing markets too; they established an Indian subsidiary in 2009 and were assembling five models there by 2012.

A stuttering world economy has stalled the growth of the Harley market and reduced the company's profitability, but the bikes themselves are better than ever, combining improved efficiency with a nod to history and heritage.

AN ASSEMBLY LINE AT A HARLEY-
DAVIDSON PLANT

▶ POLISHED TO A SHINE: HARLEYS PARKED
IN NORTH YORKSHIRE, BRITAIN, IN 2006

•2004	2005	2006•	2007•	2008•	2009	•2010	•2011	2012	•2013
New chassis and updated engine for Sportster range		35th anniversary Super Glide models	50th anniversary Sportster	New Rocker Softail models	XR1200X		XL883N Iron		Company celebrates 110 years

CHAPTER ONE

THE EARLY BIKES

1903–1929

1905 SINGLE CYLINDER

EARLY INTERNAL COMBUSTION ENGINES were underpowered, unreliable, and almost comically crude. Part of Harley-Davidson's success was its realization that increasing engine size was part of the solution to lack of power and that practical design and added strength improved reliability. But it didn't embrace change for change's sake. The evolution of the Harley engine from the first prototypes to the last of the inlet-over-exhaust valve machines of 1929 was gradual and evolutionary.

EARLY BIKE BROTHER
*Walter Davidson stands next to an early Harley single (left).
After building their first bike in 1903, it took three years
before the four founders worked full-time at Harley-Davidson.*

1905 Model No.1

MOTOR AND CYCLE. There wasn't much more to the first Harleys than these two vital ingredients. Though William Harley and the Davidson brothers used a larger engine than most of their contemporary manufacturers, the fact that pedal power was an essential supplement to the internal combustion engine on hills meant that the bicycle layout had to be retained. Harley curved the bottom frame tube under the crankcases to allow the engine to be mounted lower in the frame, resulting in superior handling. The battery ignition system, crude carburettor, belt drive, and other unrefined elements ensured that the early motorcycle wasn't really a viable means of transport, but at least the Model No.1 was a cut above the average.

Oil tank mounted within fuel tank

Rod linkage connects twist-grip control to carburettor

Carburettor float chamber

White rubber tyres were common on early machines until it was realized that black rubber hid the dirt

Solid bicycle-style front forks

One-piece cast-iron cylinder

Drive pulley

66-cm (26-in) wheel

1905 MODEL NO.1
The 1905 Model No.1 was almost identical to the bikes built in 1903 and '04, and until 1909 Harley-Davidson produced only one model, which was improved upon each year. The model number represented the year of production minus four.

"Harley's Model No.1 was essentially an engine bolted onto a bicycle frame, with pedal-power still needed when there was a steep hill to be climbed."

Lubricating oil is held in the top half of the tank; fuel is held in the bottom

Belt tensioning lever

Crude leather bicycle saddle; the saddle springs were the bike's only form of suspension

Battery case contains a rechargeable lead-plate battery to power the ignition

Belt drive pulley mounted on wheel rim

Rear hub coaster brake was operated by pedalling backwards

Ignition coil

Flat leather belt

Loop frame

Silencer restricted exhaust noise to prevent horses from being frightened

Pedal-power was often needed when the engine alone did not provide enough power

Stand used for stationary vehicle only

71-cm (28-in) tyre

SPECIFICATIONS

1905 Model No.1

- **ENGINE** Inlet-over-exhaust single
- **CAPACITY** 24.74cu. in. (405.41cc)
- **POWER OUTPUT** Unknown
- **TRANSMISSION** Single-speed, belt drive
- **FRAME** Tubular loop
- **SUSPENSION** None
- **WEIGHT** 84kg (185lb)
- **TOP SPEED** 64km/h (40mph) (est.)

1912 Silent Gray Fellow

BY THE TIME HARLEY-DAVIDSON built this X-8 single in 1912, the company was well on the way to establishing itself as a major motorcycle manufacturer and the motorcycle was a more refined mode of transport. The rugged engineering and rigorous development championed by Harley from day one had borne fruit in the form of sprung forks and magneto ignition, and the company wasted no time emphasizing that cubic inches were the key to increased power. The original 1903 Harley had a 24.74cu. in. (405cc) engine, rising to 26.8cu. in. (440cc) in 1906, and 30cu. in. (494cc) in 1909. In 1913 it gained a further 5cu. in. (82cc). The Harley single became a valued and dependable machine which earned it the nickname "Silent Gray Fellow".

1912 SILENT GRAY FELLOW
This bike was a direct development of the original 1903 model and continued in production until 1918. Though it still had belt final-drive, an atmospheric inlet valve, and no gearbox, these developments were just around the corner.

Atmospheric inlet valve is kept closed by this light spring

Valanced front mudguard

Control cables replaced rod linkages in 1909

White rubber tyres were a period feature

Leading-link front suspension

Canvas mudflap

Loop frame curves under the engine, allowing it to be positioned lower for optimum weight distribution

SPECIFICATIONS

1912 Silent Gray Fellow

- ENGINE Inlet-over-exhaust, single-cylinder
- CAPACITY 30cu. in. (494cc)
- POWER OUTPUT 6.5bhp @ 2,700rpm
- TRANSMISSION Single-speed, belt drive
- FRAME Tubular loop
- SUSPENSION Leading-link forks, rigid rear
- WEIGHT 89kg (195lb)
- TOP SPEED 72km/h (45mph)

Twist-grip throttle control

Wide handlebars

The sprung seat post was a nice touch on a bike with no rear suspension

First year of valanced mudguard

Pedals start the engine and set the bike in motion as there is no starter or gearbox

Rear brake operated by back-pedalling

Sloping frame tube allowed a lower seat height and was first used on 1912 models

Sprung leather saddle

Rear mudguard

Technical advances

The optional rear hub clutch on this model meant that the bike could be stopped without stalling the engine, and the optional Schebler carburettor hugely improved reliability over early models.

Rear stand

Battery box for coil ignition

Rear hub clutch operated by lever

Efficient silencer contributed to the bike's nickname

Clutch assembly in hub

The Early Single

THE EARLY SINGLE-CYLINDER petrol engine was under-powered and inefficient, though Harley's singles were among the best available. The "atmospheric" inlet valve relied on a light spring to keep it closed and was forced open by the pressure created from the falling piston. The system was simple, but it couldn't work properly at anything other than slow engine speeds. Increasing capacity boosted the power output, but it was no substitute for improved efficiency.

Single with Bosch magneto

A magneto was introduced as an option in 1909. This simple electric generator provided a spark for the ignition system and made the early Harley a more useable machine.

Throttle control linkage

Lead

High-tension lead

Spark plug

Iron barrel and cylinder head were cast as one piece

Atmospheric inlet valve stem and spring

Vertical fins on the cylinder head were introduced in 1911 to aid engine cooling

Carburettor throat

Harley introduced the Schebler float-feed carburettor on its bikes from 1909; the company had previously made its own

Bosch high-tension magneto was first seen on Harley singles in 1909

Exhaust valve stem and spring

No female frills

Some European manufacturers offered "ladies' models" with special frames and skirt-guards. Harley women

Oil feed union; a pipe supplied lubricant to the crankshaft, with pressure created by the hand-operated pump in the tank

INLET-OVER-EXHAUST

The inlet valve was kept closed with the exposed spring on the top of the cylinder. As the piston fell, it created a vacuum in the cylinder, resulting in the valve being forced open by atmospheric pressure. A charge of fuel and air mix was then sucked in through the carburettor.

The exhaust pipe was connected to a simple silencer, which could be by-passed to increase performance... and noise

THE COMPETITION

• 1911 EXCELSIOR MODEL K •

The Chicago Excelsior company was the third-biggest motorcycle manufacturer in the US until its closure in 1931. Like the Harley, this machine had belt-drive, but used the engine cases as part of the frame, as opposed to Harley's loop-frame system.

Alloy crankcase

The Harley single was just a good, solid, dependable motorcycle at a time when most of them were not.

Richard Rosenthal
(Motorcycle Historian)

The timing gear case conceals the four gears that drove the magneto; models with battery ignition were not equipped with gears

Engine case bolt

Alloy engine case bears the legend "Harley-Davidson, Milwaukee"; the city's other notable product was, and is, beer

Rugged and dependable
In an era of unreliable and uncomfortable motorcycles, the Harley single stood out as a solid workhorse capable of covering long distances. The well-made engine got some of the credit, but Harley's sprung seat-post was a welcome feature for the often appalling road conditions.

1915 KT Board Racer

HARLEY-DAVIDSON **DID NOT** officially participate in racing until 1914, when it decided to exploit the potential benefits of publicity and development that could be derived from racing success. Board-track racing was reaching new levels of popularity, with promotors able to attract huge paying crowds to the meetings, so Harley's decision to enter into competition made a lot of sense. And the move paid off almost immediately, as the Harley race team began to achieve significant results in 1915 on bikes such as this KT. In September 1915, an F-head Harley set a 100-mile (161-km) record of 143.46km/h (89.11mph) on a board track in Chicago. All this augured well for the launch of the famous eight-valve racer (*see pp.46–47*) a year later.

SPECIFICATIONS

1915 KT Board Racer

- **ENGINE** Inlet-over-exhaust, V-twin
- **CAPACITY** 61cu. in. (1000cc)
- **POWER OUTPUT** 15bhp
- **TRANSMISSION** Three-speed, chain drive
- **FRAME** Tubular loop
- **SUSPENSION** Leading-link front forks, rigid rear
- **WEIGHT** 147kg (325lb)
- **TOP SPEED** 130km/h (80mph)

Abbreviated mudguard is one of a number of weight-saving components

Basic lightweight saddle provided little comfort

Fuel filler-cap

Inlet-valve pushrod

The brake on this bike is a luxury; most board racers didn't have one

Lightweight wheel hub

Magneto

Pedalling forwards starts the bike, pedalling backwards operates the rear brake – just like on an American bicycle

Window in the timing gear case allowed the rider to see if the oil pump was working

1915 KT BOARD RACER

Board racers were spindly, frail-looking machines that were stripped of surplus equipment. There was no gearbox and usually no brakes, though this bike is fitted with a rear drum. Their appearance belied their astonishing strength and performance – these bikes could be run flat-out for considerable distances, with 161-km (100-mile) races not uncommon on the banked wooden tracks.

Maywood Speedway Park, 1915
Maywood Park was a typical board-track venue. Tracks were constructed by placing thin planks on a wooden frame. With use, the boards became covered in oil and rubber, gradually making them more slippery and dangerous. Despite the initial success of this form of racing, injury and death were not uncommon and the deaths of spectators in the early 1920s saw the sport go into terminal decline.

Cut-outs in the fuel tank gave clearance for the rocker gear and allowed the bike to sit lower

Dropped handlebars enabled the rider to adopt a racing crouch

Braced fork yoke

"Clincher" wheel rim

Fuel tank with integrated oil tank

Spark plug located in the valve "pocket"

Front engine mounting

Springs for the leading-link forks contained in the tubes

Shortened exhaust headers come straight out of the cylinder and apparently produced more power... and noise

Thin, high-pressure tyre resulted in minimal friction and maximum speed

Leading-link front fork

1915 KR Fast Roadster

THE IDEA OF A RACE BIKE on the road has always been attractive to motorcyclists. Modern bikers relish the power, handling, and brakes of competition-developed machinery and pioneer motorcyclists were no different. Harley's Fast Roadster was based on the board-track racer (*see pp.32–33*) but fitted with mudguards, a chainguard, and conventional handlebars. Who needed a gearbox or lights? It was built for amateur racers at a time when Harley-Davidson's factory race team was starting to taste success; the K-series won a number of 100- and 300-mile (161- and 483-km) races for Harley in 1915. With just over 100 built, this model is now very rare.

1915 KR FAST ROADSTER
The "close coupled" frame on the KR was shorter than that fitted to other models such as the F (*see pp.38–39*) because no gearbox was fitted. A short wheelbase traditionally offers better handling at the expense of comfort and stability.

The metal tank was made up of three reservoirs; two contained fuel and one on the front-left held oil

Hand oil pump

Control cables made of single-strand piano wire with a wound metal outer cable, leather-sheathed for protection

"Clincher" wheel rims were used with beaded tyres which required very high pressures to stay on the rims

Clutch pedal

Loop frame

Leading-link front fork

Canvas mudguard

The Fast Roadster had sufficient power to make the bicycle-style pedals on earlier bikes unnecessary

SPECIFICATIONS
1915 KR Fast Roadster

- ENGINE Inlet-over-exhaust, V-twin
- CAPACITY 61cu. in. (1000cc)
- POWER OUTPUT 15bhp
- TRANSMISSION Single-speed competition gearbox, chain drive
- FRAME Tubular loop
- SUSPENSION Leading-link front forks, rigid rear.
- WEIGHT 147kg (325lb)
- TOP SPEED 130km/h (80mph)

Twist-grip for the ignition advance retard mechanism

Lever to operate the clutch; it could also be pedal-operated

Nickel-plated handlebars

Wide handlebars
One of the civilizing features which the Fast Roadster acquired from its conventional road-going stablemates was a set of pulled-back handlebars. These offered a combination of comfort and control on the road. Racing handlebars would have been suitable only for short trips to the osteopath.

Seat springs

Footboards with rubber mats were positioned to allow the rider to stand in rough conditions, which was most of the time

Clutch connecting rod

Lightweight sprung saddle doesn't have the sprung seat-post present on the basic road model

Renault Grey was the colour of all Harleys in 1915

Clutch

Primary drive cover protected the rider's feet from oil and from toe-chewing chains

Rear stand

The 45° F-Head V-Twin

HARLEY-DAVIDSON SOON realized that the easiest way to significantly increase engine size was to add an extra cylinder. The company built a prototype V-twin in 1907 and four years later the first production V-twins rolled out of the factory. The engine effectively joined two singles on a common crankshaft and cases. If the angle of the "V" was narrow, the new engine could be used in the same frame as a single. Harley chose a 45° "V", and a motorcycling classic was born. The arrival of the mechanical inlet valve on the V-twin was also important, allowing engine revs to be increased and thus release more power.

Harley's trademark is born
The appearance of the 45° V-twin effectively provided the blueprint for the Harley twin of today. From 1915 it was refined and improved rather than radically altered.

Thread for rocker arm assembly

Fins to aid cooling

Inlet and exhaust valves face each other in the

Cylinder head was cast together with the barrel and so could not be removed

Carburettor manifold connects the two inlet ports and is the ideal set-up for a single carburettor

Exhaust valve stem

Inlet pushrod fits to the rocker

Adjustment sleeve

Rocker arm assembly for the inlet valve fits to a threaded insert in the cylinder head

Inlet valve cage

Cast-iron was used for the cylinders because of its heat dissipation qualities and its resistance to wear

Threaded exhaust port exits beneath

Cylinder barrel stud

Engine mounting lug is cast into the crankcase

Alloy engine case

F-HEAD SET-UP

These early V-twins were known as F-heads because the inlet valve was positioned in the cylinder head and the exhaust valve was on the side of the cylinder, creating an "F" formation. This incomplete engine is believed to be from a factory race bike.

V-twin operation

To make a V-twin, the two rods connecting the crankshaft to the pistons have to sit on the same shaft. Harley used "male and female" rods to solve the problem.

This end joins to the piston

Connecting rod

The "mated" rods join to the crankshaft

The Harley-Davidson trademark

This circular case contains the camshaft

Timing gear case covers the drive for the magneto and the oil pump

Pushrod spring collar retains the spring and some lubricant

Bulge in the timing gear case conceals the mechanical oil pump

An inspection window filled this hole, allowing the rider to check the oil pump

"The V-twin opened up America for ordinary riders. It was a giant step forward for the Harley rider."

BRUCE LINDSAY
(MOTORCYCLE RESTORER)

THE COMPETITION

• 1914 YALE V-TWIN •

Harley wasn't the only manufacturer to choose the 45° engine layout for its bikes. The Consolidated Manufacturing Company of Toledo, Ohio, built Yales from 1903–15 and this 61cu. in. model had a 45° V-twin engine and mechanically operated inlet valves.

2000s | 1990s | 1980s | 1970s | 1960s | 1950s | 1940s | 1930s | 1920s | 1910s | 1900s

1915 Model F

A WAY FROM THE RACE TRACKS, the introduction of a number of
innovative new features in 1915 meant that this was a significant
year in the development of Harley-Davidson's road bikes. It could
even be said that it was the year when the motorcycle came of age as
a practical machine. As far as Harley was concerned, there were three
main innovations: a three-speed gearbox, a mechanical oil pump, and
electrical lighting, with the Model F boasting two out of the three.
The gearbox made the bikes faster and also gave them better hill-
climbing ability and improved low-speed running. The motor-driven
oil pump guaranteed better lubrication and improved engine life,
and electrical lighting meant that journeys at night could now
be undertaken at times other than when the moon was full.

1915 MODEL F
For 1915 Harley-Davidson listed five V-twin
motorcycles with a combination of single-
or three-speed transmission and with or
without an electrical system. The Model F
had three gears but no electric lights and
sold for $275. There was also a V-twin
commercial tricycle available in the 1915
range which had a box and two front wheels
instead of conventional motorcycle forks.

Spring system
for saddle

Basic
saddle

Rear number
plate holder

Parcel rack

Rear mudguard

Spark plug
in valve
"pocket"

Oil breather pipe
is used to lubricate
the primary
drive chain

Foot-operated
silencer cut-out is
used to bypass the
silencer for improved
performance

Rear drum brake,
operated by
right-foot pedal

Exhaust
pipe

A policeman's friend

Police departments were quick to see the benefit of using high-performance motorcycles to chase errant motorists in low-performance automobiles and Harley V-twins became the models of choice. Their 97km/h (60mph) top speed put them among the fastest bikes around. This department is mounted on 1915 Model Js, which was the model up from the Model F in that it had electric lighting.

SPECIFICATIONS
1915 Model F

- **ENGINE** Inlet-over-exhaust, V-twin
- **CAPACITY** 61cu. in. (1000cc)
- **POWER OUTPUT** 11bhp
- **TRANSMISSION** Three-speed, chain drive
- **FRAME** Tubular loop
- **SUSPENSION** Leading-link front forks, rigid rear
- **WEIGHT** 147.5kg (325lb)
- **TOP SPEED** 97km/h (60mph)

Exhaust-valve spring cover

Cast-iron frame headstock

Oil tank is incorporated into the fuel tank, with this side of the tank containing fuel

Valanced front mudguard

Front number plate; indicates this bike was exported to the UK

CR 4732

Rear brake pedal

Oil-pump inspection window

Footboards were introduced from 1914 when power outputs were sufficient to make pedal assistance unnecessary except for starting

Block-pattern tyre

1928 JD

HARLEY RARELY RUSHED CHANGE, and it always knew the value of cubic inches. The history of the 45° F-head V-twin goes back to the original prototype twin of 1907, and by 1928 it was approaching its sell-by date. In 1922 Harley created the JD model by increasing capacity from 61 to 74 cubic inches. The result was a high-performance machine capable of outrunning almost any other vehicle on the road in the 1920s. No wonder these models were popular with US police departments. When Harley dropped the big F-head twins and replaced them with side-valve machines in 1930, many riders considered it a step backwards. At first, the new side-valves were slower and no more reliable than the trusty F-head.

Colour choice
Olive Green was the standard paint finish in 1928, but buyers could pay extra for colours such as Black, White, Cream, Police Blue, Coach Green, Maroon, Fawn Grey, or Azure Blue.

Cylindrical toolbox also contains a puncture repair kit

Foot clutch

Number plate mounting bracket

Parcel rack

Leather saddle mounted on top of Harley's patented sprung seat-post

Battery box

Rear stand

Contracting band rear brake is in addition to internal expanding band brake

Driving gears for optional speedometer

Tubular cradle frame

1928 JD

The single camshaft JD model was a high-performance machine that consistently outsold every other Harley between 1923 and 1930. This was partly due to its popularity with police departments. Sporting riders who wanted even more performance could opt for the two-cam JDH model, with its race-derived engine.

Rear-view mirror was an optional extra

Wide handlebars

Speedometer

Double-sided tank contains fuel and oil

Last year of single headlight as the 1929 model had dual bullet lights

Electric air horn

Cylindrical toolbox

Valanced mudguard

Thick 63.5x9.8-cm (25x3⅞-in) block-tread tyre helped to soak up the bumps

Rear brake operating rod

Pushrods are operated by a single camshaft

Silver-painted cast-iron cylinder barrel

Front drum brake, which became standard on US bikes from 1928

SPECIFICATIONS
1928 JD

- **ENGINE** Inlet-over-exhaust, V-twin
- **CAPACITY** 74cu. in. (1213cc)
- **POWER OUTPUT** 9.5bhp @ 4,500 rpm
- **TRANSMISSION** Three-speed, hand shift
- **FRAME** Tubular cradle
- **SUSPENSION** Leading-link front forks
- **WEIGHT** 166kg (365lb)
- **TOP SPEED** 121km/h (75mph)

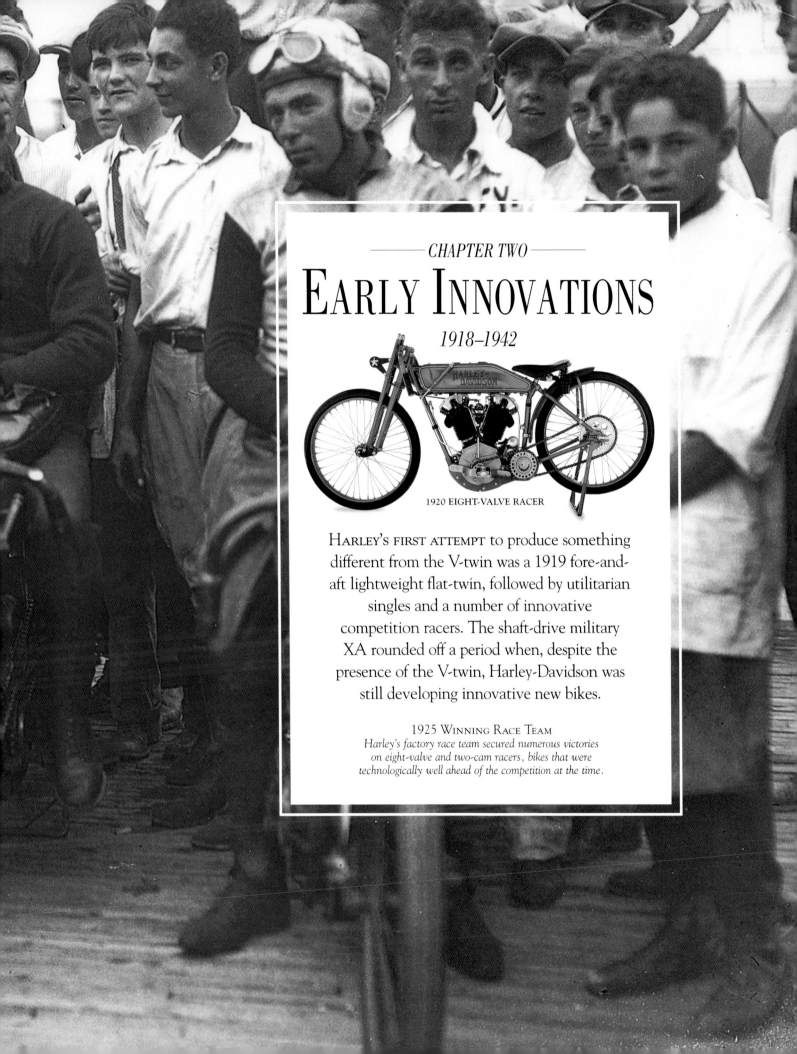

CHAPTER TWO

EARLY INNOVATIONS

1918–1942

1920 EIGHT-VALVE RACER

HARLEY'S FIRST ATTEMPT to produce something
different from the V-twin was a 1919 fore-and-
aft lightweight flat-twin, followed by utilitarian
singles and a number of innovative
competition racers. The shaft-drive military
XA rounded off a period when, despite the
presence of the V-twin, Harley-Davidson was
still developing innovative new bikes.

1925 WINNING RACE TEAM
*Harley's factory race team secured numerous victories
on eight-valve and two-cam racers, bikes that were
technologically well ahead of the competition at the time.*

1918 Model J Sidecar

HARLEY-DAVIDSON FIRST ADDED sidecars to its model range in 1914, and later offered specially tuned engines for sidecar use. Before then, standard bikes such as this Model J just had a sidecar bolted onto them. A sidecar meant motorcycle riders could now transport their family, large parcels, or even a nervous crinolene-clad girlfriend, for whom the sidecar was a poor substitute for a proper motor car. The sidecar peaked in the years leading up to the 1920s, with some Harley examples even used on the battlefields of World War I, but the Model T Ford made the car cheaper, and from around 1920 the sidecar became a minority interest for the eccentric enthusiast.

1918 MODEL J SIDECAR

Harley's big F-head V-twin was ideal for pulling a sidecar and the company began offering sidecars as an option in 1914. From then until 1925 Harley's sidecars were built by the Rogers Company, but when Rogers ceased production Harley started building its own chairs. Production has continued, but they are now built in small numbers.

Hand-operated horn

Acetylene lighting was a period addition for bikes not fitted with electric lighting at the factory

Olive Green paint scheme was standard for 1918

Valanced front mudguard

Whitewall tyre

Leading-link front suspension

61cu. in. F-head engine was offered with a special sidecar tune

Foot pedal for clutch

Hand shift lever for three-speed gearbox

SPECIFICATIONS

1918 Model J Sidecar

- **ENGINE** Inlet-over-exhaust, V-twin
- **CAPACITY** 61cu. in. (1000cc)
- **POWER OUTPUT** Unknown
- **TRANSMISSION** Three-speed, chain drive
- **FRAME** Tubular loop
- **SUSPENSION** Leading-link front forks
- **WEIGHT** 147kg (325lb)
- **TOP SPEED** 89km/h (55mph) (est.)

Sidecars could be fitted with a hood or a tonneau cover

Access door

Leaf spring provided some degree of suspension for the passenger

Footboard

A traditional design

Period sidecar production was influenced by the horse-drawn buggy. The body was mounted to the chassis by springs that isolated the passenger from the worst jolts of the road surface.

Hand lever for clutch

Speedometer cable

Sprung saddle

Upholstered sidecar seat

Parcel rack allowed the passenger's luggage to be transported

Rear light is linked to the acetylene supply by a pipe

Stand retaining clip

Rear stand was used for changing wheels as punctures were common

Chainguard

Pressed-steel primary drive case with Harley-Davidson logo

Exhaust pipe

71-cm (28-in) "clincher" tyre; early tyre sizes measured to the outside of the tyre, so this rim actually measures 56cm (22in)

1920 Eight-Valve Racer

HAVING COMMITTED ITSELF TO bike racing in 1914, Harley soon began to take the sport seriously. Special eight-valve racing twins were introduced in 1916; these were built in very limited numbers until 1927 for the exclusive use of the factory's own race team. Four versions of the machine were produced over an 11-year period, giving serious credibility to Harley as a racing-bike manufacturer. The race team secured numerous victories on the eight-valve racers and earned itself the nickname, "The Wrecking Crew". The sight and sound of these, quite literally, fire-breathing machines must have been incredible as they reached speeds of around 193 km/h (120 mph) on the steeply banked wooden tracks where they were used.

1920 EIGHT-VALVE RACER
The cylinders and heads on the eight-valve racers were the work of British engineer Harry Ricardo and featured a hemispherical combustion chamber that had been developed on aeroplane engines during WW1. The bike shown here is a 1920 version with distinct open-port cylinder heads that have no exhaust headers. It is possibly one of only eight built, with very few of these still in existence. On the rare occasions when they are sold, they command substantial prices.

Springs under the saddle are the only form of rear suspension

Leather racing saddle

Exposed valvegear

Shortened racing mudguard

"Clincher" wheel rim

Rear sprocket could be changed to alter the gearing

Footrest is a bicycle-style pedal, but serves no other purpose

Countershaft

Oil pump

SPECIFICATIONS

1920 Eight-Valve Racer

- **ENGINE** Overhead-valve, V-twin
- **CAPACITY** 61cu. in. (1000cc)
- **POWER OUTPUT** 15bhp
- **TRANSMISSION** Single-speed, direct drive
- **FRAME** Tubular loop Keystone racing frame
- **SUSPENSION** Leading-link front forks, rigid rear
- **WEIGHT** 314kg (692lb)
- **TOP SPEED** 193km/h (120mph)

Twist-grip throttle

Fork spring tube

Carburettor air intake

Dropped handlebars forced the rider into a racing crouch

Friction damper makes suspension movement more controllable

Left twist-grip controls the ignition advance retard

Footrest

(You've got to) brake-free

The eight-valve racer had no gearbox or brakes. Riders slowed their machines using a combination of the throttle, the engine-kill button, and old-fashioned boot leather. Harley riders, however, were up to the task, winning a number of prestigious races this year.

Throttle cable runs inside the handlebars

Spoked racing wheel

Compression-release lever

Open exhaust port

Oil feed pipe to the front cylinder; crank rotation forced oil back to the rear cylinder

Compression-release mechanism can be used to kill the engine or to allow the clutchless bike to be pushed with a dead engine

Engine mounting plate

Suspension linkage

Thin high-pressure tyre for minimum friction

The Eight-Valve

Two INLET VALVES AND TWO EXHAUST valves per cylinder allowed gases to flow into and out of the engine in greater quantity than in the traditional four-valve V-twin. The resulting increase in power was exactly what was needed for a successful racing engine to be used in Harley-Davidson's newly formed factory race team. Harley wasn't the first manufacturer to use this technology, but the company's eight-valve racers carved a massive reputation based on numerous racing victories.

Single speed but extra power
This profile shows the gearing on the eight-valve racer. This version has no clutch, gearbox, or brakes, and could better 161km/h (100mph).

Rocker arm

Open exhaust port followed period aircraft engine style, though some eight-valves were fitted with short pipes

Cast-iron cylinders each have a capacity of 30.50cu. in., to

Throttle control linkage

Air intake trumpet for single carburettor

Petrol tap connects to fuel tank

Oil feed to front cylinder

Carburettor

Bosch magneto

External pushrod

Rear cylinder exhaust valve and spring

Exposed valvegear

Rod linkage

Valve lifter arm releases compression in the cylinder

mounting lug

VISUALLY SIMILAR

The eight-valve Harley engine used the same crankcases as the conventional F-head racers (*see Fast Roadster, pp.34–35*). It was the cylinders and heads that were special.

Dirt-track winner
The eight-valve era was the period that American racing moved from board-track motordromes to oval dirt tracks, which were originally used for horse-racing.

Polished alloy timing gear case cover

Engine mounting bolt

Oil delivery pipe to cylinder

Mechanical oil pump is supplemented by a hand pump on the tank

"The performance of the eight-valve moved bike racing to a new level, from the board tracks to the longer horse-racing ovals of America."

GEORGE BARBER
(MOTORCYCLE COLLECTOR)

THE COMPETITION

• 1920 INDIAN TRACK RACER •
Indian had been at the forefront of eight-valve technology and had been building racing twins since 1912, though by the time Harley introduced its version, Indian was developing a side-valve racer.

1900s | 1910s | 1920s | 1930s | 1940s | 1950s | 1960s | 1970s | 1980s | 1990s | 2000s

1926 Model B

AFTER THE COMPARATIVE FAILURE of the Sport Twin of 1919–23, Harley had another crack at the lightweight market by releasing a range of single-cylinder bikes for the 1926 model year: the A, B, AA, and BA. The design was entirely conventional, and inspired by Indian's contemporary Prince as well as typical British machines of the period. The bikes were available with side-valve or overhead-valve engines and the racing versions that followed were nicknamed "Peashooters" due to the unique pitch of the exhaust; the name was eventually applied to all the models. These were ideal machines for impoverished commuters and delivery riders who accepted underwhelming performance as long as the bike was cheap to buy and run.

SPECIFICATIONS
1926 Model B

- **ENGINE** Side-valve, single cylinder
- **CAPACITY** 21cu. in. (346cc)
- **POWER OUTPUT** 10bhp
- **TRANSMISSION** Three-speed, chain drive
- **FRAME** Tubular loop
- **SUSPENSION** Leading-link front forks, rigid rear
- **WEIGHT** 119kg (263lb)
- **TOP SPEED** 97km/h (60mph)

Olive Green with maroon striping was the standard paint finish on all Harley bikes up until 1933

Tail light; the budget-priced Model A wasn't fitted with lights

66x8.5-cm (26x3⅓-in) "balloon" tyre

Bicycle-style seat features Harley's traditional telescopic sprung mounting for increased comfort

Toolroll

Rear stand; a side-stand could be fitted at extra cost

Silencer

The battery allowed the bike to run lights; buyers who chose the magneto option had no lights

Exhaust pipe

1926 MODEL B

The model shown here is a B, with side-valve engine and battery ignition option. Harley-Davidson intended these singles primarily for export markets and initially they were successful. Unfortunately, the worldwide recession meant that the British imposed severe import tariffs and the European market collapsed. The model was discontinued in 1929, though existing stock continued to be sold the following year.

Standard handlebars; "speedster" bars were optional

Headlight

Suspension springs

Klaxon

Side-valve revival
The side-valve model was revived between 1932 and 1934, probably as much to use up stocks of parts as it was to sell what Harley claimed was its cheapest ever model.

Clutch actuation mechanism operated by left foot-pedal

Rubber mudflap

Switch panel

Gear lever

"Clincher" wheel rim

Rear brake pedal

Compression release lever

Side-valve cylinder head designed by Harry Ricardo

Suspension linkage

No front brake was fitted until 1928

1926 Model S Racer

A NEW 350CC RACING class was created soon after Harley unveiled its "Peashooter" racer in the summer of 1925. The bike was based on its new 21cu. in. ohv single-cylinder economy road bike. To make it competitive for dirt-track racing the bike had a shortened frame and simple telescopic forks that were triangulated for greater strength. The legendary Joe Petrali was among several riders who achieved success on Peashooters as Harleys swept the board in the new class. Petrali was one of the best riders in the history of American bike racing and in 1935 he won all 13 rounds of the US dirt-track championships on a works Peashooter.

1926 MODEL S RACER

Harley produced its Peashooter racing bikes in limited numbers for a few years and, as well as success at home, they were also raced successfully in Britain and Australia. However, the appearance of the British JAP-powered machines in the 1930s effectively made all competitors redundant and the Peashooter disappeared from the racing circuit.

Dropped racing handlebars

Engine lubrication relies on a hand oil pump

Flimsy telescopic forks are braced for extra strength

Knobbly treaded tyre is designed to provide maximum grip on dirt-tracks

Exhaust pipe

Canvas fork gaiter protects the fork slider

"Clincher" wheel rim

Left-hand footrest for use on straights

Carburettor air intake

Footrest

Racing modifications

All non-essential components were ditched from the standard road model, including the springer forks, saddle spring, brakes, and gearbox. The bikes ran in a single gear and the clutch was only used for starting. Races on oval dirt tracks were run anti-clockwise and the left foot was used to stablilize the bike in turns.

SPECIFICATIONS
1926 Model S Racer

- **ENGINE** Overhead-valve, single cylinder
- **CAPACITY** 21cu. in. (346cc)
- **POWER OUTPUT** 12bhp
- **TRANSMISSION** Single-speed, belt drive
- **FRAME** Tubular loop
- **SUSPENSION** Telescopic front forks
- **WEIGHT** 109kg (240lb)
- **TOP SPEED** 113km/h (70mph) (est.)

Earlier versions of the bike had a shorter, rounded tank

Unsprung leather saddle was not designed for comfort

Lightweight frame

Cut-down rear mudguard

Mudguard stay

Magneto

Footrest mounting plate also serves as a basic chain-guard

Exposed primary chain drive

Drive is via primary reduction gear and a countershaft, with no clutch or gearbox

68½-cm (27-in) tyre

1930 Hill Climber

THE INGREDIENTS OF AN AMERICAN hill-climb bike appear simple, even if the reality is rather more complicated. The essential element is power, and in the case of this machine a methanol-burning eight-valve engine was enough in 1930 to make it a competitive bike. A long wheelbase and weight at the front to prevent the bike tipping over backwards are both essential, as is grip, which is why this bike's rear tyre is wrapped in chains. These crude facts belie the level of expertise involved in handling these machines and once again it was Joe Petrali who took the honours for Harley-Davidson. Between 1932 and 1938, he won six national hill-climbing titles on a Harley.

SPECIFICATIONS
1930 Hill Climber

- **ENGINE** Eight-valve, V-twin
- **CAPACITY** 74cu. in. (1213cc)
- **POWER OUTPUT** Not available
- **TRANSMISSION** Competition single-speed gearbox
- **FRAME** Tubular cradle
- **SUSPENSION** Leading-link forks, rigid rear
- **WEIGHT** 147kg (350lb) (est.)
- **TOP SPEED** Determined by the gearing chosen for the hill-climb course

Cut-down rear mudguard

Sprung saddle in low position for easier handling

Large-diameter rear sprocket to give lower gearing and better climbing ability

Contracting band rear brake

Exposed valvegear meant regular maintenance was required

Chains for traction on steep slopes

Gearbox only provides one gear and neutral

Tubular cradle frame

Kick-starter

Sloping footboard keeps the rider's weight forward

1930 HILL CLIMBER

This unrestored bike is typical of the ingenious hill-climbing machines of the period. The frame is from a JD model circa 1929 and the forks are from a 1928 45cu. in. bike. The engine cases are from a JDH (*see p.41*), with JE model flywheels; special barrels and overhead-valve cylinder heads are from a single-cylinder Harley. Modern hill-climb racers still have a similar look to this rugged machine and the difficulty of trying to convert power into climbing ability remains the same.

Racing rules

In hill-climbing, riders launch their machines at impossibly steep hills. If riders make the summit then time decides the winner, but if no rider reaches the peak, then the one who has reached the highest point wins.

Company colours

The Harley-Davidson race teams were easily recognizable by their orange and black jerseys. These colours would later be used as the livery for Harley's racing bikes.

Race jersey from the 1930s

Racing handlebars

Filler cap for small-capacity fuel tank

Schebler racing carburettor

Headstock forging is drilled to reduce weight

Heavy-duty racing wheel

Right-hand section of tank contains oil

Shortened exhaust header pipe allowed maximum power from the engine

Oil feed pipe

J-series engine was especially tuned for racing

JDH engine case has two cams

Blanked-off oil-pump drive; lubrication was by hand pump

Leading-link front fork

Ribbed front tyre

1942 XA

IT IS WELL DOCUMENTED THAT Harley supplied thousands of
traditional 45° V-twin WLA (*see pp.68–69*) and WLC models
to the Allied military during World War II, but the company also
produced a small number of BMW-style machines for the war effort.
The XA used a transversely mounted side-valve flat-twin cylinder
engine, had shaft drive to the rear wheel, a four-speed gearbox, and
plunger rear suspension. While it was built to the special specification
of the US military, the arrival of the immensely successful four-wheel
drive Willys Jeep changed the agenda as far as military motorcycle
use was concerned and only 1,000 XA bikes were ever made.

1942 XA

Although the WLA was a good all-round
military bike, the US army asked Harley-
Davidson to produce a shaft-drive machine
and Harley turned to the enemy for
inspiration. BMW's R75 was virtually
cloned and a test batch of 1,000 XA's were
produced. As were a batch of prototype
shaft-drive Indians, the idea being that the
better of the two bikes would be awarded a
contract. Neither satisfied the army, which
ordered extra WLAs instead, thus ending
the XA's brief life.

Leather saddlebag

Rear rack would often be
used to carry a field radio

Plunger rear
suspension unit

Tubular cradle frame

Oil bath
air cleaner

Heavy duty
saddle
spring

Kick-
starter

Curved,
flat metal
mudguard

Bevel gear
casing

46-cm (18-in)
wheel

Neutral location lever

Four-speed gearbox
and Harley's first
foot-shift

Brake pedal

"*The XA was a prototype shaft-driven machine built for the US army that was ultimately only produced in limited numbers because of the success of the Willys Jeep as a battlefield vehicle.*"

Thompson sub-machine gun

Left handlebar twist-grip operates the throttle as the rider's right hand needed to be free to use the gun

Harley's first production telescopic forks are fitted on this XA

Leather rifle holster

Front mudguard

Heavy duty tyre for all-terrain riding

Bashplate protects the engine

Wet sump lubrication system requires no external oil tank

It was claimed that the fins on the engine block kept the oil temperature 38°C (100°F) cooler than on the WLA

Security padlock

Front drum brake

18-cm (7-in) ground clearance

SPECIFICATIONS
1942 XA

- **ENGINE** Horizontally opposed side-valve twin
- **CAPACITY** 45cu. in. (738cc)
- **POWER OUTPUT** 23bhp @ 4,600rpm
- **TRANSMISSION** Four-speed, shaft drive
- **FRAME** Tubular cradle
- **SUSPENSION** Leading-link front forks, plunger rear
- **WEIGHT** 244kg (538lb)
- **TOP SPEED** 105km/h (65mph) (est.)

CHAPTER THREE
SIDE-VALVES
1929–1969

1944 U NAVY

THE SIDE-VALVE ENGINE holds a special place in American automotive history. Popular with Henry Ford on his Model T and with rival manufacturers Indian before Harley began using it in 1926, it was cheap to make, rugged, and reliable. Limited peformance meant it was soon superseded by overhead-valve units, but Harley continued to use the trusty side-valves long after other manufacturers had given up on it.

A MILITARY MACHINE
Side-valve units were used by many Allied forces during World War II, their easy maintenance making them ideal for battlefield conditions.

1933 VLE

HARLEY INTRODUCED THE V-series in 1930, 14 years after rivals Indian had made their first side-valve big twins, but the bike suffered a number of teething problems. The first two months' production had to be recalled so that frames, flywheels, engine cases, valves, springs, and kick-start mechanisms could be changed. The work was carried out for owners free of charge, but it was a costly exercise that did little for the reputation of the V-series. After the shaky start, the side-valves evolved into rugged, fast, dependable bikes and a VLE even went on to establish the American production bike speed record in 1933 of 167km/h (104mph).

1933 VLE
The VLE was the high-compression model in the series, with magnesium-alloy pistons providing the extra power. While only 3,700 bikes were built by Harley in 1933, this still accounted for 60 per cent of all motorcycles sold in the US that year.

Bird tank graphic detail was on 1933 models only

Horn fitted to toolbox

Mandarin, gold, and black was one of five new colour schemes introduced in 1933

Heavy-duty front forks introduced on the V-series from 1932

Mudguard stay

Magnesium-alloy pistons distinguish this VLE from a VL

Removable iron cylinder head

Front drum brake

Brake cable

Schebler die-cast carburettor

1930 VL

Introduced in August 1929 for the 1930 model year, this is an example of one of the all-new bikes brought in to replace the F-head V-twins. New features included the duplex primary chain, the steering head lock and the I-beam forged fork legs. Twin headlights and the klaxon horn were carried over from the 1929 model. The bike's colour scheme is the traditional olive green with vermilion striping edged in maroon and centred in gold. Drop centre wheel rims were another feature introduced with the VL.

Clutch on the VL

SPECIFICATIONS
1933 VLE

- **ENGINE** Side-valve, V-twin
- **CAPACITY** 74cu. in. (1213cc)
- **POWER OUTPUT** 22bhp
- **TRANSMISSION** Three-speed (optional reverse), hand shift
- **FRAME** Tubular cradle
- **SUSPENSION** Leading-link front forks, rigid rear
- **WEIGHT** 177kg (390lb)
- **TOP SPEED** 105km/h (65mph)

> *"The V-series were reliable side-valve V-twins that consistently out-sold every other range of Harley-Davidsons during the early 1930s."*

Chrome air filter was fitted from 1932

Leather saddle with new seat-post springs for the V-series; a "buddy seat" as well as other pillion accessories could be ordered as optional extras

Battery box

Though parts such as the chainguard came in black, the whole bike could be fully chromed for an extra $15

Tail light

Rear stand

Enclosed primary drive case with automatic oiling prolonged chain life and kept the rider's boots clean

"Drop-centre" wheel rims allowed modern beaded tyres to be fitted

48x10-cm (19x4-in) "balloon" tyres were an optional extra

1935 RL

WHEN THE ORIGINAL **D-SERIES** Harley 45s were introduced in 1929, they were nicknamed the "three-cylinder Harleys" because their vertically mounted generators resembled an extra cylinder. Harley-Davidson produced these bikes in response to the success of the popular Indian Scout, but the D-series was not considered a success and it was replaced, in 1932, by the new R-series. The critical change was the new frame, which now featured a curved front downtube and allowed the fitting of a conventional horizontal generator in front of the engine. These 45s were available in four versions: the basic R model, the high-compression RL, the RLD, and sidecar RS. The Rs were replaced by the W-series in 1936. While the European market considered a 750cc machine to be a big bike, the R-series were the smallest bikes in Harley's range in the mid-1930s.

SPECIFICATIONS
1935 RL

- **ENGINE** Side-valve, V-twin
- **CAPACITY** 45cu. in. (738cc)
- **POWER OUTPUT** 22bhp (approx.)
- **TRANSMISSION** Three-speed, hand shift
- **FRAME** Tubular cradle
- **SUSPENSION** Leading-link front forks
- **WEIGHT** 177kg (390lb) (approx.)
- **TOP SPEED** 105km/h (65mph)

Even with a sprung seat post, the lack of rear suspension made for a bumpy ride

Airflow tail light was introduced for the 1935 model year

Fold-up rear mudguard section allows easy rear-wheel changes

Tubular cradle frame

Battery box

6-cm (2½-in) diameter "gas-deflecting" silencer end

Quick-detach rear hub

Exhaust pipe painted in special high-temperature black paint

New constant mesh three-speed gearbox

1935 RL

This bike, with its diamond graphics and airflow tail light dates from 1935, though the engine number indicates that it is a 1932 motor. This kind of contradictory evidence is not uncommon when dealing with many years of history. When the R-series was introduced in 1932, the D-series 45 unit was totally re-worked, with modifications to the flywheels, crankcases, barrels, pistons, conrods, and oil pump. There were only a few minor internal changes to the engine between 1932 and 1935.

Left hand-grip ignition control

Speedometer

Air filter

Wide leather saddle

Crash bar

Footboard

Rear stand

A narrow bike
One of the benefits of the V-twin engine design is its narrow width, keeping the weight of the machine close to the centre line. The stand was fitted until Harley-Davidson adopted rear suspension.

Diamond graphic tank detail was used in 1934 and '35

Exposed suspension springs

Horn replaced toolbox in 1935

Two-tone Teak Red and black paint finish

Lightweight cover conceals the oil pump; the gear train that drives the cams, the oil pump, and the generator are hidden deeper

Mudflap

I-beam fork leg

Mudguard stay

The Flathead V-Twin

SIMPLICITY IS THE APPEAL of the side-valve, or flathead, engine. Though easy to make and maintain – there are no moving parts in the cylinder head that need to be lubricated – the downside is inefficiency. The inlet and exhaust tracts make convoluted curves so gasses have to take a long route in and out of the cylinder, resulting in poor performance and economy. However, from the 1920s to the 1950s simplicity triumphed over efficiency and the side-valve became the iconic American engine for both cars and motorcycles. Proof of its durability is found in the Servi-Car (see pp.74–75), which used side-valves until 1973.

Brief twin encounter

Although side-valves were used on the short-lived Sport Twin and on some singles, the 45cu. in. unit, as seen here on the RL, was its most famous application.

Spark plug; Harley made its own rebuildable spark plugs at the start of the side-valve era

No moving parts in the cylinder head allows the engine height to be low

Cylinder head contains specially shaped combustion chamber

Iron barrel

Valve cover conceals the valve stem, spring, and tappet adjuster

Inlet port

Inlet ports meet at the centre of the V, so only a short carburettor manifold is necessary

Alloy cylinder head with vertical cooling fins; early side-valves had iron heads

Exhaust port exits downwards; difficult gas flow limited the

Ribbed aluminium timing gear cover was introduced from 1937, designed to help cool the unit and make it more efficient

Well-used oil filler

In the side-valve era, continual engine lubrication was vital. The RL still used the constant loss system in which oil was burnt or blown out of the engine without recirculating.

Filling up the oil tank and using the extra hand-operated oil pump when necessary were essential riding rituals

"Rugged and reliable, these are the classic American V-twins. If you want to ride around the world, the best choice is a side-valve Harley-Davidson."

STEVE SLOCOMBE
(HARLEY-DAVIDSON RESTORER)

Outer casing contains the camshaft and timing gears

CONFIGURATION EXPLANATION

Exhaust and inlet valves are situated adjacent to the cylinder, hence the side-valve name, and because the valve stems have to be parallel, four separate cams are required. The inlet and exhaust ports are effectively L-shaped and it is these convoluted tracts that make the side-valve such an inefficient engine layout.

Connection to oil tank

Ignition timer fits in this hole

The oil pump is driven from the rear exhaust valve camshaft gear

THE COMPETITION

• 1930 INDIAN SCOUT •
Not so much competition as inspiration, the side-valve Indian Scout 101 was built from 1928–31 and was the benchmark 45cu. in. V-twin. It is widely regarded as the best bike Indian ever built.

THE FLATHEAD ERA – 1930 TO 1973

1900s | 1910s | 1920s | 1930s | 1940s | 1950s | 1960s | 1970s | 1980s | 1990s | 2000s

1941 WLD Sport Solo

HARLEY-DAVIDSON HAD originally followed Indian when the latter had produced its first 45 cu. in. side-valve machine in 1927. Initially, the Indian 45s were the most highly regarded, but by the time Harley introduced its W-series in 1937, it was the Milwaukee-built bikes that enjoyed the better specification and reputation. Replacing the R-series – with which they had much in common – the three models in the original line-up were the basic W, this high-compression WLD, and the competition model WLDR. The main difference over the Rs was in the new styling, which mimicked the classy 61 Knucklehead (*see pp.78–79*) that had been introduced the previous year. Just like their big brother, the 45s now had teardrop tanks with an integrated instrument panel and curved mudguards, creating a quality range that further established Harley as the market leader.

Passing light

"Aeroplane"-style speedometer

Safety bar

Footboard

Small is beautiful
The Ws were Harley's smallest machines of the period and matched the 45s put out by Indian. In terms of quality control, Harley had been ahead for some time.

1941 WLD SPORT SOLO
The 1941 model shown here is rare because by this date most of Harley's production was devoted to military machines (*see WLA, pp.68–69*). The 45s were basic, robust machines that made them ideal for converting to military bikes.

Fold-up rear mudguard section allowed easy wheel removal

The large saddle helped to compensate for the lack of rear suspension

High-compression alloy cylinder head

New tail light introduced in 1939

Rear stand

Introduction of 40-cm (16-in) wheel in 1940 improved the ride quality

New streamlined toolbox

Exhaust guard was a factory-fitted extra

SPECIFICATIONS
1941 WLD Sport Solo

- **ENGINE** Side-valve, V-twin
- **CAPACITY** 45cu. in. (738cc)
- **POWER OUTPUT** 25bhp (est.)
- **TRANSMISSION** Three-speed, chain drive
- **FRAME** Tubular cradle
- **SUSPENSION** Leading-link front forks, rigid rear
- **WEIGHT** 314kg (692lb)
- **TOP SPEED** 155km/h (96mph)

Tubular forks were added to the WLD in 1940

Throttle cable runs inside handlebar

Optional extras
By the time this bike was built Harley was offering a range of factory-fitted accessory packages. Extras on this WLD include chrome spotlights, chrome trim on the mudguards, and a front fender light.

Chrome headlight shell

Handlebar grip

Fuel tank

New recirculating lubrication system meant that the oil was contained on the left side of the fuel tank

Footboard

Rubber mudflap

Running light

Valanced mudguard

Horizontal fins on timing case differentiate R- and W-series engines

Exhaust downtube

Safety bars were an optional extra

Front and rear wheels are interchangeable

1942 WLA

THE MOTORCYCLE WAS A USEFUL vehicle for military dispatch and escort duty and had been used in these roles almost since its invention. Harley-Davidson had supplied a number of machines to the US military towards the end of World War I and, despite the fact that rivals Indian actually contributed more bikes, the company pulled off a bit of a coup when the the first US serviceman to enter Germany in 1918 was photographed riding a Harley. The outbreak of World War II created a huge demand for two-wheeled transport, with the military needing machines that would survive abuse and rugged terrain, and would also be simple to ride and repair. The WLA, based on the civilian WL models (*see pp.66–67*), fitted the bill perfectly. Together with the similar WLC model, manufactured for the Canadian armed forces and with only detail changes from the WLA, Harley-Davidson built over 80,000 of these models for the Allied war effort. Other Harley-Davidsons supplied to the military were the XA (*see pp.56–57*) and the U (*see pp.70–71*).

SPECIFICATIONS
1942 WLA

- **ENGINE** Side-valve, V-twin
- **CAPACITY** 45cu. in. (738cc)
- **POWER OUTPUT** 23bhp @ 4,600rpm
- **TRANSMISSION** Three-speed, chain drive
- **FRAME** Tubular cradle
- **SUSPENSION** Leading-link front forks, rigid rear
- **WEIGHT** 261.5kg (576lb)
- **TOP SPEED** 105km/h (65mph)

1942 WLA
The huge numbers of military Harleys made during World War II mean that the WLA is relatively common in classic bike circles. Although many are presented in their original trim, many owners have "civilianized" them by painting them in different colours and dispensing with their military accessories.

Matt paint finish with no chrome or polished alloy

Leather pannier

Sturdy back rack

The seat was positioned further forward than on the WL

Hand pump for the tyres

Tail lights have blackout covers fitted

Pressed-steel rear mudguard

Rear stand clips onto rear mudguard

Black finish exhaust with "Fishtail" silencer

Toolbox

Extended bashplate protects the gearbox and exhaust as well as the engine

Windscreen fitted with canvas fairing

Rear-view mirror

Instrument console

Rubber grip handlebars

Fuel filler-cap

Points case

Footboard

Canvas leg-shield

"The rugged side-valve WLA was the most successful military motorcycle ever built, with over 80,000 seeing action for the Allied forces during World War II."

Thompson 45mm calibre machine gun

Leather machine-gun holster

Blackout lighting made night riding interesting

Small windscreen

Front brake lever

Horn

Ammunition case

Canvas leg-shield

Daunting front
Given this imposing view of the WLA, it's hard to believe that the military considered these bikes easy to ride, but the side-valve unit proved to be very reliable.

Mudguard is cut-down and raised to prevent clogging in muddy conditions

Synthetic material replaced rubber for tyres as the war continued

Chunky block-tread tyre

Front drum brake

Ground clearance was increased by extending the forks – originally on the civilian WL model – by over 5cm (2in)

1944 U Navy

THE U MODEL WAS INTRODUCED in 1937 as a replacement for the V-series 74 and 80cu. in. twins. The redesigned engine, which had a recirculating lubrication system, was fitted into a chassis taken from the 61E Knucklehead (*see pp.78–79*) that had been introduced the previous year. The styling of other components including the fuel tank and running gear was also based on the sublime Knucklehead. Side-valve fans got an improved engine with a four-speed gearbox in a much more modern-looking package, and these large-capacity side-valve machines proved to be especially useful for sidecar work. With the outbreak of World War II Harley began supplying large numbers of machines to the Allied war effort, mainly 45cu. in. bikes (*see WLA, pp.68–69*) but also some 74cu. in. U models. This example was supplied to the US Navy and used on shore duties in Guam.

SPECIFICATIONS
1944 U Navy
- **ENGINE** Side-valve, V-twin
- **CAPACITY** 74cu. in. (1213cc)
- **POWER OUTPUT** 22bhp
- **TRANSMISSION** Four-speed, hand shift
- **FRAME** Tubular cradle
- **SUSPENSION** Leading-link front forks
- **WEIGHT** 177kg (390lb)
- **TOP SPEED** 120km/h (75mph)

> *"The U model was styled on the all-new Knucklehead, but incorporated a revised version of Harley's trusty side-valve unit."*

Twin tail lights are blacked-out

Leather pannier fitted to pressed-steel rear rack

Tubular cradle frame

Leather seat is padded with horse hair

Oil tank

Rear mudguard

Rear stand

Black-painted exhaust with "Fishtail" silencer

Toolbox with ribbed lid

Gearbox

Tubular metal kick-starter pedal

1944 U Navy

The U-series bikes were simple and rugged, making
them ideal for use in a military capacity. Modifications
on this bike include blackout lighting and a rifle holster.
War-time shortages meant that rubber handgrips were
substituted by plastic and the kick-starter pedal was
nothing more than a bare metal tube. While the 80cu.
in. version was phased out in 1941, the 74cu. in. model
remained in production until 1948.

Horn

Air filter

Ammunition
case

Front
drum
brake

Second choice
*Very few U models were used by the US
military during World War II. Production
figures for 1944 show that only 580 Us rolled
out of the factory compared to 11,531 WLAs.*

Thompson 45-
calibre machine gun

Matt paint finish
in US Navy colour

US Navy insignia
on "teardrop" tank

Leather machine
gun holster

Blackout light

Military
specification
mudguard has
no valances

U.S.N.

T.P.14

Valve-spring/
tappet covers

Ribbed steel
footboard

Heat-treated
front forks

Points case

41-cm
(16-in)
wheel

1949 WR Racer

I N **1934** THE RULES OF AMERICAN RACING were changed to encourage the participation of amateur riders on cheaper, production-based motorcycles. Though influenced by the fact that Harley-Davidson and Indian's 45cu. in. twins were comparatively cheap and popular at the time, the change meant that Harley had to put out some new models to meet the challenge of the class. In 1937 Harley offered the tuned WLDR, but the real response came in 1941 when the WR (flat-track) and WRTT (TT) models were introduced. These pure racing machines were supplied without any extraneous equipment – the WR, for example, came with footrests rather than boards, a lightweight frame, and no brakes. More importantly, the engine was much more powerful than the basic W models (*see pp.66–69*) on which the bike was based.

SPECIFICATIONS
1949 WR Racer

- ENGINE Side-valve, V-twin
- CAPACITY 45cu. in. (738cc)
- POWER OUTPUT 38bhp
- TRANSMISSION Three-speed, hand shift
- FRAME Tubular cradle
- SUSPENSION Leading-link front forks
- WEIGHT 136kg (300lb)
- TOP SPEED 177km/h (110mph) (est.)

The WR came with a choice of 46- or 48-cm (18- or 19-in) wheels

Shortened rear mudguard

Tubular cradle frame

This style of tank detail was introduced in 1947 and continued on the W-series through to 1951

Leather saddle pivots from the tank

Heavy-duty saddle springs

Frame bracing strut

Different sprockets allowed gearing changes

Rear drum brake was not an original component

Folding footpegs were fitted to the WR; WRTT models came with footboards, brakes, and a different frame

1949 WR RACER

The WR was available with a variety of components so riders could adapt the bike to suit their needs. Small fuel tanks could be fitted for short races, large ones for longer events; sprockets and tyres also came in different sizes. Harley's real innovation with the WR was to empower amateur racers by offering them such a wealth of options, resulting in the growth in popularity of amateur bike racing.

Post-war racing victories
Harley-Davidson had phenomenal racing success in the years immediately after World War II, especially in events such as this 100-mile (161-km) road race in 1947. Harley's racing stars of the period included Babe Tancrede, winner of the Laconia 100-mile (161-km) race in 1947 and Jimmy Chann, who won the Grand National Championship in 1947, '48, and '49, as well as winning the 1949 Langhorne 100-mile (161-km) race.

Red extended control grip is a nice period touch

Exposed suspension springs

Oil filler-cap

Cast-iron headstock is drilled to reduce weight

Thick dirt-track racing tyre

Right side of fuel tank actually contains engine oil

Aluminium cylinder head

Exhaust retaining spring

Two-into-one exhaust system provided optimum power

Vertical Wico magneto was derived from a unit originally intended for tractor engines

Strengthened spokes on racing wheel

Leading-link front suspension

1969 GE Servi-Car

First introduced in 1932, series G Servi-Cars were popular with US police departments until the 1970s. They were often ridden by meter maids on parking patrol and were geared for low-speed use. The rider would drive the bike slowly past parked cars while marking the cars tyres using chalk on a stick. When the officer returned an hour later, any cars with a chalk mark on their tyre would receive a ticket. Many Servi-Cars were fitted with a left-hand throttle so that the rider's right hand was free to use the chalk. They were engineered to be user friendly as they were used by unskilled riders.

SPECIFICATIONS

1969 GE Servi-Car

- **ENGINE** Side-valve, V-twin
- **CAPACITY** 45cu. in. (738cc)
- **POWER OUTPUT** 22bhp
- **TRANSMISSION** Three-speed forward, one-speed reverse
- **FRAME** Tubular cradle with additional rear subframe
- **SUSPENSION** Telescopic front forks, swingarm rear
- **WEIGHT** 271kg (598lb)
- **TOP SPEED** 105km/h (65mph)

Radio aerial

Fibreglass was used for the box construction from 1967, replacing sheet metal and wood

Leather solo saddle

The gargantuan storage box was advertised as being able to carry loads of up to 227kg (500lb)

41-cm (16-in) pressed-steel wheel with chrome hubcap

Rear sub-frame provides necessary support for the box and extra wheel

Generator

1969 GE SERVI-CAR

The 45cu. in. side-valve engine was gradually updated throughout the Servi-Car's 42-year production run, but it remained essentially the same unit used on the pre-war machines. The Servi-Car was used as a guinea pig for Harley's first electric starter in 1964; once proved, the system was fitted to the Electra Glide (*see pp.90–91*) the following year.

Wing mirror

Parking brake lock

Windscreen is height-adjustable

Police light

Indicator

Lever-operated siren

Aluminium headlight nacelle is painted black

Instrument panel

Chrome headlight peak

Right side of the fuel tank contains lubricating oil

Practical machine
Three wheels meant this was a safe bike to ride and, with its enormous carrying capacity, it appealed to general goods traders as well as police forces.

Dynamo-operated siren would take over a minute to wind down

HARLEY-DAVIDSON

Cast-iron cylinders and heads

Engine design remained almost unchanged from W-series solo machines (*see pp.64–67*)

Electric starter case

Deeply valanced mudguard with chrome trim

Telescopic forks are the same as those used on the big-twins

Front drum brake

OHV BIG-TWINS

1936–1984

1936 61EL "KNUCKLEHEAD"

KNUCKLEHEAD, PANHEAD, AND SHOVELHEAD can only be used as terms of endearment when discussing Harley-Davidson motorcycles. These were the nicknames given to the overhead-valve engines that powered Harley's big-twins from 1936 to 1984. Another great name in this chapter of Harley history is the Electra Glide, probably the single most famous motorbike in the world. Harley's big-twins really were the true embodiment of the American motorcycle.

STAR BIKES
Peter Fonda, seen here in the film The Wild Angels, *went on to star in the quintessential Harley-Davidson chopper film,* Easy Rider.

1936 61EL

Some people consider the 61 "Knucklehead" to be the bike that put Indian out of business; others claim it was the bike that saved Harley-Davidson. Either way, this was Harley's first proper production overhead-valve twin and, introduced in 1936, it was a ground-breaking machine. The crucial new feature on the bike was its all-new overhead-valve Knucklehead engine which, for the first time on a Harley, also had a recirculating lubrication system. But the 61 wasn't just about improved technology – it was also one of the best-looking bikes that Harley ever built and elements of its design can be seen in the cruisers of today. The teardrop fuel tank, curved mudguards, and elegant detailing gave the bike a tight, purposeful, and modern look. Although the 61EL suffered delays in development and teething troubles in production, it became one of the best-loved Harleys ever made.

SPECIFICATIONS
1936 61EL

- **ENGINE** Overhead-valve, V-twin
- **CAPACITY** 61cu. in. (1000cc)
- **POWER OUTPUT** 40bhp @ 4,800rpm
- **TRANSMISSION** Four-speed, chain drive
- **FRAME** Twin downtube tubular cradle
- **SUSPENSION** Leading-link front forks, rigid rear
- **WEIGHT** 234kg (515lb)
- **TOP SPEED** 161km/h (100mph)

Shape of the alloy rocker boxes gives the engine its Knucklehead name

Harley's patented sprung saddle

Air-flow streamlined tail light

46-cm (18-in) rear and front wheels are interchangeable

Teak Red and black colour scheme was one of five offered for 1936

Twin downtube cradle frame

Rear stand

Exhaust fitted with Burgess "fishtail" silencer

Oil tank is wrapped around the battery

Four-speed gearbox

Kick-starter pedal

1936 61EL

The 61 incorporated a four-speed, constant mesh gearbox and a cradle frame. These features, combined with the new engine block, gave the bike improved performance and reliability over its side-valve predecessor. The 61 was produced in three models: 61E (medium compression), 61EL (Special Sport solo), and 61ES (medium compression sidecar). A 74cu. in. version of the Knucklehead engine (available in F, FL, and FS models) was introduced in 1941 (*see pp.82–83*).

Twist-grip throttle control

Large-diameter headlight

Control cables run inside the handlebars

Gear lever

Winged-face horn with chrome cover

Crash bar was a standard fitting

More innovations
The 61 carried Harley-Davidson's first four-speed, constant mesh gearbox, yet another feature that in technological terms pushed Harley ahead of its rivals Indian.

Beautifully sculpted fuel tank incorporates the instrument console

Front suspension springs

Teardrop fuel tank

Friction suspension damper

Stylish curved mudguard

Diagonal air intake only used on 1936 models

Points case was in this position on the big-twins until 1970

Folding footboard

Chrome molybdenum fork legs replaced the forged I-beams on the side-valve bikes

Colour-co-ordinated wheel rim

The Knucklehead

THE KNUCKLEHEAD ENGINE, so named because of the shape of its rocker covers, came with two significant new features when it was introduced in 1936. The first was overhead valves, which boosted power from the V-twin unit, and the second was a single camshaft arrangement that would be used on Harley's big-twins for the next 60 years. The Knucklehead was also the first Harley-Davidson to incorporate a recirculating oil system, where oil was constantly fed through the engine rather than just burnt off.

1936 61E

As well as the the 61EL, the Knucklehead was also fitted to the 61E. The difference between the models was that the EL had a high-compression Knucklehead unit, whereas the E had medium-compression.

From above, the cylinders reveal a crude valve-spring enclosure and partly exposed rocker-arm shafts

Exhaust port

Contact breaker case

Rocker shaft retaining nut; the other end is bolted to the cylinder head

Carburettor manifold

Pushrod tube

Oil-feed pipe; oil was returned to the crankcases via the pushrod tubes

Alloy cases on the top of the cylinder heads enclose the rockers

Cooling fins on cylinder barrel

2000s
1990s
1980s
1970s
1960s
1950s
1940s
1930s ▶
1920s
1910s
1900s

Ribbed timing gear case

Engine case screw

New dry sump lubrication system meant that oil recirculated rather than just burnt off

THE COMPETITION

• 1938 CROCKER •

The Crocker was produced in limited numbers in California, but it was one of the few bikes capable of out-running a good Knucklehead. It was built in the classic style of an American V-twin and was available in the traditional red, white, and blue colour scheme.

Single camshaft was superior to the twin and four-cam systems used by Harley in the past

"Right there is the engine that put the Indian Motorcycle Company out of business."

LAURIE MAYERS
(KNUCKLEHEAD OWNER)

Aerodynamic fairing and fork

Disc wheel

Crankcase bolt

Oil pump

The Knucklehead originally had a capacity of 61cu. in., but a 74cu. in. version became available from 1941

WHY KNUCKLEHEAD?

Clench your fist, look at the back of your hand, and you'll see why this was called the Knucklehead. The polished nuts that retain the rocker arms are the knuckles and the pushrod tubes are the tendons running down the back of the hand. With its overhead valvegear and recirculating lubrication system, the Knucklehead was a giant leap forward for Harley-Davidson.

Aerodynamic body shell

Nationwide publicity
In March 1937, this streamlined Knucklehead achieved a record speed of 220km/h (136.183mph) when ridden by Joe Petrali at Daytona Beach, Florida. With the Knucklehead released just the year before, it was confirmation of the new engine's pedigree.

1941 74FL

THE HARLEY-DAVIDSON PHILOSOPHY of making a good idea bigger was applied to the Knucklehead engine in 1941 when capacity was increased to 74 cubic inches, though the 61cu. in. model remained in production. As well as the larger engine, the frame was stronger and adjustments had been made to the transmission since the Knucklehead first appeared in 1936 (*see pp.78–81*). Despite regular revamps, the evolution of Harley's big overhead-valve engine has been continuous and gradual, and there is a direct link between today's big-twins and the 1936 model. From 1942, production of the Knucklehead was badly disrupted by the war, with Harley redirecting its efforts to producing military bikes, and the FL wasn't back in production in significant numbers until 1946. It remained largely unchanged until the Knucklehead was replaced by the Panhead (*see pp.86–87*) in 1948.

SPECIFICATIONS
1941 74FL

- **ENGINE** Overhead-valve, V-twin
- **CAPACITY** 74cu. in. (1213cc)
- **POWER OUTPUT** 48bhp @ 5,000rpm
- **TRANSMISSION** Four-speed, hand shift
- **FRAME** Tubular cradle
- **SUSPENSION** Leading-link front forks
- **WEIGHT** 243kg (535lb)
- **TOP SPEED** 169km/h (105mph)

Smooth brown cowhide leather seat

Knucklehead rocker cover

Fold-up rear section allows easy wheel removal

Skyway Blue was one of five colours in the Harley range for 1941

Black painted "boat-tail" rear light

Battery is situated in the middle of the horseshoe-shaped oil tank

Rear stand

New, quieter, "speed-lined" silencer was introduced for 1941

Streamlined toolbox designed by Raymond Loewy

Chromed exhaust pipe covers

1941 74FL

Comparing the profile of this 1941 Knucklehead with the 1936 bike (*see pp. 78–79*), it is clear to see how much the model had developed in only five years. The streamlined toolbox, round air filter and speed-tuned exhaust all contribute to a more modern appearance, aided by the input of designer Raymond Loewy. With design credits that included the Greyhound Scenicruiser bus and the Studebaker Avanti, Loewy was one of the most influential designers of the 20th century.

Wide handlebars

Filler-cap for 3.8-litre (1-gallon) reserve fuel tank

Imposing front
The chrome horn with embossed winged motif was introduced on the original 1936 Knucklehead and, combined with the high-mounted headlight, gave the FL a handsome front profile.

Foot-operated clutch lever

"Cat's eye" instrument console

Suspension springs

Metal tank badge introduced in 1940

Chrome horn

Wheels measuring 41 cm (16 in) were optional from 1940 and gave improved ride comfort over the old larger style

New vane-type oil pump replaced double-gear unit

18-cm (7-in) diameter circular air cleaner

Chrome mudguard trim

Whitewall tyre

1951 74FL Hydra-Glide

HARLEY HAD BEEN KEEPING ITS riders comfortable using the springer leading-link fork (introduced 1907) and the sprung seat-post (introduced 1912) for years. By 1949, though, the merits of hydraulically damped telescopic forks were obvious and from that year they were fitted to the 61 and 74cu. in. twins; hence the name Hydra-Glide. Another development had taken place the previous year with the arrival of the Panhead engine (*see pp.86–87*) to replace the Knucklehead. Though regarded as a classic, the Knucklehead had been prone to oil leaks and the new unit sought to address this problem – the Panhead moniker referred to the large rocker covers that enclosed the valvegear and kept the oil inside the engine. Combined with the new hydraulic valve-lifters, these modifications all amounted to reduced wear on the engine and completed another successful chapter in the history of Harley's big-twins.

SPECIFICATIONS
1951 74FL Hydra-Glide

- **ENGINE** Overhead-valve, V-twin
- **CAPACITY** 74cu. in. (1213cc)
- **POWER OUTPUT** 55bhp @ 4,800rpm
- **TRANSMISSION** Four-speed, hand shift
- **FRAME** Tubular cradle
- **SUSPENSION** Hydraulically damped telescopic forks, rigid rear
- **WEIGHT** 271kg (598lb)
- **TOP SPEED** 164km/h (102mph)

1951 74FL HYDRA-GLIDE
The L designation denotes this as a high-compression model, and the 74FL was Harley's biggest-selling model in 1951, with over 6,000 units sold. Optional foot-shift and hand-lever clutch were introduced in 1952 on the new FLF model.

First-aid kit came as part of the police option package

Mudguard-mounted fire extinguisher

Panhead rocker cover

Radio equipment stored in this wooden pannier

Solo leather saddle still uses the sprung seat-post first seen in 1912

Tail light

Rear stand

41x13-cm (16x5-in) tyre

"Mellow-tone" silencer was introduced from 1950 and designed to reduce levels of exhaust noise

Horseshoe-shaped oil tank with battery in centre

Four-speed gearbox

Exhaust downtube

Windscreen is height-adjustable

Tinted lower windscreen section

Large-diameter headlight sits in a pressed-steel upper fork panel

Hydraulically damped telescopic forks from which the Hydra-Glide gets its name

Policeman's favourite
This particular bike was used by the Willowick Police Department, Ohio. Harley sold large numbers of bikes to police forces and offered a standard police accessory group costing $78.75 in 1951.

Pursuit light

Mudguard-mounted police sign

Silver-grey police paint finish

Chrome mudguard trim

Eight-rib timing gear cover new for 1951

New chrome tank badge with script lettering and bar

Black spoked wheel and rim

One-piece front safety guard

20-cm (8-in) front drum brake

The Panhead

THERE WASN'T MUCH WRONG with the Knucklehead (*see pp.80–81*), but the Panhead is proof that you can improve on a good idea. Though the new engine was essentially a Knucklehead bottom end with a revised top section, there were a number of significant changes on the Panhead. Fully enclosed valvegear made the engine quieter and cleaner, and hydraulic valve-lifters cut down on maintenance. In addition, new aluminium cylinder heads were capped with large pan-shaped rocker covers which gave the bike its name.

Official choice
With the demise of Indian in 1953, Harleys became the only choice for police departments. Many Americans got their first close look at a motorcycle as they explained their slip-ups to a Harley-mounted highway patrol officer.

Rocker covers are lined with felt to reduce noise

Exhaust port

Points unit; timing

Air filter cover

Inlet manifold

New aluminium cylinder head

Pressed-steel rocker cover

Exhaust port; exhaust pipe is fitted to the heads

gear case

The Panhead came in both 61 and 74cu. in. capacities, though the smaller engine was phased out in 1953; there was also a choice of medium- or high-compression units

Crankcase bolt

Hydraulic valve-lifters positioned at the bottom of the pushrod

Oil pressure gauge is an addition to this modified engine

Screw regulates oil pump's delivery rate

Feed pipe to oil tank

THE COMPETITION

• 1951 INDIAN CHIEF ROADMASTER • The Indian Chief may have been one of the most stylish bikes ever built, but technologically it was way behind the Panhead. Side-valves and a crude three-speed box were no match for the ohv four-speed Harley.

REVISION RATHER THAN REVAMP

The similarities between the Pan and the Knuckle are obvious, but the later engine has a much cleaner appearance. However, the Panhead was revised in 1955 when larger engine casings were fitted.

"The Panhead was classic Harley-Davidson thinking – take something that works [the Knucklehead] and make it better."

CLIVE WESSLER
(PANHEAD OWNER)

Pan handling

Cowboys would have been happy to cook their beans in these pans and it's obvious how the engine got its name. The alloy collar slips over the pan and a series of screws secure it to the cylinder head.

2000s | 1990s | 1980s | 1970s | 1960s | 1950s | 1940s | 1930s | 1920s | 1910s | 1900s

1960 FLH Duo-Glide

BY THE LATE **1950s**, HARLEY'S big-twins had captured a section of the market for big, comfortable, large-capacity tourers. Weight wasn't an issue, but comfort and dependability were. In 1958 Harley finally added rear swingarm suspension to its "Panhead" big-twin and celebrated the addition with the Duo-Glide model name. By the time that this model was built in 1960, almost no two Harleys were the same, as owners tended to load their machines with extra components in order to individualize the looks and improve the comfort and capabilities of their bike. Harley offered a range of accessory groups and colour schemes, which meant that buyers could specify the extras they wanted on their machine when they ordered it from the dealer. These accessory-laden machines came to be known as "dressers".

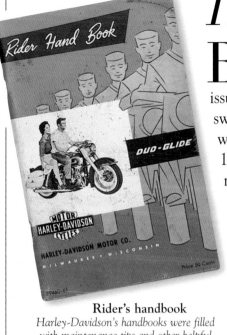

Rider's handbook
Harley-Davidson's handbooks were filled with maintenance tips and other helpful hints. In addition, the comprehensive network of knowledgeable Harley dealers would always provide assistance if things went wrong.

Number-plate holder

Round tail light

This model is painted in the optional colour scheme of Hi-Fi Red with Birch White tank panels

Safety guards

Fibreglass rear panniers were an optional extra

Chrome silencer

Cast-iron rear brake is hydraulically operated

Luggage carrier

Chrome-covered shock absorber, with the rear suspension giving the Duo-Glide its name

Passenger grab-rail

Heavy-duty saddle combined with the new rear suspension made this a perfect touring bike

Kick-starter

Vertical toolbox

Saddle springs were retained despite the new rear suspension

Windscreen redesigned this year to incorporate new fork nacelle

Wing mirror

"Arrow-flite" tank badge

Red tinted lower windscreen section

Ball-ended handlebar lever

New aluminium fork nacelle

SPECIFICATIONS
1960 FLH Duo-Glide

- **ENGINE** Overhead-valve, V-twin
- **CAPACITY** 74cu. in. (1213cc)
- **POWER OUTPUT** 55bhp @ 7,200rpm
- **TRANSMISSION** Four-speed, hand shift
- **FRAME** Tubular cradle
- **SUSPENSION** Hydraulically damped telescopic forks, rear swingarm
- **WEIGHT** 304kg (670lb)
- **TOP SPEED** 160km/h (100mph)

1960 FLH Duo-Glide

The FLH designation had been introduced in 1955 for the top-of-the-range models after a revamp of the "Panhead" had produced a more efficient block resulting in greater horsepower. The H indicated that the engine had polished ports and "Victory" camshafts, which Harley claimed gave a 10-per cent power increase.

Chrome fork shroud

Single front drum brake

Chrome mudguard bars

Trumpet horn was fitted as standard

Ribbed timing case cover

Exhaust has a chrome cover

Rear brake pedal for new hydraulic system

Elaborate mudguard detailing

Whitewall tyre

1965 74FLHB Electra Glide

IN THE EARLY 1960S ELECTRIC starters were being offered by the emerging Japanese manufacturers on even their smallest machines, so Harley felt obliged to fit them on its 1200cc machines. The system was developed for the three-wheeled Servi-Car (*see pp.74–75*) in 1964 and, having proved its reliability, was fitted to the FLH the following year to create the Electra Glide. A larger battery and 12-volt electrical system was needed to run the starter, so the oil tank on the FLH had to be redesigned. Harley continued to fit the kick-starter alongside the new system for a while so that riders could impress their friends with their one-kick starting technique (and when it didn't work they could press the button).

1965 74FLHB ELECTRA GLIDE
While 1965 was the first year of the famous Electra Glide, it was also the last year for the Panhead engine. This example is a hand-shift model, which Harley continued to offer as an option until 1973. The foot clutch is on the left side, the shift-lever is on the left side of the tank, and the front brake is on the left-side handlebar. This bike is still in regular use and covers thousands of miles every year.

Sprung seat post

Kick-starter pedal was retained on early Electra Glides

Chrome passenger grab rail

Alloy rear mudguard support

Rear number plate

Tail light

"Fishtail" silencer

Two-into-one exhaust system; a two-pipe system was an option

Chrome shock absorber cover

High-output battery situated on the right side of the frame; oil tank was moved to the left

Electric starter button

Wing mirror

Wide-diameter handlebar grips

12-volt headlight

Polished alloy headlight nacelle

Optional front spotlight

Front brake lever

Instrument console

SPECIFICATIONS
1965 74FLHB Electra Glide

- **ENGINE** Overhead-valve, V-twin
- **CAPACITY** 74cu. in. (1213cc)
- **POWER OUTPUT** 60bhp @ 5,400rpm
- **TRANSMISSION** Four-speed, hand shift
- **FRAME** Tubular steel cradle
- **SUSPENSION** Hydraulically damped telescopic forks, rear swingarm
- **WEIGHT** 355kg (783lb)
- **TOP SPEED** 158km/h (98mph)

"The 1965 FLH bikes were the first Harley big-twins to be fitted with electric starters and the only Electra Glides powered by the Panhead engine."

Indicators fitted from 1963

Electra Glide front mudguard script

This style of tank badge was used from 1963 to 1965

Crash bar

Rear brake pedal

Panhead engine fitted on the Electra Glide for 1965 only

41x13-cm (16x5-in) tyre provided superior ride quality

Front drum brake

1971 FX Super Glide

Though Harley-Davidson frowned on the customizers who chopped and modified its machines in the 1960s – and certainly didn't approve of the influence of the film Easy Rider – the company introduced its own tribute to the customizing trend in 1971. The FX Super Glide mated a kick-start 74cu. in. engine with the forks and front wheel from a Sportster to give the bike a chopper-inspired look. Styled by Willie G. Davidson, grandson of co-founder William A. Davidson, the idea was to combine the grunt of the big F-series engine with the lean looks of the X-series Sportsters. But although the Super Glide concept proved to be a winner in the long run, the unique bodywork on the 1971 model was too much for customers of the time and '72 models came with a more conventional seat and mudguard.

SPECIFICATIONS

1971 FX Super Glide

- **Engine** Overhead-valve, V-twin
- **Capacity** 74cu. in. (1213cc)
- **Power output** 65bhp @ 5,400rpm
- **Transmission** Four-speed, left foot-shift
- **Frame** Tubular cradle
- **Suspension** Telescopic front forks, swingarm rear
- **Weight** 254kg (559lb) (with half a tank of fuel)
- **Top speed** 174km/h (108mph)

"Boat-tail" design was only made in 1971

Fibreglass seat unit was developed by Harley's golf-cart division

Only a small battery is needed because the FX is not fitted with an electric starter

13.25-litre (3½-gallon) two-part fuel tank

Shovelhead rocker cover

SUPER GLIDE

Silencer

The wheel rim is a non-standard alloy version

Two-into-one exhaust system

Chromed kick-starter spring cover

Kick-starter

Single chromed
wing mirror

Fuel filler-cap for
the right-side of
the two-part tank

1971 FX Super Glide

This bike is an unrestored and in-use
example of the much sought-after 1971
Super Glide, with the "Sparkling America"
red, white, and blue colour scheme and
"boat-tail" seat unit. These one-year-only
elements to the bike have ensured that the
'71 is now a collector's piece. This style of
seat was also an option on 1971 Sportsters.

Sportster-style
headlight with
"eyebrow"

Buckhorn,
custom-style
handlebars

Circular
tail light

Primary
drive casing

Fold-up
footrest

Light switch and
speedometer are
mounted in the
tank-top dash

Rear profile
*The slim rear profile of the Super
Glide is only compromized by the
bulbous primary drive casing.
Even so, the FX looked like no
other bike Harley had produced.*

41-cm
(16-in)
rear wheel

Non-standard
rubber fork
gaiter

Brake
cable

Sportster
front fork

"Ham can"
air filter

Chrome cover for
master cylinder
operating the rear brake

"Cone" alternator cover
was used on the Shovelhead
engine from 1970

Single leading-shoe
front drum brake

48-cm (19-in)
front wheel

The Shovelhead

THE KNUCKLEHEAD LOOKED LIKE knuckles, the Panhead looked like pans, so the Shovelhead looked like… but you have to squint and use your imagination. Introduced in 1966, the Shovelhead's new cast-alloy rocker boxes on the revised cylinder heads gave the engine its distinctive shape. It was quieter, cleaner, more efficient, and a bit more powerful than the Panhead (see pp. 86–87). The bottom end of the engine was almost identical to that on the Panhead until a revamp in 1970 changed the electrical supply from generator to alternator power.

Shovelhead chopper

The Shovelhead engine is at the heart of the classic chopper. It is possible to build up a cloned Harley engine just using parts from after-market suppliers.

Alloy rocker cover replaces the one-piece cover used on the Panhead

Nine cooling fins indicate that this is a 74cu. in. model; 80cu. in. versions

Rocker cover looks like a shovel turned upside down

Large "ham can" air filter

Carburettor

Rocker shafts are retained by recessed bolts

Pushrod tube

Exhaust pipes are fitted with two screws and a collar

1984 FLHX Electra Glide

AFTER **18** YEARS IN PRODUCTION the Shovelhead engine was replaced in 1984 by the new, but externally similar, Evolution engines (*see pp.144–45*). The FLHX was the swansong of the Shovelhead Electra Glides, a special limited-edition model (apparently only 1,250 were made) available in black or white with wire-spoked wheels and full touring equipment. Cynics would say that this was a good excuse to use up the last of the old-style engines, while others might argue that an engine with the reputation and life span of the Shovelhead deserved a celebratory parting shot. Either way it was the end of an era.

1984 FLHX ELECTRA GLIDE

The 80cu. in. Shovelhead engine had been introduced in 1978 and the long-established 74cu. in. version had been discontinued in 1981, three years before the 80's demise. Both had been sterling power units but had been somewhat left behind by the new technologies being developed by foreign competition. But ultimately the FLHX was a fitting last shell for the Shovelhead block, ending an era where the old workhorse had become synonymous with the whole concept of Harley touring bikes.

Passenger backrest

Safety relector

"King and queen" seat gives the pillion passenger a raised view

Larger (by 15 per cent) panniers were introduced in 1983

Luggage rack

Battery box

Circular indicator

Harley-Davidson Motor Co. Special Edition Electra-Glide

"Fishtail" exhaust silencer

Rear disc brake first appeared on the Electra Glide in 1973

Box section steel swingarm

Folded-up passenger footboard

Height-adjustable
windscreen

Square wing
mirror

Windscreen
support frame

Handlebar-
switchgear

Alloy
headlight
peak

Gold stripes and
red pinstriping
are unique to
the FLHX

Passing
light

SPECIFICATIONS
1984 FLHX Electra Glide

- **ENGINE** Overhead-valve, V-twin
- **CAPACITY** 80cu. in. (1312cc)
- **POWER OUTPUT** 65bhp (est.)
- **TRANSMISSION** Four-speed, left foot-shift, belt drive
- **FRAME** Tubular cradle
- **SUSPENSION** Telescopic front forks, swingarm rear
- **WEIGHT** 341kg (752lb) (with half a tank of fuel)
- **TOP SPEED** 145km/h (90mph)

*"The FLHX Electra Glide
was a limited-edition model
that had, at its heart, the last
of Harley's Shovelhead units."*

Indicator

Chromed fork shroud

Wire-spoked wheel

Special Edition Electra-Glide

Huge airbox
advertises the FLHX's
80cu. in. capacity

Flexible mountings
reduce engine
vibration

Front disc brake,
first introduced on
the 1971 Electra Glide

Crash bar

Whitewall
tyre

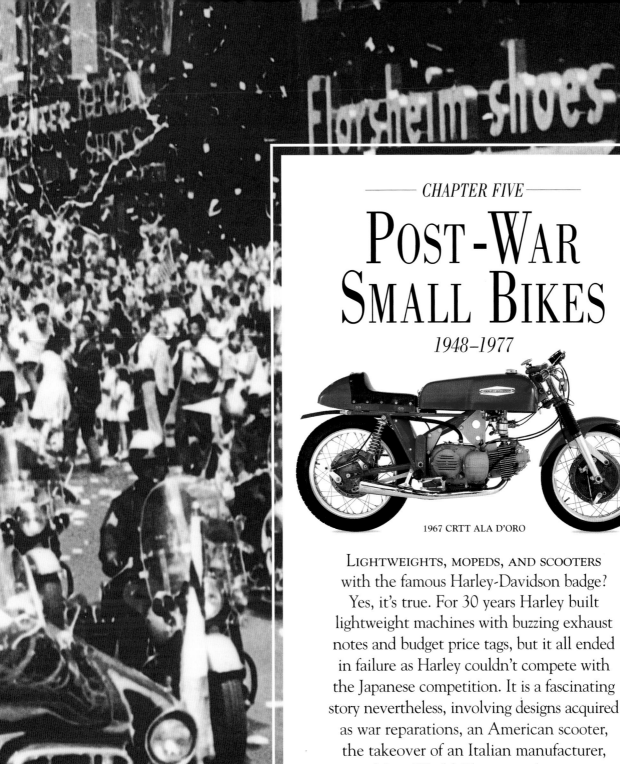

CHAPTER FIVE

POST-WAR SMALL BIKES

1948–1977

1967 CRTT ALA D'ORO

LIGHTWEIGHTS, MOPEDS, AND SCOOTERS with the famous Harley-Davidson badge? Yes, it's true. For 30 years Harley built lightweight machines with buzzing exhaust notes and budget price tags, but it all ended in failure as Harley couldn't compete with the Japanese competition. It is a fascinating story nevertheless, involving designs acquired as war reparations, an American scooter, the takeover of an Italian manufacturer, and four World Championship wins.

HARLEY-DAVIDSON CONVOY

The Apollo 11 astronauts get a Harley-Davidson convoy through the streets of New York in 1969. The 1960s was the decade when Harley-Davidson produced its widest range of small motorcycles.

1955 ST

HARLEY'S LITTLE 125cc TWO-STROKE first appeared in the range for the 1948 season. The design was based on the German DKW, which was made available to Harley, and to the British BSA group, as part of war reparations. Harley gave the bike its own styling details, which were based on those used on the bigger models. The new bike was designated the Model S and a 165cc version was introduced for 1953. Throughout its seven-year production run the ST retained a three-speed gearbox and rigid rear, so by the time it reached the end of its life it must have appeared very old fashioned. From 1960 Harley offered a new model based on the same engine (see *Bobcat pp.104–05*) but even these didn't get rear suspension until 1963.

<table>
<tr><td colspan="2" align="center">SPECIFICATIONS</td></tr>
<tr><td colspan="2" align="center">1955 ST</td></tr>
<tr><td>• ENGINE</td><td>Two-stroke single</td></tr>
<tr><td>• CAPACITY</td><td>165cc</td></tr>
<tr><td>• POWER OUTPUT</td><td>7bhp</td></tr>
<tr><td>• TRANSMISSION</td><td>Three-speed</td></tr>
<tr><td>• FRAME</td><td>Tubular cradle</td></tr>
<tr><td>• SUSPENSION</td><td>Telescopic forks, rigid rear</td></tr>
<tr><td>• WEIGHT</td><td>77kg (170lb)</td></tr>
<tr><td>• TOP SPEED</td><td>89km/h (55mph) (est.)</td></tr>
</table>

1955 ST

The basic design of the ST may have been German, but Harley Americanised it by using the company's own style of motorcycle parts. The fuel tank, mudguards, seat, headlight, and other details were all derived from those fitted to bigger machines in the Harley range. It may not have been a big-twin, but it was a Harley-Davidson.

"Peanut" fuel tank shape was created for the original 125 and survives in the Sportster

Battery case with horizontally mounted ampmeter

Tassled leather saddle

"V" Harley badge used on the ST from 1955–56

Bullet-shaped tail light

Rear brake linkage

Chromed steel wheel rim

Exhaust retaining bracket

Folding rubber-covered footrest

Cast-alloy carburettor cover

> "The ST was descended from the German DKW bike acquired by Harley after World War II as part of reparations."

German origins
DKW's influence was global in the years after World War II. Small two-strokes featuring the gear pedal and kick-starter on the same axis – a DKW trademark – were produced in at least six different countries.

Windscreen support

Lightweight "Tele-Glide" front forks first appeared in 1951

Fuel filler-cap unscrews and contains a cup for measuring oil

Optional leather panniers

Fork yoke panel incorporates the speedometer

Left foot-shift lever

Kick-starter lever

Prop stand

Headlight style and mounting are derived from the Hydra-Glide (see pp.82–83)

Mudguard stay

Tinted windscreen

Chrome front mudguard trim is non-standard

Crash bars were optional

Light switch

Exhaust pipe

Valanced mudguard

Small drum brake copes with the sedate performance and light weight of the ST

Footrest

Silencer

48x8.3-cm (19x3¼-in) wheel

Extra refinements
This example is fitted with non-standard, but period, screen and panniers and has additional chrome trim on the mudguards.

1964 AH Topper

T HE AMERICAN SCOOTER MARKET had flourished in the 1950s,
but the arrival of the 165cc Topper scooter to the Harley range in
1959 heralded the end of the boom. Scooter buyers wanted bikes that
were easy to ride and, though the Topper met this criterion, its boxy
styling was no match for the attractive curves of the contemporary
Italian Vespa and Lambretta scooters. Intriguingly, a sidecar option was
offered. The Topper was dropped from the Harley catalogue after the
1965 season, much to the pleasure of die-hard Harley enthusiasts.

SPECIFICATIONS
1964 AH Topper

- **ENGINE** Two-stroke, single cylinder
- **CAPACITY** 165cc
- **POWER OUTPUT** 9bhp
- **TRANSMISSION** Automatic
- **FRAME** Steel frame
- **SUSPENSION** Swingarm front and rear
- **WEIGHT** 90kg (200lb)
- **TOP SPEED** 105km/h (65mph)

Lift-up seat with under-seat storage

1964 was first year of rear badging

Hand-pulled recoil starter

Exhaust pipe

Fibreglass body panels in two-tone paint scheme

Passenger footrest

"Scootaway" transmission has chain final drive

Large silencer muted the 165cc two-stroke engine

Front brake lever on the left handlebar had a lock on it so it could also be used as a parking brake

Handlebars were more streamlined than on previous versions

Horn grille

Apart from this Fiesta Red and white, the only other paint finish on offer in 1964 was black and white

Horn

Revised grips fitted for the 1962 model year

Legshields and front mudguard were constructed of metal

1964 AH TOPPER
While the Topper may have been a bit lacking in style, it was no worse than most other American-built machines of the era. A centrifugal clutch and belt-drive system with variable diameter pulleys provided automatic gear change and the two-stroke engine had a reed valve in the induction system. Quirkily, it was started with a pull cord, like a lawn mower.

White painted headlight with chrome trim

Each wheel has 13-cm (5-in) brakes

Commuter runaround
With the Topper Harley-Davidson was trying to appeal to the urban buyer who needed a stress-free form of transportation, and it achieved this with some measure of success.

Rear brake pedal

Footboard with rubber mat

30-cm (12-in) pressed-steel wheel

Exhaust mounting bracket

Unconventional right-hand propstand

Swingarm front suspension has a shock absorber on this side only

1966 BTH Bobcat

THE AMERICAN MOTORCYCLE MARKET was shaken up in the 1960s by the arrival of vast numbers of Japanese machines. In 1963 Harley introduced the BT Pacer, a revamp of its old 165 (*see pp.100–101*) with a new frame – finally incorporating rear suspension – and a new 175cc engine. A further rework for 1966 produced the Bobcat, a one-year-only model whose styling reflected the fashion for off-road biking at the time. This was the final version of the DKW-derived two-stroke and the last Harley lightweight to be built in America – Harley's acquisition of Aermacchi in 1960 meant production shifted to Italy after 1966. Though a valiant attempt, it failed to match its well-equipped and competitively priced Japanese contemporaries.

SPECIFICATIONS
1966 BTH Bobcat

- **ENGINE** Single cylinder, two-stroke
- **CAPACITY** 175cc
- **POWER OUTPUT** 10bhp (est.)
- **TRANSMISSION** Three-speed, chain drive
- **FRAME** Tubular cradle
- **SUSPENSION** Telescopic front forks, swingarm rear
- **WEIGHT** Not known
- **TOP SPEED** 105km/h (65mph) (est.)

Rear light housing follows lines of moulded body

The tank cover/ mudguard unit was a one-piece resin moulding

Solo and dual seat options were available

Horn

High-level exhaust pipe

Pressed-steel chainguard

49-tooth rear sprocket could be switched to an 84-tooth version for off-road use

Pressed-steel swingarm

Horizontal springs for rear suspension

Heat shield

1966 BTH Bobcat

The Bobcat was the last in a long line of Harley two-strokes produced from 1948. The Model 125 was released that year in response to the need for an economical bike for the post-war climate and over the next few years a succession of variants followed, with engine sizes ranging from 125 to 175cc. These included the Hummer, Pacer, Scat, Ranger, and Super 10.

Large-diameter twist-grip

7.5-litre (1⅝-gallon) fuel tank is hidden under the fibreglass bodywork

Central speedometer

Chrome-trimmed headlight

Hexagonal tank badge

Single-downtube frame

Brake cable

Fork slider telescopes into the upper section of the simple forks

One of six mudguard stays

Alloy engine/gearbox unit

46-cm (18-in) wheel

Brake lever

Single mirror

Holiday Red paint finish came as standard, as did Indigo Metallic; Sparkling Burgundy was an optional colour

Steel mudguard

Monocoque for the future

Though the Bobcat was only produced for one year – about 1,150 models rolled out of the factory – its legacy was the all-in-one body concept used on the first Super Glides a few years later.

Footrest

46x9-cm (18x3½-in) tyre

Narrow front drum brake

1966 Sprint H

H ARLEY BOUGHT A SHARE IN THE Italian Aermacchi company in 1960 and this Harley-badged Aermacchi 250 joined the range the following year under the Sprint moniker. It was unlike any other Harley-Davidson and wary dealers treated the model with caution. The single-cylinder 246cc engine had wet sump lubrication, a cylinder positioned almost horizontally, and pushrod-operated valves. Unusually, the crankshaft rotated in the opposite direction to the wheels. Although the Sprint was a nice enough machine, it was pushed to keep up with comparable Hondas of the period. Production of the Italian four-strokes continued until 1974, by which time a 350cc model had joined the 250.

SPECIFICATIONS

1966 Sprint H

- **ENGINE** Overhead-valve, single cylinder
- **CAPACITY** 246cc
- **POWER OUTPUT** 28bhp
- **TRANSMISSION** Four-speed, chain drive
- **FRAME** Tubular spine
- **SUSPENSION** Telescopic front forks, swingarm rear
- **WEIGHT** 127kg (280lb)
- **TOP SPEED** 145km/h (90mph) (est.)

Frame brace reinforces the critical area between the swingarm and the suspension top-mounting

Canister air filter

Dual seat

Pressed-steel mudguard is rigidly mounted to the frame

Circular tail light

Number-plate mounting

Alloy wheel hub

Low-level exhaust system; earlier Sprint H models used a high-level system

Wet sump engine case

Right-hand propstand

Right-foot gearshift

1966 SPRINT H

The Sprint H was originally a trail model sold with a high-level exhaust pipe and mudguard for this popular section of the American market. The Sprint C was the roadster version. But by the time this bike was produced, a lower pipe and conventional guards were also fitted to the H. The Sprint was arguably Harley's most competent and successful small bike.

"The Sprint was one of Harley's Italian acquisitions after it bought into the Aermacchi company and was produced for 14 years."

Handlebar grip

Brake cable

Hexagonal tank badge was introduced in 1966

Steering damper

Elongated headlight shell contains the speedometer

Chrome trimmed headlight

High-level handlebars

Telescopic fork

Footrest

Font brake

Fork gaiter

9.8-litre (2⅖-gallon) fuel tank

Rocker inspection cover

Horizontal cylinder finning provided improved cooling

Dell'Orto carburettor with remote float bowl

Camshaft end cover

46x7.6-cm (18x3-in) front tyre

Handlebar fashions
While high handlebars were popular with American buyers, European riders preferred a sportier look, so Sprints that stayed in Europe had lower bars.

46-cm (18-in) wheel with chrome rim

Single leading-shoe front brake

1966 M-50 Sport

MOPEDS ALWAYS SOLD WELL IN EUROPE, but were less well suited to America, with its expanse of wide-open spaces and culture of long-distance motorcycle touring. Despite this, Harley's Italian connection resulted in the arrival of a 49cc two-stroke moped with a step-through frame and a three-speed gearbox for 1965. The addition of a conventional motorcycle fuel tank and a stylish seat justified the "Sport" moniker the following year. However, poor sales forced Harley to drop the M-50 after 1968 and the company never attempted mopeds again. Which was a relief to many Harley traditionalists.

1966 M-50 SPORT
Apparently Aermacchi built 10,500 M-50 Sports in 1966, though not many were brought to America. Even with a list price of $225, the ones that did get to the USA didn't sell quickly. Another 15cc was added in 1967 to create the M-65 Sport, resulting in a claimed 62 per cent power increase. The advertising copy stated that these bikes were "fun for young America at any age", but the reality was that America was distinctly unimpressed.

Racing-style seat

Circular tail light

Miniscule Dell'Orto carburettor

Steel mudguard unit and streamlined rear light mounting

Brake actuating arm

43x5-cm (17x2-in) tyre

Expansion chamber exhaust

Tubular spine frame

Right-hand throttle with large-diameter grip

Front brake cable

Pressed-steel, elongated headlight shell with chrome trim

Rubber-mounted 9.5-litre (2½-gallon) fuel tank

HARLEY-DAVIDSON

Horn

Spark plug cap

Ignition coil

Shroud surround for telescopic fork

Pressed-steel front mudguard

Gear-change cable connects the left twist-grip to the change mechanism

Mudguard stay

Three-speed gearbox

Alloy cylinder head has an integral engine mounting point from which the engine is connected to the spine frame

Minimalist brakes match minimalist performance

Chrome wheel rim

SPECIFICATIONS
1966 M-50 *Sport*

- **ENGINE** Single cylinder, two-stroke
- **CAPACITY** 49cc
- **POWER OUTPUT** Unknown
- **TRANSMISSION** Three-speed with twist-grip change
- **FRAME** Tubular spine
- **SUSPENSION** Telescopic front forks, swingarm rear
- **WEIGHT** 127kg (280lb)
- **TOP SPEED** 48km/h (30mph)

"The M-50 was the smallest-capacity bike ever to carry the Harley-Davidson badge, but was really more at home in Italy than the United States."

1967 CRTT

THE BASIC DESIGN OF THIS Italian-built overhead-valve single was penned by Alfredo Bianchi and was originally based on a 175cc unit that powered Aermacchi's distinctive Chimera road bike. Also known as the Ala D'Oro ("Golden Wing"), a number of racing versions of the bike were produced from 1961, in 250, 350, and 402cc formats. Although the layout was the same, the race bikes differed from the road-going bikes in many respects. Engine cases were sand-cast and incorporated the provision for a dry clutch and crankshaft-driven magneto ignition.

1967 CRTT
The CRTT was only produced for one year, with just 35 rolling out of the factory. By 1967, the Italian company was pleased with the way things were going with its American partner. In 1964, for example, 75-per cent of its production was being exported to the US for distribution by Harley and the range of bikes being produced was expanding.

Aerodynamic seat unit

Engine breather pipe

Exposed rear suspension springs

Quick-release rubber strap for fuel tank

Twin leading-shoe rear brake

Gear-change pedal

"Megaphone" exhaust increases power and, as the name suggests, noise

Ventilation slots help to keep the dry clutch cool

"Though never an international Grand Prix winner, the CRTT was a successful national level racer – at least until eclipsed by more powerful Japanese two-strokes."

Rev counter

Fuel filler-cap

Steering damper

Rev-counter cable

Elongated fibreglass fuel tank

Brake cable splitting box

HARLEY-DAVIDSON

Fork gaiter

Italian Ceriani telescopic forks and front brakes were the best available components of the period

Brake cable

Dell'Orto carburettor

Short-stroke engine was an option

Horizontal engine cooling fins

Magneto cover and other engine casings are sand-cast magnesium alloy on these Italian-built race bikes

Flanged alloy wheel rim

Twin leading-shoe front drum brake

SPECIFICATIONS
1967 CRTT

- **ENGINE** Air-cooled, overhead-valve, horizontal single
- **CAPACITY** 248cc
- **POWER OUTPUT** 35bhp @ 10,000rpm
- **TRANSMISSION** Five-speed, chain drive
- **FRAME** Tubular spine
- **SUSPENSION** Telescopic front forks, swingarm rear
- **WEIGHT** 111kg (245lb)
- **TOP SPEED** 185km/h (115mph)

1975 250SS

I N THE MID-1970S HARLEY RELEASED a range of modern-looking single-cylinder two-strokes built in Italy at the Aermacchi factory. These replaced its ageing line-up which included the four-stroke Sprint (*see pp.106–07*). Offered in both street (SS) and trail (SX) styles, the bikes came in 125 and 175cc variants from 1974, and a 250cc model from 1975. The 250 may have looked a neat bike, but once again it couldn't match the strong Japanese competition of the time. The SX had some success and was produced until 1978, but only 1,417 SSs were sold in 1976 and this model was dropped soon after its release. Along with the whole Aermacchi subsidiary, which Harley decided to relinquish in 1978.

1975 250SS

The 250SS and its smaller siblings had brief production runs as Harley-Davidsons, but continued under another name after Harley sold Aermacchi in 1978. The factory and production rights were bought by Cagiva, which went on to acquire the famous Ducati and MV Augusta marques. This was not before the company achieved considerable success with the lightweight two-strokes that it acquired from Harley-Davidson.

Streamlined tail-light mounting

Dual seat

Tubular cradle frame

Battery housing

Rear mudguard

46-cm (18-in) rear wheel

Snail cam chain adjusters allow simple chain-tension adjustment

Conical rear hub design gives maximum strength with minimum weight

Chrome silencer

Rear brake pedal

Two-stroke engine

Wing mirror

Separate oil tank is in the top tube of the frame

Speedometer and tachometer

Clutch lever

Styling contained a hint of traditional Harley, but the result was mainly a clean 1970s lightweight look

Fuel filler-cap for 10.6-litre (⅓-gallon) fuel tank

AMF Harley-Davidson

Headlight switch

Betor front fork

Brake cable

Safety reflector

Exhaust retaining spring

Speedo cable

Exhaust downtube

Dell'Orto carburettor

Five-speed gearbox

13.5-cm (5⅓-in) leading-shoe drum brake; later models had disc brakes

48-cm (19-in) front wheel

Chromed steel rim

SPECIFICATIONS
1975 250SS

- **ENGINE** Two-stroke, single-cylinder
- **CAPACITY** 243cc
- **POWER OUTPUT** Unknown
- **TRANSMISSION** Five-speed, chain drive
- **FRAME** Tubular cradle
- **SUSPENSION** Telescopic front forks, swingarm rear
- **WEIGHT** 111kg (245lb)
- **TOP SPEED** 137km/h (85mph)

"The 250SS was Harley's attempt to update its Sprint range but was a commercial failure due to the high quality of contemporary Japanese bikes of the same size."

1976 RR250

MOST TRADITIONAL HARLEY riders may not realize that the company won a string of World Championships in the mid-1970s, and if they do they probably don't really care. The bikes that gave Harley the titles were as far removed from the traditional V-twin as it's possible to get. These high-revving two-stroke twins were developed in Italy to take on the Japanese manufacturers in international road-racing championships. Ridden by Italian ace Walter Villa, the twins won three straight 250cc World Championships in 1975, '76 and '77, and a 350cc version also took that title in 1977.

SPECIFICATIONS
1976 RR250

- ENGINE Two-stroke twin-cylinder
- CAPACITY 246cc
- POWER OUTPUT 53bhp
- TRANSMISSION Six-speed, chain drive
- FRAME Tubular cradle
- SUSPENSION Telescopic front forks, swingarm rear
- WEIGHT 109kg (240lb)
- TOP SPEED 225km/h (140mph)

Knee cut-out

Aerodynamic seat hump

Moulded racing seat

Ignition coil

Rear shock-absorber mounting

Rear shock-absorber

Box section swingarm

Fuel tap

Tubular cradle frame

Twin leading-shoe rear drum brake is cable-operated

Eccentric swingarm mountings provide chain adjustment

Right-foot gear-change with reversed lever

Exposed dry clutch

1976 RR250

The RR250 was a production version of the bike
that won four World Championships for Villa. The
two-stroke twin dominated racing in the 125, 250,
and 350cc classes at that time, though in most
cases the bikes had a Yamaha sticker. When
Kawasaki developed its disc-valve racers in the late
1970s, however, the RR250 was soon outclassed.

Water
temperature
gauge

Rev-counter
mounting isolates
the instrument
from vibration

Large-capacity fuel tank;
two-stroke racers are not
noted for their economy

Fuel filler-cap

Racing
handlebars

Fairing
support
bracket

Ceriani
telescopic fork

Large-
capacity
radiator

Water-cooled
cylinder jacket

Expansion chamber exhaust
pipe allows the two-stroke
engine to realize its full power

Water-pump casing also
conceals the tachometer drive

Scarab front
brake calliper

Bare essentials
*Racing machines have minimal
instrumentation, allowing
the rider to concentrate
on the job in hand, and the
RR250 is no exception. The
large, white-faced rev-counter
gives all the information needed to
time gear-changes to perfection.*

Rear shock
absorber

Footrest

Exhaust
pipe

Road-racing
grooves in tyre

Lightweight
mudguard

Borrani alloy
wheel rims
are flanged for
extra strength

46-cm (18-in)
Dunlop racing
tyre

CHAPTER SIX

SPORTSTERS

1952–2010

1972 XRTT RACER

THE HARLEY-DAVIDSON SPORTSTER
is the motorcycle in its purest form – just a
handsome V-twin engine, a minimalist chassis,
wheels, handlebars, and a fuel tank. It represents
the true experience of motorcycling, a visceral
embodiment of the things that make us love
motorcycles. The Sportster is the longest-
running production motorcycle in the world,
having been around since 1957. In that time it
has been uprated and improved without altering
the essential ingredients that make it what it is.

RACING PEDIGREE
*Harley Sportsters have been winning races ever since
their introduction, with bikes ranging from the KRTT to the
XR750 taking the honours on tracks all over the world.*

1952 Model K

IN THE EARLY 1950s American motorcylists wanted more from their motorcycles. They were buying faster, better handling and better looking British imports rather than Harley's traditional 45cu. in. V-twins. In 1952 Harley hit back with the K model, its first significant new machine since the Knucklehead of 1936 (*see pp.78–79*). While the bike incorporated several novel features on a 45cu. in. side-valve block, it still could not match the performance of the smaller-capacity British machines. Increasing capacity to 54cu. in. on the KH in 1954 helped, but there was only so much that could be done with the side-valve layout. The solution came in the form of the OHV XL Sportster (*see pp.120–21*).

Rubber-mounted "buckhorn" style handlebars

Single mirror

Ignition and light-switch mounting

Hydraulically damped telescopic forks with chrome shrouds

Large-diameter headlight with chrome shell

Painted steel mudguard

20-cm (8-in) diameter drum brake

1952 MODEL K
Innovations on the K included an engine and gearbox as one unit, swingarm rear suspension on the cradle frame, and telescopic forks. The British style of hand clutch and right foot-shift replaced Harley's usual foot clutch and hand gear-change.

SPECIFICATIONS
1952 Model K

- **ENGINE** Side-valve, V-twin
- **CAPACITY** 45cu. in. (738cc)
- **POWER OUTPUT** 30bhp (est.)
- **TRANSMISSION** Four-speed, chain drive
- **FRAME** Tubular cradle
- **SUSPENSION** Telescopic front forks, swingarm rear
- **WEIGHT** 181kg (400lb)
- **TOP SPEED** 136km/h (85mph) (est.)

"The forerunner of Harley's Sportster series, the Model K was nevertheless an underpowered bike."

Brake lever now mounted on the right

Clutch operated by lever on handlebar

Panniers came as part of a Harley accessory group for the Model K

Crash bar was an optional fitting

Air horn

Classic Harley design
While the K model was not in itself a great success, its styling has been used on Harley-Davidsons ever since; note the striking visual similarities between this bike and the 1999 model 1200 Sportster (see pp.134–35).

20.5-litre (4½-gallon) fuel tank

Cast-alloy cylinder head

Battery case with access door; the oil tank is on the other side

Saddle incorporates sprung seat-post despite the bike also having swingarm rear suspension

Swingarm rear suspension

Tail light

Rear brake pedal

Passenger footrest

Alloy primary drive case

48-cm (19-in) wheel is higher and narrower than on previous models

Cast-iron rear drum brake

1957 XL

HARLEY FINALLY FITTED OVERHEAD cylinder heads to its smaller V-twin in 1957 to create the Sportster, a model that was to become one of the longest surviving production motorcycles in the world. The Sportster combined the good looks of the earlier K (*see pp.118–19*) and KH models with enough power to match the performance of contemporary imported bikes. Although capacity remained at 54cu. in., the same as for the KH, the larger bore and shorter stroke resulted in increased horsepower. It meant that American buyers could now invest in a domestic product without suffering the indignity of being blown away by their Triumph- and BSA-mounted friends. As with the bigger twins, the factory offered a variety of accessories including the screens, racks, panniers, crash bars, and spotlights fitted to this 1957 model. Other owners went the opposite way and stripped superfluous parts off their machines to improve both looks and performance.

SPECIFICATIONS

1957 XL

- **ENGINE** Overhead-valve, V-twin
- **CAPACITY** 54cu. in. (883cc)
- **POWER OUTPUT** 32bhp @ 4,200rpm
- **TRANSMISSION** Four-speed, chain drive
- **FRAME** Tubular cradle
- **SUSPENSION** Telescopic front forks, swingarm rear
- **WEIGHT** 210kg (463lb)
- **TOP SPEED** 148km/h (92mph) (est.)

1957 XL

When the Sportster was introduced it was intended for touring riders as well as those for whom performance was important. As a result, panniers and racks were included as factory extras, to allow Sportster riders to dress up their bikes.

The number plate mounted above the rear light remains a Harley feature

Optional panniers and luggage rack were available for those who wanted to tour on their Sportster

Sprung saddle

Tank holds 2.8 litres (¾ gallon) of oil

16.6-litre (4⅖-gallon) fuel tank with two-tone finish

Circular tail light

46-cm (18-in) wheel

Two-into-one exhaust system exits through a simple silencer

Bicycle-style pedal on kick-starter

Swingarm rear suspension

Four-speed gearbox

Windscreen was a Harley-Davidson optional extra

Rear-view mirror

Blue-tinted lower windscreen section

The Sportster look
The classic Sportster look developed from these early models when an optional 8.5-litre (2¼-gallon) "peanut" fuel tank was introduced on XLC Sportsters in 1958. Once that was in place, the look remained the same up to this present day.

"The XL was the first true Harley Sportster, with overhead-valves providing the power and revised styling providing the looks to compete with the British competition."

Round plastic tank emblem was only used in 1957

Speedometer is mounted in the metal fork shroud

Additional passing light

When the Sportster range was expanded in 1958, the XLC featured cut-down mudguards and no lights

Optional crash bar

Trumpet horn

Chromed spokes and wheel rims

Ribbed front tyre

Two-into-one exhaust system

Iron cylinder head and barrel; alloy heads were not fitted until the 1980s

British-style right footshift

Single, leading-shoe drum brake engaged by lever on right handlebar

1961 KRTT

ALONG WITH THE INTRODUCTION of the new K-series road bike in 1952 (*see pp.118–19*) Harley-Davidson also released a racing version, designated the KR. The bike's engine had all the tweaks you would expect in a competition power unit, while looking externally similar to the K. There were big valves, racing cams, and new bearings, as well as re-shaped ports and a revised cylinder head. Riders like Brad Andres, Joe Leonard, Carroll Resweber, George Roeder, and Roger Reiman achieved many wins on the side-valve KR racers in the 1950s and 1960s. Because of the variety of track surfaces and conditions found in American racing, both sprung and rigid versions of the KR's frame were produced.

Rev-counter

Large fuel tank for long-distance races

Alloy wheel rim is lighter and stronger than the usual steel examples

Telescopic forks are based on those used on the road-going Sportster and K-series machines

Clip-on handlebar is used on long straights to reduce drag

Magneto

Tubular frame cradle

Ventilated brake drum

1961 KRTT
The basic KR was intended for dirt-track racing and so did not come equipped with brakes or suspension. This TT version had both and was ridden to victory at Daytona in 1961 by Roger Reiman at the first 200-mile (322-km) race to be held at the new banked oval track.

Wide bars for
dirt-track racing

Number 55 was
Roger Reiman's
race number at
Daytona in 1961

Tank breather-pipe

Simple saddle is still
sprung despite the rear
suspension now fitted
to Harley bikes

Side-valve success
While the standard road-going K-series was discontinued for 1957, the racing KRs had continued success with this engine layout until the late 1960s.

Air filter

"Despite the limitations of the side-valve layout, the KR racers continued Harley's tradition of success on the race track."

SPECIFICATIONS
1961 KRTT

- **ENGINE** Side-valve, V-twin
- **CAPACITY** 45cu. in. (750cc)
- **POWER OUTPUT** 50bhp
- **TRANSMISSION** Four-speed, chain drive
- **FRAME** Tubular cradle
- **SUSPENSION** Telescopic front forks, rear swingarm
- **WEIGHT** 145kg (320lb)
- **TOP SPEED** 233km/h (125mph)

Race number plate

Cut-down alloy
mudguard

Brake pedal has
been drilled to reduce
the bike's weight

Mudguard
support

Pressed-steel
primary drive cover

Tyre is screwed to the
rim for added security

Block tread
race tyre

1972 XRTT

ROAD-RACING WAS A RARITY IN America in the 1960s. Most racing action was on dirt tracks for which the XR and KR models were conceived, but Harley decided to build a road-race version of the XR. Unlike the flat-track bike, it was fitted with a front brake and a large-diameter four-leading shoe drum, which was combined with a rear disc as on the dirt bike. Most machines had the disc-drum combination the other way around. Although the XRTT was a useful machine, its success was in the most part due to its most famous rider, Cal Rayborn, who often beat machines of greater power on this XRTT.

SPECIFICATIONS
1972 XRTT

- **ENGINE** Overhead-valve, V-twin
- **CAPACITY** 45cu. in. (750cc)
- **POWER OUTPUT** 90bhp @ 8,000rpm
- **TRANSMISSION** Four-speed, chain drive
- **FRAME** Tubular cradle
- **SUSPENSION** Telescopic front forks, swingarm rear
- **WEIGHT** 147kg (324lb)
- **TOP SPEED** 209km/h (130mph) (est.)

Aerodynamic seat hump reduces drag

Special frame allows lower seat height

Knee cut-out allows aerodynamic riding position

Oil tank is under rider's seat

Cal Rayborn

Rear disc brake as used on flat-track bike

46-cm (18-in) rear wheel with lightweight flanged alloy rim

Carburettors run without air cleaners to increase power

Reversed gearshift has upside-down pattern change, with up for down and down for up

Short racing exhaust is positioned high on the bike to improve cornering clearance

1972 XRTT

Differences on the TT models from the dirt-track bikes included a modified frame, a larger capacity fuel tank, and an aerodynamic seat and fairing. Despite Cal Rayborn's notable efforts, these road-race versions of the XR did not have as much success as the dirt-track models.

Rider's chin-rest pad

Centrally mounted rev-counter is the bike's only instrument

Bikini fairing

Polished alloy fork yoke

Aerodynamic front fairing

Classic chassis

The XRTT chassis was derived from that used earlier on the K-series road racers (see pp.122–23). These frames continued to give service until the early 1980s, when they were used on Harley's "Battle of the Twins" racer.

Exhaust from rear cylinder

Underslung rear brake calliper

Front cylinder exhaust pipe

Brake cable

Ribbed pattern racing tyre

Fairing painted in Harley-Davidson racing colours

Clip-on handlebars clamp directly onto the fork leg

Cerani four leading-shoe drum brake with huge ventilation slots to aid cooling

Tyre is screwed to the rim for added security

1978 XLCR

In 1977 Harley introduced a new variation of the Sportster. The XLCR – it can't have been an accident that it sounded like "excelsior" – was designed by Willie G. Davidson, and the CR stood for café racer. Harley's model was a blend of 1960s café racer – a name given to stripped, tuned, road-going hot rods used for blasting from bar to bar – with some of the styling cues of the XR flat-track racers. The frame and the exhaust pipes were new and would be used on the rest of the Sportster range the following year, but the engine was a stock XL1000. The really important stuff was the bodywork and the black finish. The XLCR looked great, but never sold in the numbers that were hoped for and was dropped after only two years.

SPECIFICATIONS
1978 XLCR

- **ENGINE** Overhead-valve, V-twin
- **CAPACITY** 61cu. in. (1000cc)
- **POWER OUTPUT** 55bhp
- **TRANSMISSION** Four-speed, chain drive
- **FRAME** Tubular cradle
- **SUSPENSION** Telescopic front forks, box-section swingarm rear
- **WEIGHT** 213kg (470lb)
- **TOP SPEED** 169km/h (105mph)

Fibreglass tailpiece/mudguard

Triangulated frame section derived from the XR750

Solo seat; a dual seat was also available in 1978

Battery housing cover

15-litre (4-gallon) fuel tank

Rear drive sprocket

Rear shock absorber mounting placed close to axle

Rear-set footrest and brake pedal linkage

Brake pedal

Redesigned rear frame allows the oil tank (on other side of the battery) to be tucked in

1978 XLCR

One of the reasons behind the bike's failure was that there was not enough stock to meet demand that had been generated by the pre-release publicity. Now, however, the small amount of numbers produced – about 3,200 – means that this is something of a collector's item.

A funked-up XL

Differences from the stock XL on which it was based included positioning the seat further backwards and lowering the height of the handlebars. The rear section of the frame was derived from that used on the XR750 dirt-track bikes (see pp.128–29).

Tinted windscreen

"Bar and shield" logo first used in 1910

Drag-style straight handlebars

Sculpted fuel tank

Headlight contained in fairing

Rear shock absorber

Bikini fairing

Fold-up footrest

Chromed suspension shroud

46-cm (18-in) rear wheel

Shortened racing mudguard

Oil cooler

Wrinkle finish black engine paint

Speedometer cable

"Siamese" twin exhaust system

Exhaust retaining clamp

Morris 48-cm (19-in) seven-spoke alloy wheel

Kelsey-Hayes twin front disc brakes

1980 XR750

THE HARLEY-DAVIDSON XR750 is the most successful competition bike ever produced, though for many it's more famous as the bike that jump hero Evel Knievel used for his stunts. The early bikes were introduced in 1970 with iron barrels and heads that failed miserably, so a revised alloy engined version of the bike was introduced two years later. For the first time on a production Harley V-twin, the rear cylinder had a forward-facing exhaust and rear-facing inlet port. The bike won the A.M.A. Grand National Championship in its first year and, uprated and improved over time, it is still winning races more than a quarter of a century later.

SPECIFICATIONS

1980 XR750

- **ENGINE** Overhead-valve, V-twin
- **CAPACITY** 45cu. in. (748cc)
- **POWER OUTPUT** 90bhp @ 8,000rpm
- **TRANSMISSION** Four-speed, chain drive
- **FRAME** Tubular cradle
- **SUSPENSION** Telescopic front forks, swingarm rear
- **WEIGHT** 134kg (295lb)
- **TOP SPEED** 185km/h (115mph) (est.)

Alloy oil tank is retained with springs

Small-capacity 9.5-litre (2½-gallon) tank holds just enough fuel to last a race

Lightweight fibreglass mudguard and seat base

Rear shock-absorber

Large air filter prevents dust from entering the engine

Dirt-track racing tyre

Alloy drive sprocket can be easily changed to alter the gearing

Gear-change lever is seldom used once races are underway

Fuel
filler-cap

Wide handlebars
provide extra
leverage

Spot the difference
*The first XR750 was a comparative failure.
This bike is one of the iron-engined machines
produced from 1970–71 that used the same
Harley layout of carbs and
exhaust on the same side.*

Large racing seat

High ground clearance
is essential for all dirt-
track bikes

Steering
lock stop

*"The XR750 is a Harley-Davidson
racing classic, made famous by the
exploits of Evel Knievel and acknowledged
as one of the best dirt-track race
bikes ever produced."*

Standard Harley
frame was replaced by
most tuners seeking a
performance edge

Lightweight
telescopic
fork

Alloy
wheel rim

Alloy
cylinder
and head

Fins on the
cylinder barrel
help to disperse heat

Lightweight
front hub
with no brake

1980 XR750

Compare the engine to that of a Sportster
(*see pp.126–27*) and the origins of the bottom half
are obvious. However, the all-alloy top end, with rear
racing carburettors, was unique. The crankshaft was
different too and the 750cc capacity was achieved with
a bore of 3.125 inches and a stroke of 2.98 inches.

1984 XR1000

IT SEEMED OBVIOUS. Harley's XR750 (*see pp.128–29*) was cleaning up in dirt-track racing, so why not offer a limited run of road-going examples? In 1983 Harley produced the XR1000. They fitted the alloy heads and twin Dell'Orto carburettors from the XR750 onto the bottom half of an XL1000 engine. The engine itself was fitted into a standard XLX chassis. The result was an engine that put out 10 per cent more power than the stock Sportster in standard trim, though many owners tuned the bike even more. The result was the fastest production bike Harley ever made, but buyers were not impressed – it looked almost identical to the cheapest bike in the range while costing a great deal more. The XR1000 didn't sell, but the bike is now a collector's piece.

SPECIFICATIONS
1984 XR1000

- **ENGINE** Overhead-valve, V-twin
- **CAPACITY** 61cu. in. (998cc)
- **POWER OUTPUT** 70bhp @ 6,000rpm
- **TRANSMISSION** Four-speed, chain drive
- **FRAME** Tubular cradle
- **SUSPENSION** Telescopic front forks, swingarm rear
- **WEIGHT** 213kg (470lb) (est.)
- **TOP SPEED** 193km/h (120mph) (est.)

Rear light

Alloy mudguard support

Oil tank

Non-standard Corbin seat; the XR was supplied with a solo saddle only

Classic Sportster fuel tank holds 8.3 litres (2¼ gallons)

41-cm (16-in) nine-spoke alloy rear wheel

Box section steel swingarm

Pillion footrest

Air filter

Rear brake master cylinder

Rear-view mirror

Front brake master cylinder

Speedometer and rev-counter

Low handlebars

Headlight eyebrow

Race success
In 1984, Gene Church won the Battle of the Twins race at Daytona on a heavily tuned 112bhp XR1000, retaining his title for the next two years.

High-level exhaust pipes mounted on the left-hand side

"Successes on the race track brought the XR's potential to the public's attention, to the point where it is now seen as a classic Harley."

Telescopic front fork

Though this model is painted slate grey, Harley's orange and black racing livery was optional for 1984

Slim mudguard and other components taken from the base XLX model

48-cm (19-in) nine-spoke alloy front wheel

Cast-iron cylinders are topped by alloy heads

Safety reflector

Generator mounting

New brake calliper design

25-cm (10-in) front brake discs

1984 XR1000

There was massive initial interest in the XR1000, but speed-hungry buyers expecting a new breed of Harley were disappointed. Only the few who bought the $1,000 bhp-doubling tuning kit saw the bike's real potential. Some people maintain that the XR1000 is the best bike Harley ever built.

1987 XLH883

HARLEY NEEDED HELP in the mid-1980s. It wanted to lure new customers who would resist the suspect reliability and high maintenance of a traditional Harley, but would still want the image. In addition, the company was required to meet strict new emission and noise laws. The end result was the "Evo" Sportster. It looked and sounded (once you'd taken the baffles out of the silencers) just like an old Sportster, the difference being that the all-new engine was cheap and reliable. Introduced for 1986, the XLH had an 883cc block with alloy barrels and heads. Larger 1100cc and 1200cc units followed soon after, as did belt final-drive and a five-speed box. A competitively low price tag on this base model helped attract a whole new group of buyers who wanted to sample the Harley legend.

SPECIFICATIONS
1987 XLH883

- **ENGINE** Overhead-valve, V-twin
- **CAPACITY** 54cu. in. (883cc)
- **POWER OUTPUT** 49bhp @ 7,000rpm
- **TRANSMISSION** Five-speed, chain drive
- **FRAME** Tubular cradle
- **SUSPENSION** Telescopic front forks, swingarm rear
- **WEIGHT** 213kg (470lb)
- **TOP SPEED** 169km/h (105mph)

Number plate mounted above the rear light

Rear light

After-market seat

Oil tank for dry sump lubrication system

Alloy rocker cover

41-cm (16-in) rear wheel

Dual exhaust system with twin silencers

1987 XLH883
The XLH helped pull Harley-Davidson out of trouble at a time when it was losing vast amounts of money. Its combination of quiet Evolution engine, reliability, classic design, and cheap price made it an immediate success.

Rear-view mirror

No fancy details on the instrument dial, just a speedometer

Wide-bladed control lever

Traditional Sportster handlebars

10-litre (2½-gallon) "peanut" fuel tank

The 883cc engine capacity was a return to the Sportster's original 1957 engine size

Clean lines
As well as the impressive new engine, the bike's simplicity was one of its main selling points. The single instrument dial, plain paint job, and small tank all made for a neat-looking machine that found favour with tens of thousands of new Harley buyers.

Braced steering head

Alloy fork slider

Narrow build and low seat height made the Sportster appealing to novice riders

Throttle cable

Safety reflector

Single 29-cm (11½-in) front disc brake

New federal noise regulations were satisfied by adding a balance tube between the twin exhaust pipes

The large "ham can" air filter was first introduced on the Sportster in 1966 and still gets in the way of the rider's right leg

This model has traditional wire wheels, but cast spoked wheels were offered as an optional extra

Chrome wheel rim

1999 XL1200S

Though the Sportster engine has been through various guises and capacities over the years, it has always remained true to its original layout. In a sense, the XL1200S harks back to the XLCH Sportster of the late 1950s and early 1960s, a bare-boned bike intended for fast fun. A 1200cc version of the alloy Evolution engine (*see pp.144–45*) was introduced in 1988, and 11 years later it has received only detail changes. The Sportster Sport has uprated suspension and improved power output over the basic model to justify its S designation. In addition, the engine is fitted with twin-plug heads and has increased compression and revised camshafts in comparison with the base model. There's no doubt that the XL1200S is a true return to form.

1999 XL1200S

When the 1200 Sport was originally released in 1996, it was the first road-going Harley to feature adjustable sporting suspension. Other additions such as the 13-spoke wheels and twin-plug heads turned this into Harley-Davidson's most adventurous model. Three years on, the minimalist 1999 bike is arguably the most stylish and competent Sportster that Harley has ever made.

12.5-litre (3⅓-gallon) fuel tank larger than on previous Sportsters

Gas reservoir rear shock absorber is adjustable for pre-load and damping

Low profile seat

Oil tank filler-cap

Tail light

41-cm (16-in) spoked alloy rear wheel

Large-diameter sports silencer

Belt drive pulley

Belt drive-pulley; belt final drive has been used on Sportsters since 1991

Brake master cylinder

Dual exhaust system

Five-speed gearbox

Rear-view mirror

Twin instrument dials

"V" tank graphic detail harks back to the early 1960s

Headlight peak

Head shock

Ignition lock

Adjustable front fork

Pressed-steel mudguard

Cylinder head incorporates twin-spark plug ignition system

Dual-piston brake calliper

48-cm (19-in) tyre

Engine mounting point

Exhaust downtube

13-spoke alloy wheel

Twin drilled brake discs

SPECIFICATIONS
1999 XL1200S

- **ENGINE** Overhead-valve, V-twin
- **CAPACITY** 73cu. in. (1200cc)
- **POWER OUTPUT** 69bhp
- **TRANSMISSION** Five-speed, belt drive
- **FRAME** Tubular cradle
- **SUSPENSION** Adjustable telescopic front forks, swingarm rear with gas shocks
- **WEIGHT** 314kg (692lb)
- **TOP SPEED** 174km/h (108mph)

"The XL1200S continues Harley's tradition of innovation in its Sportster range by incorporating twin plugs in its cylinder heads and a fully adjustable suspension system."

2003 XL883R

HARLEY'S LONG HISTORY OF flat-track racing success has never been a rich seam of inspiration for production models. The XLCR (*see pp.126–27*) and XR1000 (*see pp.130–31*) were both influenced by the all-conquering XR750 (*see pp.128–29*), but neither was a commercial success. In 2002 the factory tried again with the 883R. The new model was little more than a pared-down version of the base model Sportster fitted with black cowhorn handlebars and a two-into-one exhaust. Despite the limited modifications, it was an inspired addition to the range. Compared to many modern machines the 883R's handling is unrefined, but it is a hugely involving bike to ride in town, or on country roads where its limited performance isn't an issue.

2003 XL883R

The six-model Sportster range is derived from one frame, two engines, a couple of different fuel tanks, and a variety of handlebar shapes and colour schemes. Yet the different models can feel markedly different. The 883 is seen as an entry-level model, but the racetrack credibility of the orange and black livery – it is inspired by factory racers – helps make the R version attractive to flat-track fans.

12.5-litre (3⅓-gallon) fuel tank will allow an uninterrupted ride of over 240km (150 miles)

Simple rear shock absorber is adjustable for pre-load only

Stepped dual seat provides a level of back support

Tail light

41-cm (16-in) rear wheel

Drive belt pulley

Large-diameter sports silencer

Satin black oil tank

Oil filler-cap

Curved two-into-one exhaust system

Fuel
filler-cap

Short-stem rear-
view mirror

Centrally mounted
speedometer

"Bullet"-style
indicator

29.6° steering
head

Fork shroud

Safety reflector

Four-piston front
brake calliper

Air filter

Chromed exhaust
downtube

48-cm (19-in)
front wheel

Twin drilled
29-cm (11½-in)
brake discs

HARLEY-DAVIDSON
883

Sportster

SPECIFICATIONS
2003 XL883R

- **ENGINE** Overhead-valve, V-twin
- **CAPACITY** 54cu. in. (883cc)
- **POWER OUTPUT** 45bhp @ 6,000rpm
- **TRANSMISSION** Five-speed,
  belt drive
- **FRAME** Tubular cradle
- **SUSPENSION** Telescopic front forks,
  swingarm rear
- **WEIGHT** 245kg (540lb) (dry, claimed)
- **TOP SPEED** 166km/h (103mph)

"In a world bored by retro-kitsch, this is the real deal – not some new-VW Beetle pastiche of an old design. This is a new design."

2010 XR1200X

HARLEY'S **XR750** is an iconic race bike that has dominated American dirt track racing since 1972. However, Harley were never able to effectively translate the image of the XR to a road bike. They attempted this in 2008 when the XR1200, a more aggressive version of the Sportster, was introduced. The new bike was originally intended for European markets, though it was subsequently sold in America too. Based on the 1200 Sportster, the XR1200 featured a tuned engine, uprated suspension, improved brakes, and sports tyres.

<table>
<tr><td colspan="2">SPECIFICATIONS
2010 XR1200X</td></tr>
<tr><td>• ENGINE</td><td>Overhead-valve, V-twin</td></tr>
<tr><td>• CAPACITY</td><td>1250cc</td></tr>
<tr><td>• POWER OUTPUT</td><td>90bhp @ 7,000rpm</td></tr>
<tr><td>• TRANSMISSION</td><td>Five-speed, belt drive</td></tr>
<tr><td>• FRAME</td><td>Tubular cradle</td></tr>
<tr><td>• SUSPENSION</td><td>Telescopic fork front, swingarm rear</td></tr>
<tr><td>• WEIGHT</td><td>187kg (412lb)</td></tr>
<tr><td>• TOP SPEED</td><td>201km/h (125mph)</td></tr>
</table>

Rack and backrest are factory options

Seat echos styling of XR750

Oil-cooled cylinder heads

Oil tank

Rear suspension units have adjustable damping

Twin exhausts echo styling of XR750 racers

43-cm (17-inch) rear wheel

Alloy swingarms

Raised footrests give improved cornering clearance

Mirrors have unobtrusive black finish

13.25-litre (3½-gallon) fuel tank

XR1200X

For 2010 an X was added to the model number of the XR1200. The bike was fitted with better quality suspension and offered with a black paint finish. Showa multi-adjustable suspension featured remote reservoir "piggy back" shock absorbers and "upside down" forks for greater chassis rigidity.

Analogue revcounter is centrally mounted, with smaller digital speedo to one side

"In the Sportster's half century of history, the fastest and best-handling version of the model that Harley ever built was the XR1200"

Showa forks

Twin disc brakes are fitted

Two-into-one-into-two exhaust system

Vibration-isolating front engine mounting

Four-piston front brake calliper

46-cm (18-inch) front wheel

CHAPTER SEVEN

RECENT BIG-TWINS

1984–2010

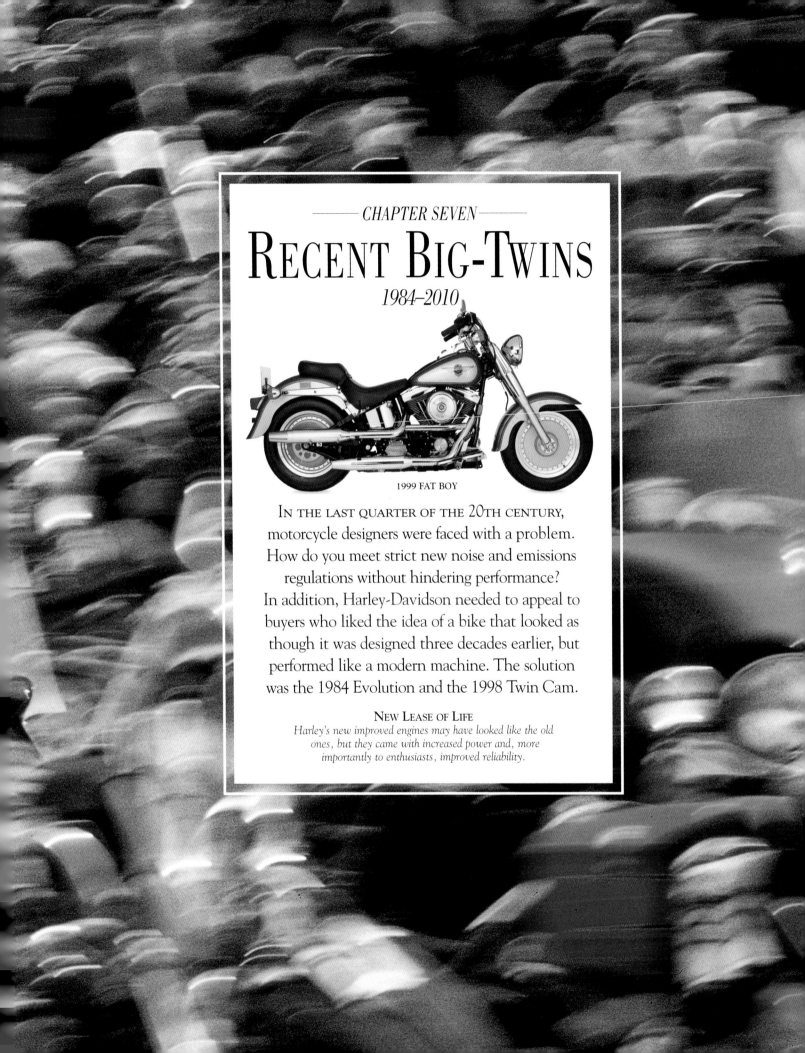

1999 FAT BOY

IN THE LAST QUARTER OF THE 20TH CENTURY,
motorcycle designers were faced with a problem.
How do you meet strict new noise and emissions
regulations without hindering performance?
In addition, Harley-Davidson needed to appeal to
buyers who liked the idea of a bike that looked as
though it was designed three decades earlier, but
performed like a modern machine. The solution
was the 1984 Evolution and the 1998 Twin Cam.

NEW LEASE OF LIFE
*Harley's new improved engines may have looked like the old
ones, but they came with increased power and, more
importantly to enthusiasts, improved reliability.*

1988 FLHS Electra Glide

THE FLHS WAS A NEW DERIVATIVE of the classic Electra Glide introduced in 1987. At the heart of the bike was the 80cu. in. Evolution engine and five-speed transmission that was first released in 1984. Also present on the bike was belt final-drive, which became common on Harleys from 1985. The FLHS was a return to the traditions of the earliest Electra Glides and was sold with no top box and a removable screen. Though the "Sport" tag might have been stretching a point, the trimmed-down model certainly felt more agile than the fully encumbered standard version. It also had the advantage of being considerably cheaper.

1988 FLHS ELECTRA GLIDE

The FLHS designation had been around for a few years, with the first example introduced for 1977 as a one-year-only limited edition model. Harley then decided to withdraw the sport edition of the Electra Glide for three years before returning as the 1980 FLHS. This was carried through until the end of the Shovelhead engine in 1984 and a break of a couple of years ensued before the FLHS returned as a sport version of the new Evolution Electra Glide in 1987.

Passenger backrest for added comfort during long journeys

Heavily padded rider's seat

Passenger grab rail

Oil tank

Number plate is mounted above the rear light in traditional Harley-Davidson style

Luggage rack

Large-capacity lockable fibreglass panniers have lift-up lids

Circular tail light

Safety reflector

Large silencer

41-cm (16-in) 10-spoke cast-alloy wheel

Single rear disc brake

Split exhaust system feeds silencers on each side of the machine

Gearbox as a separate unit

Detachable windscreen is one of the elements that makes this a Sport version

Rear-view mirror

Brake fluid reservoir

Rubber handlebar grip

Bar and shield tank logo

19-litre (5-gallon) fuel tank

Chrome headlight nacelle

Fog lamp

Self-cancelling indicators were new for 1988

Pressed-steel front mudguard

Evolution cylinders

Air filter

Crash bar

Footboard

Dual front disc brakes

46-cm (18-in) tyre

Alloy fork slider

SPECIFICATIONS
1988 FLHS Electra Glide

- **ENGINE** Overhead-valve, V-twin
- **CAPACITY** 80cu. in. (1312cc)
- **POWER OUTPUT** 55bhp @ 7,200rpm
- **TRANSMISSION** Five-speed, belt drive
- **FRAME** Tubular cradle
- **SUSPENSION** Telescopic front forks, twin rear shock absorbers, swingarm rear
- **WEIGHT** 314kg (692lb)
- **TOP SPEED** 161km/h (100mph)

"The Electra Glide is the most enigmatic of all Harley-Davidsons, the king of touring bikes and the undisputed leader of the pack."

The Evolution

ONE MILLION CUSTOMERS can't be wrong. That is how many Evolution engines were built in its 15 years of production from 1984 to 1999. The engine followed the traditional Harley format of a 45° air-cooled V-twin with two overhead valves per cylinder, but it was more reliable and more efficient than its predecessor, the venerable Shovelhead. The Evolution gave Harley the chance to get on with developing new bikes and new markets without having to worry about the engine. While the standard engine produced a restrained 69bhp, many owners were happy to make the bike noisier and more powerful.

FLHS Electra Glide

The Evolution was used to power an increasingly broad range of machines that covered everything from this traditional Electra Glide to the FLSTF Fat Boy.

Three-piece alloy rocker cover conceals hydraulic tappets

Alloy cylinders ran more coolly than the Shovelhead's iron ones and so were

Air filter mounting bolt

Carburettor

Circular air filter

Cylinders have a 3.5 x 4.25in bore and stroke

Exhaust port with studs for exhaust

used to return oil from the head to the crankcase; oil is forced up to the heads through the pushrods themselves

Hydraulic tappets are situated in the blocks at the base of the pushrod tubes

INSIDE THE EVOLUTION

The Evolution part of the engine was really in the new cylinders, heads, ignition, and carburation systems, which were fitted to a lower end based on the last of the Shovelheads. Alloy cylinders, improved combustion-chamber shape, and flat-topped pistons made the Evo run more coolly and more efficiently than the Shovel. An improved carburettor and a new "V-Fire III" electronic ignition system also helped.

traditional position at the rear of the timing case

Camshaft is mounted beneath the centre of the "V"

The alternator cover also hides the trigger for the electronic ignition

This was the engine that secured Harley's future. It killed the poor reputation that had developed during the difficult AMF years.

JOHN WARR
(HARLEY DEALER)

Crankshaft and bottom end are the same as on the Shovelhead

A high-quality touring bike

The Evolution arrived on the scene at a time when touring was a well-established part of motorcycle culture. Increased reliability, more miles to the gallon, and reduced weight over the Shovelhead meant the Evo was an ideal power plant for all types of touring.

Overnight the Evolution motor transformed Harley's fortunes. It came at just the right time, worked faultlessly, and really saved the Hog's bacon.

JOHN WARR
(HARLEY DEALER)

THE COMPETITION

• 1987 HONDA GL1500 GOLDWING •
In the six-cylinder GoldWing, Honda had a fierce competitor to Harley's Evo bikes. More so as the 'Wing was made in Ohio and wore its "Made in America" badge almost as proudly as the Milwaukee machines.

1900s | 1910s | 1920s | 1930s | 1940s | 1950s | 1960s | 1970s | 1980s | 1990s | 2000s

1989 FLTC Tour Glide

BY CONTRAST WITH THE trimmed-down FLHS (*see pp.142–43*), the FLTC represented the "all mod cons" end of the Electra Glide range. Harley understood that it could offer a variety of models based on similar ingredients to suit the needs of all its customers, and in the case of the FLTC – first introduced for the 1984 model year – the need was for complete luxury. The fairing has twin headlamps and is frame-mounted to improve the bike's handling. The special two-tone paint finish was used on the "Classic" (FLTC) model, but there was also a slightly cheaper FLT version with a single-colour paint finish.

SPECIFICATIONS
1989 FLTC Tour Glide

- **ENGINE** Overhead-valve, V-twin
- **CAPACITY** 80cu. in. (1312cc)
- **POWER OUTPUT** 58bhp @ 7,200 rpm
- **TRANSMISSION** Five-speed, belt drive
- **FRAME** Tubular cradle
- **SUSPENSION** Telescopic front forks, swingarm rear
- **WEIGHT** 332kg (732lb)
- **TOP SPEED** 177km/h (110mph) (est.)

Top box adds to the already expansive luggage capacity

Passenger armrest

Massive twin headlights allow safe night riding

Additional side reflectors

Footboard

Self-cancelling indicator

Silencer

Rear disc brake

Oil tank

Whitewall 46-cm (18-in) tyre

Sidecar companion
The FLTC was an ideal bike for a sidecar and buyers could order one from Harley. Numbers were never high, however, with 15 produced in 1989 out of a total FLTC production figure of 603.

Rocker cover badge
The sentiment expressed on this replacement for the standard air filter – and also inscribed on the passenger footboard – is typical of the die-hard Harley-Davidson fanatic.

Smoked windscreen creates a calm pocket of air for a relaxed ride

40-watt stereo system; a CB radio came with the "Ultra" package

Handlebar-mounted controls can adjust the stereo volume

Two-tone paint finish

Deep-cushioned, solidly mounted seat

"The FLTC was the top-of-the-range Electra Glide, and included features such as a 40-watt music system, twin headlights, and all the luggage space you could want."

1989 FLTC TOUR GLIDE CLASSIC
The Tour Glide Classic was based on the FLT which first appeared in 1980. This significant new model had a revised frame which incorporated a vibration-isolated engine and a box-section spine, these features being adopted by all Electra Glides from the mid-1980s. The FLTC weighed over half a tonne when carrying two riders and a full load.

Fibreglass fairing mounted to the frame rather than the forks to improve stability

Highway peg mounted on safety bar where rider can rest feet

Safety reflector

Folded-up passenger footboard

Two-into-one exhaust system

Five-speed gearbox

Old-style footboards add to rider comfort

Chrome mudguard trim

Ten-spoke alloy wheel

1989 FXR Super Glide

HARLEY'S SUPER GLIDE WAS revised in 1982 with the introduction of the FXR, the base model in an expanded range of Super Glide-derived bikes. The FXR got an 80cu. in. engine, a new frame, and many other changes, but it vanished in 1984 when the new Evolution engine appeared. It re-emerged in 1986 in a similar guise and continued until 1994, when the Dyna-framed Super Glide (*see pp.154–55*) replaced it. Though the bike has been modified over the years, the original Super Glide concept of a big-twin engine in a cruiser/custom chassis has remained constant. A good idea is timeless.

1989 FXR SUPER GLIDE

Harley offered a range of factory-fitted optional extras for the FXR that included twin front disc-brakes, a solo seat, Sportster fuel tanks, and spoked wheels. A tuning kit was also available that boosted power output to over 80bhp. However, this example has been given a number of non-factory extras by its owner; note the handlebar tassles, the "slash-cut" silencers, the screen, and the panniers.

> *" The FXR was a continuation of Harley's successful Super Glide theme of placing the biggest V-twin engine of the range in a cruiser chassis."*

Passenger backrest

"King and queen" seat

Non-standard pannier

Non-standard back rack and "sissy" bar

Tail light

Low, well-padded saddle

Rear mudguard

41-cm (16-in) rear wheel

The exhaust system was based on that used on the Sportster (*see pp.130–31*)

Rear disc brake

Belt final-drive was added to the Super Glide in 1987

Five-speed gearbox

Brake master cylinder

"Buckhorn" handlebars

Removable windscreen was not a standard feature on the FXR

Windscreen is height-adjustable

Handlebar-mounted indicator

Fork-mounted tool pouch is a popular owner addition

Safety reflector

Narrow front mudguard

48-cm (19-in) front wheel

After-market air cleaner

Exhaust cross-pipe

Rubber engine mounts reduce vibration

"Highway" foot peg offers an alternative leg position on long rides

Nine-spoke alloy wheel

Single front disc brake

SPECIFICATIONS
1989 FXR Super Glide

- **ENGINE** Overhead-valve, V-twin
- **CAPACITY** 80cu. in. (1312cc)
- **POWER OUTPUT** 58bhp @ 7,200rpm
- **TRANSMISSION** Five-speed, belt drive
- **FRAME** Duplex cradle
- **SUSPENSION** Telescopic front forks, swingarm rear
- **WEIGHT** 259kg (570lb)
- **TOP SPEED** 185km/h (115mph)

"When the Evolution engine appeared in 1984 it transformed the Super Glide from just another touring bike into a real market-leader."

1997 FLHRI Road King

BY THE MID-1990S IT WAS QUITE obvious that there wasn't going to be any significant "new idea" which had a Harley-Davidson badge on the tank. Harley knew what its customers wanted, and it knew what it was good at building. Hence the regular reappearance of old ideas such as the Road King, a middleweight tourer first introduced for the 1995 model year. This was a return to traditional values for the Electra Glide in much the same way that the FLHS (*see pp.142–43*) had been a decade earlier. The Road King combined improvements to the Harley package – like electronic sequential port fuel injection on the FLHRI – with the looks of the traditional Electra Glide such as whitewall tyres, spoked wheels, leather saddlebags, and plenty of chrome. And with a price tag of about $15,000, Harley-Davidson now had a bike to give the big Japanese tourers a run for their money.

SPECIFICATIONS
1997 FLHRI Road King

- **ENGINE** Overhead-valve, fuel-injected V-twin
- **CAPACITY** 80cu. in. (1312cc)
- **POWER OUTPUT** 69bhp
- **TRANSMISSION** Five-speed, belt drive
- **FRAME** Tubular cradle
- **SUSPENSION** Telescopic front forks, swingarm rear
- **WEIGHT** 314kg (692lb)
- **TOP SPEED** 155km/h (96mph)

1997 FLHRI ROAD KING

The Evolution engine had been a success since its introduction in 1984 but the Weber fuel-injection option available on the FLHRI transformed it into a different beast again. Economic on fuel, easy to start, and lower exhaust emissions all added to a new, improved riding experience.

Removable pillion seat

Removable saddlebag is made from leather covering a hard shell

Rear indicator

Oil tank has 3.8-litre (1-gallon) capacity

Large silencer

Whitewall tyre

Wire-spoked wheel

Single rear disc brake

Swingarm pivot

Passenger footboard (folded up)

Quick-detach windscreen

Electronic starter button

Wide-bladed handlebar lever

19-litre (5-gallon) fuel tank

Riding stance
The handlebars were positioned high and wide, which was good for short- to middle-distance touring but not so practical for longer journeys. The bike's narrow profile and low centre of gravity did, however, provide enjoyable riding on twisting roads.

Passing lights are now a traditional feature of the touring Harley

Footboard

Traditional valanced mudguard

Road King mudguard script

Air filter cover boasts that the bike is fitted with fuel injection

Footboard

Chrome trim

80cu. in. Evolution engine is positioned in rubber-mounting system to reduce vibration

Dual front disc brakes

1999 FLSTF Fat Boy

HARDTAILS WERE MOTORBIKES without rear suspension, a customizing trend intended to give the rear of a machine a cleaner look. In another example of Harley-Davidson being influenced by the way its bikes were being customized, the company introduced the "Softail" in 1984. Harley wanted the clean look but didn't want to inflict the discomfort of a solid chassis onto its riders, so the bike had the look of a hardtail but with rear suspension units hidden under the engine. The FLSTF Fat Boy, launched in 1990, was a further variation on this idea, with solid disc wheels and a unique exhaust system contributing to the Fat Boy look. The FLSTS Heritage Springer went even further by using the Springer forks that Harley had discontinued in 1949 when it introduced the Hydra-Glide (*see pp.84–85*).

SPECIFICATIONS
1999 FLSTF Fat Boy

- **ENGINE** Overhead-valve, V-twin
- **CAPACITY** 80cu. in. (1312cc)
- **POWER OUTPUT** 83bhp
- **TRANSMISSION** Five-speed, belt drive
- **FRAME** Tubular cradle
- **SUSPENSION** Telescopic front forks, swingarm rear
- **WEIGHT** 271.5kg (598lb)
- **TOP SPEED** 193km/h (120mph)

1999 *FLSTF FAT BOY*
The solid disc wheels are the Fat Boy's most unusual feature, but solid covers for spoked wheels have been seen on Harleys at various times in the past, normally as an after-market accessory. The distinctive headlamp and fork panel was originally on the Hydra-Glide (*see pp.84–85*).

Rear mudguard is almost identical in style to that on the Hydra-Glide

Tail light

Ultra-low contoured seat is just 67.3cm (26½in) above road level

Rear disc brake

Softail swingarm has concealed suspension units

Low silencer hides the horizontally mounted shock absorber

Passenger footrest

Chromed oil tank

Wing mirror

Handlebar-mounted indicator

Front brake lever

Wide-spaced handlebars

Electric starter

Indicator

15.9-litre (4⅛-gallon) fuel tank

" The Fat Boy's unique styling has made it the best-selling Harley of the 1990s and the perfect partner for Arnold Schwarzenegger in the 1991 film Terminator II. "

Footboard

Instrument console

Chrome headlight

Tidy front
Placing the speedometer and warning lights in the dash on the fuel tank gives the Fat Boy a very uncluttered front, which is part of its appeal.

Headlight is mounted to a metal panel on the forks as on the 1948 FL

Two-tone Lazer Red and black paint finish

Metal shrouds conceal the fork legs on the FL-style front end

Safety reflector

Footboard

Dual exhaust system

Evolution engine was replaced by the Twin Cam (*see pp.152–53*) on year 2000 Softail models

41-cm (16-in) alloy disc wheel

Dunlop Elite "fat" tyre

1999 FXDX Super Glide

FOR THE NEW MILLENNIUM, Harley figured that it needed a new, more powerful, and more purposeful engine to replace the Evolution power unit which had provided such good service since 1984. This being Harley, it didn't want too much change all at once, so the new Twin Cam engine (*see pp.156–57*) could be, and was, slotted straight into the existing big-twin chassis. The new unit made its debut in 1998 on selected 1999 models, including the Super Glide Sport. Harley claimed a hefty 24-per cent power increase – to a still unspectacular 68bhp – for the new engine, largely as a result of an increase in revs and an increase in capacity to 88cu. in. Whatever, the new power enabled the Super Glide Sport to hit solid three-figure top speeds, and sustain them – an ability uncharacteristic for a Harley.

SPECIFICATIONS
1999 FXDX Super Glide

- ENGINE Overhead-valve, V-twin
- CAPACITY 88cu. in. (1450cc)
- POWER OUTPUT 68bhp (est.)
- TRANSMISSION Five-speed, belt drive
- FRAME Tubular cradle
- SUSPENSION Telescopic front forks, swingarm rear
- WEIGHT 279kg (615lb)
- TOP SPEED 177km/h (110mph)

1999 FXDX SUPER GLIDE SPORT
Harley first used a black engine finish on the XLCR (*see pp.126–27*) back in 1977, and although a black finish on engines and exhausts helps to dissipate heat, its popularity is more for cosmetic reasons. The matt finish on the FXD gives the engine a mean and purposeful look.

Sport version has a slimmer seat than the base FXD model

Battery case

Tail light

Ignition and parking light switch

41-cm (16-in) wire-spoked wheel with Dunlop Elite tyre

Single rear disc brake

Non-standard exhaust pipes release more power... and noise

Wing mirror

Electronic speedometer and rev-counter

Lower, black handlebars fitted on this Sport model

Handlebar-mounted indicator

Front brake lever

Essential components
The Super Glide is a no-flab motorcycle unburdened with unnecessary features. The front aspect is limited to the essentials of the bike and no more.

Small-diameter headlight

Fuel filler-cap

Fuel gauge

Chrome trimmed headlight

Fork yoke

18.57-litre (5-gallon) fuel tank

28° steering head

Fork shroud

Footrest

Buyers could choose from Aztec Orange Pearl, Diamond Ice Pearl, or Vivid Black paint finishes

Steering lock

Lightweight front mudguard

Safety reflector

Front brake calliper

Engine mounting point

88cu. in. Twin Cam engine with wrinkle black paint finish

Chromed exhaust downtube

Chrome wheel rim

Twin front disc brakes

Connector

Power cable

Chain-driven efficiency
Removing the cam cover allows a view of the exposed chain-drive to the cams. Replacing the gear-drive used on earlier engines reduced noise and manufacturing costs.

The Twin Cam was put through over 4 million test kilometres (2½ million miles) before its release

Exhaust port with stud for exhaust

Oval air-filter cover conceals the fuel-injection system

Two-piece alloy rocker cover

New aluminium cylinders have shorter stroke and larger bore than the Evolution

Exhaust port

Polished

The Twin Cam

TRADITION DICTATED THAT Harley engineers would ignore overhead camshafts, multi-valve cylinder heads, and other innovations when designing a new engine for the next millennium. And so it turned out. Though sophisticated fuel-injection and ignition systems provide a nod to the future, the 1999 Twin Cam still relies on the trusty 45° overhead-valve layout. The Twin Cam was a cleaner, more integrated design than the Evolution engine that preceded it (see pp 144-45) and it provided a platform for future development; engine capacity grew from 88 cu.in. to 96 cu.in. and then 103 cu.in.

area is increased by 50 per cent compared to the Evolution engine

Oil filter boss

Electrical cable

Engine mounting point

TIDIER BY DESIGN

Only 21 of the 450 component parts are carried over from the previous Evolution engine design, resulting in about ten per cent more torque. However, the 45° V-twin format ensures there's no mistaking that it's still a Harley-Davidson.

COMPETITION BIKE

•1999 DUCATI MONSTER•

The Italian Ducati company uses the air-cooled two-valve V-twin layout to good effect on its Monster range, which provides an alternative approach to the non-sporting motorcycle.

"The Twin Cam 88 is smooth, powerful, and very efficient. It is truly an air-cooled V-twin engine for the 21st century and destined to become a classic amongst riders."

JOHN WARR
(HARLEY DEALER)

Oil line connection

Gearbox mounting face

Inlet tract sensor

"We always walk a fine line between technical improvements and maintaining the look, sound, and feel. The new Twin Cam 88 is an example of how successfully we can do this."

WILLIE G. DAVIDSON
(VICE-PRESIDENT OF STYLING, HARLEY DAVIDSON INC.)

Alloy crankcase

Rocker cover

Electronic control

Sophisticated electronics provide the Twin Cam with supreme performance. Sensors supply information to the engine management system, which works out optimum fuel-injection settings for a given speed and load.

Pushrod tube

Ignition timing sensor

Connector

Crankcase

Power cable

2000s
1990s
1980s
1970s
1960s
1950s
1940s
1930s
1920s
1910s
1900s

1999 FXDWG Wide Glide

T**HE WIDE GLIDE IS A** chopper-style machine inspired by the bikes featured in the film Easy Rider. With the huge customizing culture in the US, the Wide Glide was intended to give buyers the chopper look straight from the Harley-Davidson factory. The Wide Glide was an immediate hit when it first appeared in 1980 – the widened fork yokes giving the bike its name – and soon became an established part of the Harley range. The Super Glide Dyna chassis is fitted with custom features that all come as standard, and for 1999 the bike incorporated the new 88cu. in. Twin Cam engine (*see pp.156–57*).

SPECIFICATIONS
1999 FXDWG Wide Glide

- **ENGINE** Overhead-valve, V-twin
- **CAPACITY** 88cu. in. (1450cc)
- **POWER OUTPUT** 79bhp
- **TRANSMISSION** Five-speed, belt drive
- **FRAME** Tubular cradle
- **SUSPENSION** Telescopic front forks, swingarm rear
- **WEIGHT** 271.5kg (598lb)
- **TOP SPEED** 193km/h (120mph)

1999 FXDWG WIDE GLIDE
The Dyna frame has a unique, computer-designed engine mounting system that uses flexible mountings and clever engineering to further reduce the effects of vibration on the motorcycle. The backbone of the frame is a rectangular section which is welded to a cast steering head.

Padded passenger backrest

"King and queen" seat with the pillion higher than the rider was another custom feature adopted by the factory

"Bobbed" rear mudguard

Rear indicator

Seat height is a modest 67.95cm (26¼ in)

41-cm (16-in) wire-spoked rear wheel with chrome rim

"Staggered short duals" exhaust system

Chrome battery box

Five-speed gearbox

"The Wide Glide has been updated ever since its introduction in 1980 and is now a true mix of classic custom styling with the most up-to-date Harley technology."

High-rise "Ape-hanger" handlebars

Handlebar controls feature wide-bladed levers and Harley's unique self-cancelling indicators

The "sissy bar", or passenger backrest was intended to reassure nervous pillions

Chromed speedometer binnacle

Custom-style chrome headlight with single mounting point

Made in the USA badging
Harley customers around the world were getting a real piece of Americana when they bought their motorcycle. The company were happy to reassure them that they had made the right decision.

Widened fork yokes give the bike its name

Optional two-tone colour scheme

53-cm (21-in) front wheel with skinny tyre

Safety reflector

Forward-mounted foot controls

"Dyna" frame with vibration-isolating engine mountings

Chrome air filter displays the bike's 88cu. in. capacity

Single 29-cm (11½-in) front disc brake

Dunlop Elite tyre

2003 FXSTB Night Train

INTRODUCED IN 1997, this variant of the Softail frame featured a pared-down custom look, a low profile seat, and flat, drag-racing handlebars. Originally fitted with the 1340cc Evo engine, the Night Train was given the 1450cc Twin Cam engine for the 2000 model year. With Harley-Davidson quick to notice new trends among motorcycle customizers, the model reflected a move away from candy paint finishes and exuberant use of chrome to a simpler appearance and predominantly black finish. The Night Train represents typical Harley policy of re-packaging a variety of components in different ways to create a large number of models around one engine, three types of frame, and a raft of wheels, fuel tanks, handlebars, and seats.

SPECIFICATIONS
2003 FXSTB Night Train

- **ENGINE** Overhead-valve, V-twin
- **CAPACITY** 88cu. in. (1450cc)
- **POWER OUTPUT** 69bhp (est.)
- **TRANSMISSION** Five-speed, belt drive
- **FRAME** Tubular cradle
- **SUSPENSION** Telescopic front forks, swingarm rear
- **WEIGHT** 305kg (673lb)
- **TOP SPEED** 193km/h (120mph)

2003 FXSTB NIGHT TRAIN
Riding a Harley is an experience. "You roll on the throttle and hear the engine roar", claims the marketing material for the Night Train. "Before long, the same primal urge that made cavemen go out and hunt woolly mammoths overtakes you." The reality may be less intriguing, but it is certainly an enjoyable ride.

Tail light

Low-profile seat

Rear disc brake

41-cm (16-in) solid rear wheel

"Staggered shorty duals" exhaust system

Softail swingarm unit

Passenger footrest

Twin Cam engine

Wing mirror

19.7-litre
(5¼-gallon)
fuel tank

Classic styling
*The slim rear view and considerable length of
the Night Train are classic Harley-Davidson
styling features. By mounting the instruments
in a tank-top console, the handlebars are kept
clear to give a better view of the small,
custom-style chrome headlight.*

"Riser"
handlebar
mountings

Central instrument console
incorporates speedometer,
warning lights, and
ignition switch

Small,
custom-style
headlight

Indicator

Flat, drag-racing
handlebars

Classic
"bobber"-
style rear
mudguard

Chrome
silencer

Front brake
calliper

Lightweight
front mudguard

Hydraulic
brake hose

Forward control
rear brake pedal

The engine's crinkle finish is
contrasted by the deep gloss
black on the cycle parts

53-cm (21-in)
spoked front wheel

2010 FLHR Road King

THE FL RANGE OF MACHINES can be traced all the way back to the original FL of 1941, and the current Road King plays on that heritage whilst also being a capable touring motorcycle for the 21st century. A ride-by-wire throttle, combined with digital fuel injection, constantly balances performance, economy, and emissions. At the same time, chassis improvements – a stiffer chassis with better suspension quality and improved geometry – means that the bike is easier to manoeuvre, and with a bike as big and heavy as this one, that is a really important consideration.

FLHR ROAD KING

In 2009 the Road King and its more luxurious stablemate, the Electra Glide, were given all-new chassis, resulting in better handling and superior ride quality. Improved engine mountings minimized vibration without losing the looks and riding character of the previous models, while better brakes were a welcome addition, and an anti-lock braking system was also an option.

Rack provides additional luggage capacity

One-piece dual seat

Chrome rocker covers

Passenger footboards fold when not in use

Panniers have 64-litre (2.26-cu. ft) capacity

40-cm (16-in) rear wheel

Two-into-one-into-two exhaust system

Six-speed gear box

Quickly detachable windscreen

Speedo mounted in tank-top console

Compass (non-standard)

27-litre (6-gallon) fuel tank gives a range of nearly 483-km (300 miles)

Passing lights

Indicators

Traditional deeply valanced mudguard

28-spoke, 43-cm (17-in.) alloy wheel

96-cu. in. (1584cc) Twin Cam engine

Air cleaner

Four-piston brake calipers

SPECIFICATIONS
2010 FLHR Road King

- **ENGINE** Overhead-valve, V-twin
- **CAPACITY** 96cu. in. (1584cc)
- **POWER OUTPUT** 68bhp
- **TRANSMISSION** Six-speed, belt-drive
- **FRAME** Tubular cradle
- **SUSPENSION** Telescopic front forks, swingarm rear
- **WEIGHT** 352kg (775lb)
- **TOP SPEED** 185km/h (115mph)

CHAPTER EIGHT

V-Rod

2001–2010

2003 VRSCA V-ROD

WHEN HARLEY-DAVIDSON introduced the V-Rod engine – officially called the "Revolution" – it came as something of a shock. Suddenly here was a Harley with overhead camshafts, water-cooling, and genuine performance. And the futuristic appearance of the V-Rod was also a surprise. Just when we thought that Harley had explored every variant of the cruiser look, the company invented something completely different.

A NEW DIRECTION
The radical nature of the V-Rod was the result of Harley responding to calls for significantly higher performance in an age of increasing noise and pollution restrictions.

2003 VRSCA V-Rod

HARLEY ENTHUSIASTS LOOKING for more performance from their bikes were finally rewarded in 2001 with the introduction of a radical new machine. The V-Rod was that rare thing in the history of the Milwaukee giant – a new model owing nothing to earlier machines. At the heart of the bike is an all-new 60° V-twin unit featuring overhead camshafts, four valves-per-cylinder, and water cooling, all innovations on a Harley engine. The chassis is long and low, with drag-bike-inspired looks and a unique finish in brushed and polished alloy. The V-Rod's astonishing performance and radical new look is in itself exciting, but the promise it suggests for a new generation of Harley-Davidson motorcycles is remarkable.

SPECIFICATIONS
2003 VRSCA V-Rod

- **ENGINE** Dual overhead-cam, V-twin
- **CAPACITY** 1130cc
- **POWER OUTPUT** 115bhp @ 8,500rpm (claimed)
- **TRANSMISSION** Five-speed, belt drive
- **FRAME** Tubular steel perimeter
- **SUSPENSION** Telescopic front forks, swingarm rear
- **WEIGHT** 270kg (595lb) (claimed)
- **TOP SPEED** 209km/h (130mph)

2003 VRSCA V-ROD
With almost double the power of existing models, the V-Rod frame needed to be stiffer than any previous Harley frame. Large-diameter steel tubing is wrapped around the engine in what Harley call a "perimeter" design, so that the frame is a styling component.

Indicator

Brushed aluminium body panel

Upper frame rail is a single piece of tubing with multiple curves

Seat unit lifts up to expose the fuel-tank filler

Rear shock absorbers have adjustable pre-load setting

15-litre (4-gallon) fuel tank

Dual exhaust system

Chrome-plated engine case

Wing
mirror

Instrument pod
contains rev-
counter,
speedometer,
and fuel gauge

Dummy tank
*The VRSCA's fuel tank cover is a dummy and
actually conceals the airbox. The real fuel tank is
positioned under the seat to lower the bike's centre
of gravity and contribute to its handling stability.*

Distinctive
oval headlight

49mm
telescopic fork

Imposing rear view
*The rear view of the V-Rod is dominated by the
180 section rear tyre and the twin exhaust pipes,
which both exit on the same side of the bike.*

Solid disc
aluminium
wheel

Twin front disc
brakes have
292mm discs and
four-piston
callipers

Cooling
radiators are
concealed in
aluminium
cowlings

Lower frame rail can be
unbolted to aid engine removal

The V-Rod

To **MEET THE DEMAND FOR** higher performance, Harley abandoned their traditional 45° overhead-valve design in favour of a 60° cylinder configuration in 2001. Consultants at Porsche worked with Harley engineers on the new V-Rod, with much of the technology originally developed for the VR1000 (*see pp.176–77*). Liquid cooling, overhead valves, and twin camshafts in each head increased the power output. The "knife and fork" connecting rods, a feature of Harley V-twins since 1909, were replaced with side-by-side rods.

Compact design

Because the engine and gearbox are designed and built as a single unit the power plant is much more compact than those seen on previous models. The shorter unit allows space in the chassis for the fuel tank to be positioned behind the engine.

Camshaft end blanking plate

Cam chain tensioner

A shaft located between the "V" of the cylinders drives a water pump located on the

Chrome-plated horn cover conceals the fuel injection system

Chrome-plated cambox cover

Cast alloy cylinder heads have fins for visual effect

Camchain tunnel runs inside the cylinder head

Cylinder barrels are integrated with the upper crankcase

Oil filler

Chrome-plated casing conceals a compact high output alternator

UP-TO-DATE TECHNOLOGY

The V-Rod uses modern technology in manufacturing and design for optimum performance within the constraints of emissions and noise legislation, but also to make the production process economic. Wet sump lubrication, another unusual feature for a Harley, means that oil is retained at the bottom of the engine and so there is no need for a separate oil tank.

Camshaft bearing cap

Camshaft drive sprocket

Camshaft

Valve

Cylinder head gasket

Valve spring

Inlet port

Inside the cylinder head
Twin camshafts run in the alloy cylinder head and operate two inlet valves and two exhaust valves. The increased valve area compared to the two-valve engines allows higher speeds and greater power. Harley claim that the V-Rod produces 115bhp, far more than the Evo (see pp. 144–45) and Twin Cam (see pp. 156–57) units.

"*Up around 5,000rpm, where your air-cooled hog is getting flustered, the Rod takes on fresh resolve. There's real urge to be found from 6,000rpm on.*"

BEN MILLER (BIKE MAGAZINE)

COMPETITION BIKE

•2003 YAMAHA ROAD WARRIOR•
Yamaha were also developing powerful cruisers at the time the V-Rod was introduced. The Road Star Warrior has an old-fashioned ohv engine which relies on huge capacity (1675cc) for its considerable power.

Water pump

Painted alloy crankcases are horizontally split

Fuel injection air inlet

Clutch and primary drive gears

Engine mounting

Fuel injection system
This cutaway drawing illustrates the V-Rod's fuel injection system, with twin vertical air inlet tracts positioned between the cylinder heads at the centre of the "V".

1993 | 1994 | 1995 | 1996 | 1997 | 1998 | 1999 | 2000 | 2001 | 2002 | 2003

2010 CVO Softail Convertible

IN 1999 THE MOTOR COMPANY responded to the growing trend for customizing standard machines by creating their own limited-edition custom models. These were dubbed CVO models, for Custom Vehicle Operations. Every year a limited number of models were given the CVO treatment, with larger capacity engines than the base models, more expensive paint finishes, non-standard accessories, and performance parts from Harley's "Screamin' Eagle" catalogue. The detailing reflected current trends in the custom world, with hand-applied pin-striping, metal-flake, and flame paint jobs being some of the finishes used. CVO models were naturally pricier than the standard bike, although fitting the parts at the factory was often more cost-effective than a retro fit.

CVO SOFTAIL CONVERTIBLE

Harley-Davidson's two traditional variants of the big-twin were the comfortable and well-equipped touring machines and the stylish cruisers. They came together in the Softail Convertible model which, with quickly detachable panniers and screen, could perform both roles: you could use it as a regular machine for short runs, or fit the screen and panniers, load up, and head out for longer rides.

Chromed mudguard support rails incorporate pannier mounts

Minimalist pillion seat for masochistic passengers

Leather solo saddle

46-cm (18-in) custom alloy wheels

Vance and Hines "Big Shot Longs" exhausts

Oil tank

Shock absorber is concealed beneath the gearbox

Chromed
handlebar
controls

19-litre
(5-gallon)
fuel tank
with
instrument
console

Small
custom-style
chrome
headlight

SPECIFICATIONS

2010 CVO Softail Convertible

- ENGINE Overhead-valve, V-twin
- CAPACITY 110cu. in. (1804cc)
- POWER OUTPUT 85bhp
- TRANSMISSION Six-speed, belt drive
- FRAME Tubular cradle
- SUSPENSION Telescopic front forks, swingarm rear
- WEIGHT 328kg (724lb)
- TOP SPEED 209km/h (130mph)

"Customizing is part of Harley-Davidson ownership – bikes don't remain the same as when they left the factory for long"

Chromed fork
shrouds echo 1950s
Harley style

Deeply valanced
FL-style mudguard

Single front
disc brake with
scalloped rotor

110-cu. in
(1804cc) Twin
Cam engine

"Screamin' Eagle"
performance air
filter

Billet alloy
brake pedal

CHAPTER NINE

SPORTS BIKES

1994–2010

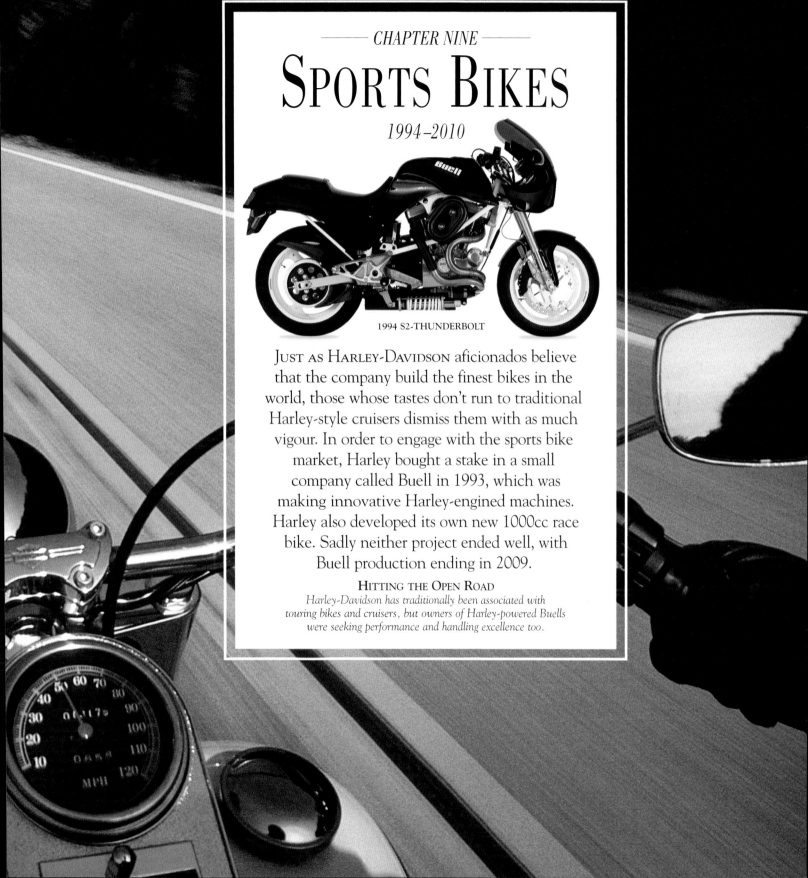

1994 S2-THUNDERBOLT

JUST AS HARLEY-DAVIDSON aficionados believe that the company build the finest bikes in the world, those whose tastes don't run to traditional Harley-style cruisers dismiss them with as much vigour. In order to engage with the sports bike market, Harley bought a stake in a small company called Buell in 1993, which was making innovative Harley-engined machines. Harley also developed its own new 1000cc race bike. Sadly neither project ended well, with Buell production ending in 2009.

HITTING THE OPEN ROAD
Harley-Davidson has traditionally been associated with touring bikes and cruisers, but owners of Harley-powered Buells were seeking performance and handling excellence too.

1986 Buell RR1000

THE FIRST **RR1000** PROTOTYPE was built in 1984 by Eric Buell, a former Harley employee, as a commission from the Vetter fairing company. Although Buell was still independent of Harley-Davidson at this point, the company would soon be incorporated into the Harley fold (*see pp.178–79*). The RR1000 used an XR1000 engine (*see pp.130–31*) fitted into Buell's patented Uniplanar chassis, which restricted engine vibration by using a system of rods, joints, and rubber mountings. Only 50 RR1000s were built before the supply of XR1000 engines dried up.

SPECIFICATIONS
1986 Buell RR1000

- **ENGINE** Overhead-valve, V-twin
- **CAPACITY** 61cu. in (998cc)
- **POWER OUTPUT** 77bhp @ 5,600rpm
- **TRANSMISSION** Four-speed, chain drive
- **FRAME** Chrome-moly, open-cradle space frame
- **SUSPENSION** Telescopic front forks, swingarm rear
- **WEIGHT** 177kg (390lb)
- **TOP SPEED** 217km/h (135mph) (est.)

Aerodynamic seat hump with integral rear light

Moulded knee cut-out

Solo seat

RR 1000
BATTLETWIN

Number-plate mounting

British-made Dymag three-spoke alloy wheel

Swingarm

Alloy rear sprocket

Brake pedal linkage

Rear brake master cylinder

Lower section of the fairing conceals a shock absorber and silencer

Air link
tube for
forks

Fuel tank
breather pipe

Flush fuel
filler-cap

Aerodynamic
smoked
windscreen

1986 BUELL RR1000 BATTLETWIN
Buell also offered a conventional 1200cc
Sportster engine version of the
Battletwin, which was designated the
RR1200. Though this model was not too
dissimilar to the RR1000, the exposed
engine on the unfaired version – the
RS1200 – resulted in an altogether more
traditional looking machine.

Bar-end wing mirror

Harley-Davidson's
orange and black
racing colour scheme

Oblong headlamp

Fairing mounting
bolt; direction
indicators also
positioned here

Italian Marzocchi
telescopic forks

Aerodynamic
shrouded front
mudguard

41-cm (16-in)
wheel reflects
period fashion
for small wheels

Bulges reflect the position
of the carburettors on the
XR1000 engine

The Buell's Harley engine
has to be advertised,
otherwise you would never
know it was a Harley unit

Massive
front disc
brakes

Pirelli
MP7 tyre

1994 VR1000

THERE ARE PROBABLY SEVERAL reasons why, in 1994, Harley decided to develop a totally new race bike. Corporate pride, the necessity to familiarize itself with new technology, and a desire to appeal to a new type of customer are among them. Whatever, the VR1000 made its debut under the spotlight at America's most prestigious road race – the 1994 Daytona 200-mile (322-km) Superbike. However, it wasn't a fairytale debut as the bike was off the pace and then blew up. Five years on, the VR1000 had still to achieve significant success despite swallowing large amounts of money and development time.

SPECIFICATIONS
1994 VR1000

- **ENGINE** Dual overhead-cam, V-twin
- **CAPACITY** 61cu. in (996cc)
- **POWER OUTPUT** 140bhp @ 10,400rpm
- **TRANSMISSION** Six-speed, chain drive
- **FRAME** Twin-spar alloy
- **SUSPENSION** Inverted telescopic front fork, single-shock rear
- **WEIGHT** 161kg (355lb)
- **TOP SPEED** 306km/h (190mph) (Daytona gearing)

Moulded racing seat

Tank cover and seat unit are a single lightweight structure

Lightweight alloy silencer

Braced swingarm

Slick racing tyre provides maximum grip on dry tracks

Drilled rear disc brake

Underslung brake calliper

Alloy chassis is constructed with twin-spars connecting the steering head to the swingarm pivot

Two-into-one exhaust system

Exposed dry clutch is cable-operated

1994 VR1000

Limited numbers of the VR1000 were offered for sale to the public to comply with Superbike racing rules that stated that a number of production versions of the competing bikes had to be produced. This was the fourth bike off the production line and was ridden to third position by Ron McGill in the 1995 Bears Series.

Quick-detach fairing fasteners allow a replacement to be fitted during a race

Rider's kit

The Harley-Davidson "bar and shield" logo features heavily on Rider Ron McGill's leathers. Racing a VR1000 as a privateer was costly and most bikes weren't campaigned for a second season.

Quick-release strap for removing the tank cover and seat unit

Fairing designed by Willie G. Davidson

Protective racing leathers

Racing handlebars

Inverted "upside-down" telescopic fork provides maximum rigidity for minimum weight

Lightweight Marchesini five-spoke alloy wheel

Racing tyre

Front brake calliper

Quick-release couplings for the fuel lines

Unique paint finish features Harley's traditional colours – orange on this side and black on the other

Braided steel pipes lead to the oil cooler

Large-diameter twin front brake discs

1994 Buell S2

I N 1993, HARLEY-DAVIDSON BOUGHT a 49 per cent stake in US sports-bike manufacturer Buell, giving Harley the potential to explore new markets without alienating existing customers. Money was now available to develop new machines and the S2-Thunderbolt was the first fruit of the new association. The bike was a development of the original Buell concept but with revised styling details and a 20 per cent power increase thanks to improvements in the exhaust and intake systems. Production of Buell bikes increased from 100 to 700 per year, helping to make the Thunderbolt much cheaper than earlier Buells.

SPECIFICATIONS
1994 Buell S2

- ENGINE Overhead-valve, V-twin
- CAPACITY 73cu. in. (1203cc)
- POWER OUTPUT 76bhp
- TRANSMISSION Five-speed, belt drive
- FRAME Tubular cradle
- SUSPENSION Telescopic front forks, swingarm rear
- WEIGHT 204kg (450lb)
- TOP SPEED 177km/h (110mph)

Self-cancelling indicator

Rear sub-frame

Dual seat

19-litre (5-gallon) fuel tank includes 2.2 litres (⅖ gallon) in reserve

Battery

Lightweight carbon-fibre hugger and belt-guard

Belt drive pulley

Marchesini three-spoke alloy wheel

Car-style silencer

Harley's belt final-drive retained on the Buell

Suspension damping adjustment dial

Horizontally mounted WP shock absorber is operated in tension

1994 BUELL S2-THUNDERBOLT

Buell sourced high-quality components from outside suppliers for the Thunderbolt, including WP forks and shock absorbers, Marchesini wheels, and Performance Machine brake callipers. Combined with some well-thought-out engineering, the end result was a bike that handled very capably, even though the 1200cc Sportster engine was slightly underpowered for the Buell's chassis.

Aerodynamic smoked windscreen

Chromed steel handlebars

Fuel breather pipe

Original Harley control lever

Instrument console

Frame-mounted bikini fairing

Headlight mounted in fairing

Rubber engine mounts reduce vibration

Short racing-style front mudguard

Two-into-one exhaust

Six-piston Performance Machine front brake calliper

34-cm (13½-in) front disc brake

Adjustable rear-view mirror

Chrome-moly tubular frame

Air vents

Two-into-one stainless steel exhaust pipes

Dunlop Sportmax front tyre

WP "upside-down" front forks

Slim profile

The Buell S2 made use of the Sportster power unit to provide the traditional benefits of the V-twin engine in a sport bike. This combination of a slim profile with good power delivery created a bike capable of competing with its contemporaries.

Knee cut-out in fuel tank

Prop stand

Rear wheel is 3.8cm (1½in) wider than front wheel

1999 Buell X1 Lightning

WHEN HARLEY BOUGHT ANOTHER chunk of Buell – taking its stake in the sports bike company to 98-per cent – in the late 1990s, the X1 Lightning followed soon afterwards. Launched in 1998 for the 1999 model year, the Lightning was more polished and refined than earlier Buells while retaining the oddball looks of the older machines. The ride was improved, the styling was tidied up, and a new electronic fuel-injection system was added to the Sportster engine. But in refining the Lightning some of the raw charm of the earlier bikes was lost.

1999 BUELL X1 LIGHTNING

Showa suspension units front and rear gave the Lightning a far superior ride over previous models, and another neat touch was the alloy seat sub-frame. Mechanically, the new fuel-injection system increased outright power and allegedly made the delivery smoother. Harley-Davidson hoped that the X1 would attract a more mainstream buyer to its sports marque.

Tail light

Number-plate light

Alloy seat support sub-frame new for 1999

Lightweight carbon-fibre hugger and belt-guard

Belt drive pulley

Chain adjuster

43-cm (17-in) wheel with Dunlop Sportmax tyre

12-volt sealed lead-acid battery

After-market silencer

Beefy swingarm

"Dynamic Digital" fuel-injection system monitors fuel mixture, air and engine temperature, and exhaust gasses

Instruments include a speedometer, tachometer, odometer, and tripmeter

17.4-litre (4⅖-gallon) fuel tank

Fuel tank breather pipe

The design of the wing mirrors was new for 1999, allowing easier adjustment

"Chin" fairing

SPECIFICATIONS
1999 Buell X1 Lightning

- **ENGINE** Overhead-valve, V-twin
- **CAPACITY** 73cu. in. (1203cc)
- **POWER OUTPUT** 101bhp @ 6,000rpm (claimed)
- **TRANSMISSION** Five-speed, belt drive
- **FRAME** Tubular cradle
- **SUSPENSION** Telescopic front forks, single-shock rear
- **WEIGHT** 200kg (441lb)
- **TOP SPEED** 225km/h (140mph)

" The Lightning incorporates one of the most advanced fuel management systems ever seen on a motorcycle. "

Indicator

Chrome trimmed headlight

"Upside down" Showa front forks are adjustable to suit different riders

Nylon airbox

Short racing-style front mudguard

Six-piston brake calliper

Belly pan

Red Snap was one of four colour schemes available; the others were Onyx Alloy, Reactor Yellow, and Carbon Black

Stainless steel two-into-one exhaust

Three-spoke cast-alloy wheel

2002 Buell XB9R Firebolt

THE FIREBOLT WAS A radical new model introduced for 2002, and it marked Buell's first serious effort at producing a genuine sports bike. It was lighter, shorter, and more focused than their previous machines, with steeper steering geometry to provide the sharper steering response required by sports riders. To make the machine more compact, Buell's traditional tubular steel frame was replaced by a twin-spar alloy chassis. The Sportster-based engine had a reduced capacity, but a shorter stroke allowed the engine to rev to nearly 7,500rpm.

SPECIFICATIONS

2002 Buell XB9R Firebolt

- ENGINE Overhead-valve, V-twin
- CAPACITY 948cc
- POWER OUTPUT 92bhp @ 7,200rpm (claimed)
- TRANSMISSION Five-speed, belt drive
- FRAME Aluminium twin-spar
- SUSPENSION Telescopic front forks, swingarm rear
- WEIGHT 175kg (386lb) (dry, claimed)
- TOP SPEED 201km/h (125mph)

Tail light

Plastic bodywork is colour impregnated so that scratches do not show

Belt drive pulley

Removable swingarm section allows the continuous drive belt to be fitted

Exhaust retaining clip

Belly pan

2002 BUELL XB9R FIREBOLT

Buell designed the Firebolt around a new chassis and managed to give the bike a distinctive and good-looking profile. The new chassis wraps around the air-cooled engine, hiding the rear cylinder head from view. A fan helps keep the engine cool by drawing air past the rear cylinder. An oil cooler is mounted on the left side of the bike below the front cylinder.

Wing mirror

Clip-on handlebars are angled and low to provide a sporting riding position

"Upside down" Showa fork

Bikini fairing

14-litre (3¼-gallon) fuel tank

Distinctive appearance
Though sharing a slim frontal aspect, the Firebolt's bug-eye headlights and frame-mounted fairing differentiate it from Buell's Lightning model (see pp.184–85).

Dunlop tyres developed for the bike are a special lightweight construction

Rim-mounted disc brake is a unique Buell feature

"Inspired by the track. Built for the streets. The Firebolt comes armed with industry-leading innovations that are as ground-breaking as its style."

2003 Buell XB9S Lightning

HAVING INTRODUCED THE radical new Firebolt for 2002 (*see pp.182–83*), Buell stripped the bike of its clip-on handlebars, frame-mounted sports fairing, and sports seat to create the aggressive-looking Lightning street-bike for the following year. The cast alloy rear sub-frame now supported a minimalist dual seat, and the higher bars and lower footrests provided a more accommodating riding position. Though these changes appear insignificant, and are relatively easy to implement, they alter the nature of the bike. The resulting model is less demanding and more practical than the uncompromising Firebolt it is based on. In terms of character and function, the Lightning has more in common with earlier Buells.

2003 BUELL XB9S LIGHTNING
A particular care over choice of materials has been exercised in the production of the Lightning. The wheels use a combination of rough-cast and polished alloy for visual effect. Colour-impregnated plastic body panels provide flashes of colour, the engine uses a combination of black and bare alloy, and the exhaust pipe headers are made from stainless steel. The details are exquisite and passers-by find plenty to look at.

> *"The Lightning feels like a BMX, a bicycle with the last two pots of a Detroit V8 rumbling away instead of pedal power."*

SPECIFICATIONS
2003 Buell XB9S Lightning
- **ENGINE** Overhead-valve, V-twin
- **CAPACITY** 984cc
- **POWER OUTPUT** 84bhp @ 7400rpm (claimed)
- **TRANSMISSION** Five-speed, belt drive
- **FRAME** Aluminium twin-spar
- **SUSPENSION** Telescopic front forks, swingarm rear
- **WEIGHT** 175kg (386lb) (dry, claimed)
- **TOP SPEED** 193km/h (120mph)

Low-profile dual seat

Cast alloy sub-frame supports the seat

Mudguard doubles as a number-plate mounting

43-cm (17-in) six-spoke rear wheel

180-mm (7-in) Dunlop tyre

Drive belt tensioning pulley

Swingarm contains the oil tank (on the other side)

Plastic cover conceals air box

Wing mirror

Front section of the frame doubles as a fuel tank

Fork-mounted twin headlights

Front forks are adjustable for pre-load and compression or rebound damping

Tubular steel handlebars

Duct channels air into the engine

Oil cooler

Minimal protection
The central bulge of the fly-screen covers the rev-counter, but the panel itself provides little in the way of weather protection for the rider.

Colour options are yellow or black

Belly pan

Six-piston front brake calliper

2010 VRSCDX Night Rod Special

THE WATER-COOLED, four-valves per-cylinder and double overhead camshaft V-Rod engine offered a level of power and performance never seen on a production Harley-Davidson, but it also offered the potential for further tuning. With support from the factory the bike became a popular choice for drag racing. The one make Harley Davidson racing series ran a V-Rod class, and the bike was extensively developed for the Pro-stock class, with the fastest machines achieving standing quarter mile times below seven seconds.

VRSCDX N*IGHT* R*OD* S*PECIAL*

The VRSCD Night Rod was introduced in 2006, its styling apparently inspired by Hot Rod cars and culture. The more powerful VRSCDX Night Rod Special, with an almost completely black finish, appeared the following year. The newer version had a 1250cc engine producing 125bhp. Power was transmitted to the road via a huge, 240-section rear tyre, while uprated brakes meant efficient slowing too.

Pillion support an optional extra

Inclined rear shock absorbers

Cylinder head finning is cosmetic detail on liquid-cooled engine

Luggage rack an optional extra

19-litre (5-gallon) fuel tank is located below rider's seat

Seat height is a modest 67cm (26.3 in)

Huge 240/40 rear tyre

Alloy swingarm

Slipper clutch

Black finish on mirror housings and other components

Handlebar switches

Stainless steel "drag style" low rise handlebar

Dummy tank cover conceals airbox

Minimalist headlight fairing

SPECIFICATIONS
2010 VRSCDX Night Rod Special
- ENGINE Dual overhead cam, V-twin
- CAPACITY 76cu. in. (1250cc)
- POWER OUTPUT 125bhp
- TRANSMISSION Five-speed, belt drive
- FRAME Tubular steel perimeter
- SUSPENSION Telescopic front forks, swingarm rear
- WEIGHT 270kg (595lb)
- TOP SPEED 209km/h (130mph)

"The 125bhp VRSCDX is the fastest-accelerating production bike that Harley have ever built. So far at least."

Forks raked at 34 degrees

300mm brake discs

Front mudguard incorporating fork brace

48-cm (19-in) slotted alloy wheel

Water pump

Brake pedal

Four-piston Brembo brake caliper

— THE COMPLETE HARLEY-DAVIDSON —

CATALOGUE

1903–2013

1999
TWIN CAM
CAM COVER

THE FOLLOWING CATALOGUE lists every production motorcycle manufactured by Harley-Davidson, from the first model in 1903 to the 2013 model range. It also includes various racing models produced by the company as one-offs or manufactured in limited production runs.

TEST DRIVING A NEW SILENT GRAY FELLOW
Harley-Davidson established a comprehensive dealership network only a few years after the Company was set up and today there are thousands of dealers worldwide.

The Complete Harley-Davidson Catalogue

The following catalogue lists the main models manufactured annually by Harley-Davidson from 1903 until the year 2003. It does not include any Buell models but does cover the Italian Aermacchi imports. Harley's philosophy during the 1980s of producing many different versions of similar models means that some limited editions and speciality models have been omitted. Note that the years given are model years so the bikes will actually have been released sometime during the previous year.

1903

The first year of Harley production, with an output of three bikes. The first bikes followed a 10.2cu. in. (167cc) prototype which used a reinforced bicycle-type frame.

THE FIRST BIKE

• ENGINE F-HEAD SINGLE

• CAPACITY 24.74CU. IN.

• NEW FEATURES LOOP FRAME AND LARGER THAN USUAL ENGINE

• COLOURS BLACK PAINT FINISH.

1904

First Harley-Davidson factory built in a 3m x 4.5m (10ft x 15ft) shed and first dealer appointed.

MODEL 0

• ENGINE F-HEAD SINGLE

• CAPACITY 24.74CU. IN.

• COLOURS BLACK PAINT FINISH. [IDENTIFICATION NUMBERING SYSTEM BEGINS WHICH SUBTRACTS FOUR FROM THE YEAR TO GET THE MODEL NUMBER FOR THAT YEAR I.E. 1904 =, MODEL 0].

1905

Factory size doubled to 3m x 9m (10ft x 30ft). Walter Davidson becomes full-time factory manager.

MODEL 1

• ENGINE F-HEAD SINGLE

• CAPACITY 24.74CU. IN.

• COLOURS BLACK PAINT FINISH.

1905 MODEL 1 SINGLE

1906

Silent Gray Fellow name first used for Harley's singles. New building at Juneau Avenue.

MODEL 2

• ENGINE F-HEAD SINGLE

• CAPACITY 26.8CU. IN.

• NEW FEATURES CAPACITY INCREASED TO 26.8CU. IN.

• COLOURS BLACK PAINT FINISH (RENAULT GRAY OPTIONAL).

1907

First experimental Harley-Davidson V-twin is built and exhibited at a motorcycle show. Harley-Davidson Motor Company officially established.

MODEL 3

• ENGINE F-HEAD SINGLE

• CAPACITY 26.8CU. IN.

• NEW FEATURES "SAGER" SPRUNG FRONT FORK (USED TO 1948)

• COLOURS RENAULT GRAY STANDARD (BLACK OPTIONAL).

1908

Walter Davidson wins the F.A.M. endurance run with a perfect score. The company now has 35 employees.

MODEL 4

• ENGINE F-HEAD SINGLE

• CAPACITY 26.8CU. IN.

• COLOURS RENAULT GRAY STANDARD (BLACK OPTIONAL).

1909

V-twin catalogued for the first time, though the model disappeared from the range the following year.

MODEL 5 SINGLES

• ENGINE F-HEAD SINGLE

• CAPACITY 30.16CU. IN.

MODEL VARIATIONS

5-A, 5-B. 5-C

MODEL 5 V-TWIN

• ENGINE V-TWIN

• CAPACITY 49.48CU. IN.

MODEL VARIATIONS

5-D

• NEW FEATURES BOSCH MAGNETO IGNITION OFFERED SCHEBLER CARBURETTOR OFFERED WIRE CONTROL CABLE USED

• COLOURS RENAULT GRAY STANDARD (BLACK OPTIONAL).

1910

Belt idler added to models to give a form of clutch control. First year of a Harley racing model and acetylene lights as an option. The company now employs 149 workers.

MODEL 6

• ENGINE F-HEAD SINGLE

• CAPACITY 30.16CU. IN.

• MODEL VARIATIONS 6-A, 6-B. 6-C

RACING MODEL

6-E

• NEW FEATURES FIRST YEAR OF "BAR AND SHIELD" TRADEMARK LOGO

• COLOURS RENAULT GRAY STANDARD (BLACK OPTIONAL).

1911

V-twin returns and remains continuously in the Harley range. Company expands to nearly 500 employees, producing over 5,500 bikes.

MODEL 7 SINGLES

• ENGINE F-HEAD SINGLE

• CAPACITY 30.16CU. IN.

MODEL VARIATIONS

7-A, 7-B, 7-C

MODEL 7 V-TWIN

• ENGINE V-TWIN

• CAPACITY 49.48CU. IN.

MODEL VARIATIONS

7-D

• NEW FEATURES MECHANICAL INLET VALVES ON V-TWIN

• COLOURS RENAULT GRAY.

1912

All models have a new frame with the top tube sloping to the rear allowing a lower saddle which is mounted on a new sprung seat-post. Clutch assembly in rear hub on models with X designation. Workforce doubles.

MODEL 8 SINGLES

• ENGINE F-HEAD SINGLE

• CAPACITY 30.16CU. IN.

MODEL VARIATIONS

8-A, X-8, X-8A

1912 X-8 SILENT GRAY FELLOW

MODEL 8 V-TWINS

• ENGINE V-TWINS

• CAPACITY 49.48 & 61CU. IN.

MODEL VARIATIONS

8-D, X-8D (49.48CU. IN. V-TWIN) X-8E (61CU. IN. V-TWIN)

• NEW FEATURES CHAIN FINAL-DRIVE FIRST USED REAR HUB CLUTCH FIRST USED

• COLOURS RENAULT GRAY STANDARD. FOUR OTHER COLOUR OPTIONS ARE NOW OFFERED AT EXTRA COST.

1913

Harley-Davidson racing department founded. First year of Model G delivery van.

MODEL 9 SINGLES

• ENGINE F-HEAD SINGLE

• CAPACITY 35CU. IN.

MODEL VARIATIONS

9-A, 9-B

MODEL 9 V-TWINS

• ENGINE V-TWIN

• CAPACITY 61CU. IN.

MODEL VARIATIONS

9-E, 9-F, 9-G

• NEW FEATURES MECHANICAL INLET VALVES ON SINGLES MAGNETO IGNITION STANDARD TWO-SPEED TRANSMISSION OPTION AVAILABLE ON DELIVERY VAN

- **COLOURS**
RENAULT GRAY STANDARD. FOUR COLOUR OPTIONS AVAILABLE AT EXTRA COST.

1914

Harley-Davidson's factory race team starts competing on various circuits. First sidecars ordered from the Rogers Company, but not officially listed as an option until following year.

MODEL 10 SINGLES

- **ENGINE** F-HEAD SINGLE
- **CAPACITY** 35CU. IN.

MODEL VARIATIONS

10-A, 10-B, 10-C

MODEL 10 V-TWINS

- **ENGINE** V-TWIN
- **CAPACITY** 61CU. IN.

MODEL VARIATIONS

10-E, 10-F, 10-G

- **NEW FEATURES**
STEP (KICK) STARTERS OFFERED, ALLOWING THE BICYCLE PEDALS TO BE ABANDONED AND FOOTBOARDS FITTED TO SOME MACHINES
TWO-SPEED TRANSMISSION AVAILABLE FOR SINGLES

- **COLOURS**
RENAULT GRAY STANDARD. FOUR COLOUR OPTIONS AVAILABLE AT EXTRA COST.

1915

From 1915–53 a sidecar version of most of the V-twin models was offered. The initial S after the model ID letters was used to identify them i.e. FS Sidecar Twin. Harley's new interest in bike racing spawns first series of racing models in both single and V-twin formats.

MODEL 11 SINGLES

- **ENGINE** F-HEAD SINGLE
- **CAPACITY** 35CU. IN.

MODEL VARIATIONS

11-B, 11-C

RACING MODELS

11-K4, 11-KF

MODEL 11 V-TWINS

- **ENGINE** V-TWIN
- **CAPACITY** 61CU. IN.

MODEL VARIATIONS

11-E, 11-F, 11-G, 11-H, 11-J

RACING MODELS

11-K, 11-KR, 11-KT, 11-KRH, 11-KTH, 11-K12, 11-K12H

- **NEW FEATURES**
THREE-SPEED GEARBOX ON TWINS
MECHANICAL OIL PUMP
ELECTRIC LIGHTING OPTION

- **COLOURS**
RENAULT GRAY STANDARD. FOUR COLOUR OPTIONS AVAILABLE AT EXTRA COST.

1915 KR FAST ROADSTER

1916

First year of eight-valve racing twins and four-valve single racers. Identification system changes this year so that the number reflects the model year, i.e. 1916 35cu. in. single is a Model 16-B. N.B. Henceforth in this catalogue models will be referred to by identification initials only.

MODEL B

- **ENGINE** F-HEAD SINGLE
- **CAPACITY** 35CU. IN.

MODEL C

- **ENGINE** F-HEAD SINGLE
- **CAPACITY** 35CU. IN.

RACING MODELS

MODEL S

MODEL E

- **ENGINE** F-HEAD V-TWIN
- **CAPACITY** 61CU. IN.

MODEL F

- **ENGINE** F-HEAD V-TWIN
- **CAPACITY** 61CU. IN.

MODEL J

- **ENGINE** F-HEAD V-TWIN
- **CAPACITY** 61CU. IN.

RACING MODELS

MODELS R & T
EIGHT-VALVE RACER (OHV)

- **COLOURS** RENAULT GRAY STANDARD. FOUR COLOUR OPTIONS AVAILABLE AT EXTRA COST.

1917

Bosch magnetos unavailable due to the war, so replaced by Dixie brand for this year only. Harley sends its first bikes for military use in WWI.

MODEL B

- **ENGINE** F-HEAD SINGLE
- **CAPACITY** 35CU. IN.

MODEL C

- **ENGINE** F-HEAD SINGLE
- **CAPACITY** 35CU. IN.

RACING MODELS

MODEL S

MODEL E

- **ENGINE** F-HEAD V-TWIN
- **CAPACITY** 61CU. IN.

MODEL F

- **ENGINE** F-HEAD V-TWIN
- **CAPACITY** 61CU. IN.

MODEL J

- **ENGINE** F-HEAD V-TWIN
- **CAPACITY** 61CU. IN.

RACING MODELS

MODELS R & T, EIGHT-VALVE RACER

- **COLOURS**
OLIVE GREEN IS NOW THE STANDARD COLOUR. ONLY YEAR OF GOLD PINSTRIPING.

1918

Last year of the 35cu. in. F-head singles. Berling magnetos replace Dixies. Model F is the best-seller for this year.

MODEL B

- **ENGINE** F-HEAD SINGLE
- **CAPACITY** 35CU. IN.

MODEL C

- **ENGINE** F-HEAD SINGLE
- **CAPACITY** 35CU. IN.

MODEL E

- **ENGINE** F-HEAD V-TWIN
- **CAPACITY** 61CU. IN.

MODEL F

- **ENGINE** F-HEAD V-TWIN
- **CAPACITY** 61CU. IN.

MODEL J

- **ENGINE** F-HEAD V-TWIN
- **CAPACITY** 61CU. IN.

1918 MODEL J SIDECAR

MODEL VARIATIONS

FUS (GOVT. USE ONLY)

RACING MODELS

MODEL R, EIGHT-VALVE RACER

A SMALL NUMBER OF MODIFIED V-TWINS ALSO PRODUCED

- **COLOURS**
OLIVE GREEN.

1919

First year of the horizontally opposed flathead twin model W, though not a great success in the US so mainly exported to overseas markets. Also first year for the "two-cam" F-head and eight-valve racers.

MODEL W

- **ENGINE** HORIZONTALLY OPPOSED FLATHEAD TWIN
- **CAPACITY** 35.64CU. IN. (584.03CC)

1919 MODEL W

MODEL F

- **ENGINE** F-HEAD V-TWIN
- **CAPACITY** 61CU. IN.

MODEL VARIATIONS

F/FS/FUS (GOVT. USE ONLY)

MODEL J

- **ENGINE** F-HEAD V-TWIN
- **CAPACITY** 61CU. IN.

MODEL VARIATIONS

J/JS

RACING MODELS

TWO-CAM EIGHT-VALVE RACER
TWO-CAM F-HEAD RACER

A SMALL NUMBER OF ADAPTED V-TWIN MODELS ALSO PRODUCED

- **COLOURS**
OLIVE GREEN.

1920

Harley factory race team parade on victory lap with a pig on a bike, so beginning the "hog" association. The company now has the biggest motorcycle factory in the world.

MODEL W

- **ENGINE** HORIZONTALLY OPPOSED FLATHEAD TWIN
- **CAPACITY** 35.64CU. IN. (584.03CC)

MODEL VARIATIONS

W/WF/WJ

MODEL F

- **ENGINE** F-HEAD V-TWIN
- **CAPACITY** 61CU. IN.

MODEL VARIATIONS

F/FS

MODEL J

- **ENGINE** F-HEAD V-TWIN
- **CAPACITY** 61CU. IN.

MODEL VARIATIONS

J/JS

RACING MODELS

Two-cam eight-valve racer
Two-cam F-head racer

1920 EIGHT-VALVE RACER

A SMALL NUMBER OF MODIFIED
V-TWINS ALSO PRODUCED

• COLOURS
Olive Green.

1921

First year for 37cu. in. CD
commercial single model, using
same chassis as (also new) 74cu. in.
big-twin but minus one cylinder.
A Harley racer is the first bike to
win a race with an average speed
of over 161km/h (100mph).

MODEL CD

• ENGINE F-HEAD SINGLE

• CAPACITY 37CU. IN.

MODEL W

• ENGINE HORIZONTALLY OPPOSED
FLATHEAD TWIN

• CAPACITY 35.64CU. IN. (584.03cc)

MODEL VARIATIONS

W/WF/WJ

MODEL F

• ENGINE F-HEAD V-TWIN

• CAPACITY 61CU. IN.

MODEL VARIATIONS

F/FS

MODEL J

• ENGINE F-HEAD V-TWIN

• CAPACITY 61CU. IN.

MODEL VARIATIONS

J/JS

MODEL FD

• ENGINE F-HEAD V-TWIN

• CAPACITY 74CU. IN.

MODEL VARIATIONS

FD/FDS

MODEL JD

• ENGINE F-HEAD V-TWIN

• CAPACITY 74CU. IN.

MODEL VARIATIONS

JD/JDS (SIDECAR TWINS)

RACING MODELS

Two-cam eight-valve racer
Two-cam F-head racer
Four-valve racer

A SMALL NUMBER OF MODIFIED
V-TWINS ALSO PRODUCED

• COLOURS
Olive Green. Only year of Olive
Green crankcases.

1922

Model CD commercial single
discontinued at the end of this year.
Harley-Davidson output picks up
again after national economic slump
of 1921 which saw sales drop by
60 per cent and many other
motorcycle manufacturers go
out of business.

MODEL CD

• ENGINE F-HEAD SINGLE

• CAPACITY 37CU. IN.

MODEL W

• ENGINE HORIZONTALLY OPPOSED
FLATHEAD TWIN

• CAPACITY 35.64CU. IN.
(584.03cc)

MODEL VARIATIONS

W/WF/WJ

MODEL F

• ENGINE F-HEAD V-TWIN

• CAPACITY 61CU. IN.

MODEL VARIATIONS

J/JS

MODEL J

• ENGINE F-HEAD V-TWIN

• CAPACITY 61CU. IN.

MODEL VARIATIONS

F/FS

MODEL FD

• ENGINE F-HEAD V-TWIN

• CAPACITY 74CU. IN.

• MODEL VARIATIONS

FD/FDS

MODEL JD

• ENGINE F-HEAD V-TWIN

• CAPACITY 74CU. IN.

• MODEL VARIATIONS

JD/JDS

RACING MODELS

Two-cam eight-valve racer
Two-cam F-head racer
Four-valve racer

A SMALL NUMBER OF MODIFIED
V-TWINS ALSO PRODUCED

• COLOURS
Brewster Green paint scheme
(INCLUDING CRANKCASES).

1923

Last year of W Series sport twins, with
production figures only in the
hundreds. Harley factory race team is
disbanded. JD model is best-seller,
with figures of over 7,000. First year of
hinged rear mudguard on big-twins.

MODEL W

• ENGINE HORIZONTALLY OPPOSED
FLATHEAD TWIN

• CAPACITY 35.64CU. IN. (584.03cc)

MODEL VARIATIONS

W/WF/WJ

MODEL F

• ENGINE F-HEAD V-TWIN

• CAPACITY 61CU. IN.

MODEL VARIATIONS

F/FS

MODEL J

• ENGINE F-HEAD V-TWIN

• CAPACITY 61CU. IN.

MODEL VARIATIONS

J/JS

MODEL FD

• ENGINE F-HEAD V-TWIN

• CAPACITY 74CU. IN.

MODEL VARIATIONS

FD/FDS

MODEL JD

• ENGINE F-HEAD V-TWIN

• CAPACITY 74CU. IN.

MODEL VARIATIONS

JD, JDS

RACING MODELS

Model T (V-TWIN RACER)
Model S (SINGLE RACER)
Two-cam eight-valve racer
Two-cam F-head racer

A SMALL NUMBER OF MODIFIED
V-TWINS ALSO PRODUCED

• COLOURS
Brewster Green paint scheme.

1924

Generally a poor year for the
company, which operates at a loss.
As a result, 1,500 employees are
laid-off. Aluminium alloy pistons
used on some models for
this year only.

MODEL F

• ENGINE F-HEAD V-TWIN

• CAPACITY 61CU. IN.

MODEL VARIATIONS

F/FE/FES

MODEL J

• ENGINE F-HEAD V-TWIN

• CAPACITY 61CU. IN.

MODEL VARIATIONS

J/JE/JES

MODEL FD

• ENGINE F-HEAD V-TWIN

• CAPACITY 74CU. IN.

MODEL VARIATIONS

FD/FDS/FDCA/FDSCA

MODEL JD

• ENGINE F-HEAD V-TWIN

• CAPACITY 74CU. IN.

MODEL VARIATIONS

JD/JDS/JDCA/JDSCA

RACING MODELS

Two-cam eight-valve racer
Two-cam F-head racer

• COLOURS
Olive Green.

1925

Last year that Harley outsources
sidecar manufacture, the company
now deciding to build its own. First
export of Harleys to Japan. Revamp of
the big-twins, with major mechanical
and design changes including Harley's
famous teardrop fuel tank. Despite the
decline in popularity of board-track
racing, Joe Petrali secures a number of
notable victories on a Harley.

MODEL F

• ENGINE F-HEAD V-TWIN

• CAPACITY 61CU. IN.

MODEL VARIATIONS

F/FE/FES

MODEL J

• ENGINE F-HEAD V-TWIN

• CAPACITY 61CU. IN.

MODEL VARIATIONS

J/JE/JES

MODEL FD

• ENGINE F-HEAD V-TWIN

• CAPACITY 74CU. IN.

MODEL VARIATIONS

FD/FDCB/FDSBS

MODEL JD

• ENGINE F-HEAD V-TWIN

• CAPACITY 74CU. IN.

MODEL VARIATIONS

JD/JDCB/JDCBS

RACING MODELS

Two-cam eight-valve racer
Two-cam F-head racer

• NEW FEATURES
WIDER, LOWER FRAME
CYLINDRICAL TOOLBOX MOUNTED
ON FRONT FORK TEARDROP-STYLE
STREAMLINED TANKS
IRON ALLOY PISTONS

• COLOURS
OLIVE GREEN.

1926

Models A and B are Harley's new
flathead singles, with optional
overhead-valve units on models AA
and BA. All road-going twins now
equipped with electrical lighting. First
year of Harley's own-production
sidecars. Over 9,000 JD models
manufactured this year, making it the
most popular Harley by far.

MODEL A

• ENGINE FLATHEAD SINGLE

• CAPACITY 21CU. IN.

MODEL VARIATIONS

A, AA (OHV ENGINE)

MODEL B

• ENGINE FLATHEAD SINGLE

• CAPACITY 21CU. IN.

MODEL VARIATIONS

B, BA (OHV ENGINE)

1926 B PEASHOOTER

MODEL F

• ENGINE F-HEAD V-TWIN

• CAPACITY 61CU. IN.

MODEL VARIATIONS

F/FE/FES

MODEL J

• ENGINE F-HEAD V-TWIN

• CAPACITY 61CU. IN.

MODEL VARIATIONS

J/JE/JES/JS

MODEL FD

• ENGINE F-HEAD V-TWIN

• CAPACITY 74CU. IN.

MODEL VARIATIONS

FD/FDCB/FDSBS

MODEL JD

• ENGINE F-HEAD V-TWIN

• CAPACITY 74CU. IN.

MODEL VARIATIONS

JD/JDCB/JDCBS/JDS

RACING MODELS

MODEL S (21CU. IN. OHV SINGLE)
TWO-CAM F-HEAD RACER
TWO-CAM EIGHT-VALVE RACER

1926 MODEL S RACER

• COLOURS
OLIVE GREEN. WHITE OR CREAM
AVAILABLE AT EXTRA COST ON TWINS.

1927

A year of minimal change, with
only minor detail modifications,
though models AA and BA do
get Ricardo cylinder heads and
a revised frame.

MODEL A

• ENGINE FLATHEAD SINGLE

• CAPACITY 21CU. IN.

MODEL VARIATIONS

A; AA/AAE (OHV ENGINE)

MODEL B

• ENGINE FLATHEAD SINGLE

• CAPACITY 21CU. IN.

MODEL VARIATIONS

B; BB/BAE (OHV ENGINE)

MODEL J

• ENGINE F-HEAD V-TWIN

• CAPACITY 61CU. IN.

MODEL VARIATIONS

J/JS

MODEL F

• ENGINE F-HEAD V-TWIN

• CAPACITY 61CU. IN.

MODEL VARIATIONS

F/FK/FS

MODEL JD

• ENGINE F-HEAD V-TWIN

• CAPACITY 74CU. IN.

MODEL VARIATIONS

JD/JDL/JDS

MODEL FD

• ENGINE F-HEAD V-TWIN

• CAPACITY 74CU. IN.

MODEL VARIATIONS

FD/FDL/FDS

RACING MODELS

MODELS S/SM/SA/SMA (21CU. IN.
OHV SINGLES)
MODEL T (V-TWIN)
MODELS FHAC/FHAD (61CU. IN
HILL-CLIMBERS)

TWO-CAM EIGHT-VALVE RACER
TWO-CAM F-HEAD RACER

• COLOURS
OLIVE GREEN. WHITE OR CREAM
AVAILABLE AT EXTRA COST ON TWINS.

1928

New high-performance JH and JDH
models are road-going versions of the
two-cam competition machines, using
a slimmer and lower chassis than the
standard single-cam J and JD models.

MODEL A

• ENGINE FLATHEAD SINGLE

• CAPACITY 21CU. IN.

MODEL VARIATIONS

A; AA/AAE (OHV ENGINE)

MODEL B

• ENGINE FLATHEAD SINGLE

• CAPACITY 21CU. IN.

MODEL VARIATIONS

B; BA/BAE (OHV ENGINE)

MODEL J

• ENGINE F-HEAD V-TWIN

• CAPACITY 61CU. IN.

MODEL VARIATIONS

J/JS/JX/JXL/JH

MODEL F

• ENGINE F-HEAD V-TWIN

• CAPACITY 61CU. IN.

MODEL VARIATIONS

F/FH/FS

MODEL JD

• ENGINE F-HEAD V-TWIN

• CAPACITY 74CU. IN.

MODEL VARIATIONS

JD/JDH (TWO-CAM)/JDX/JDXL/JDS

1928 JD

MODEL FD

• ENGINE F-HEAD V-TWIN

• CAPACITY 74CU. IN.

MODEL VARIATIONS

FD/FDH/FDS

RACING MODELS

MODELS S/SM/SA/SMA (21CU. IN.
OHV SINGLES)
MODEL T (V-TWIN)
MODEL FHAC/FHAD

(61CU. IN. HILL-CLIMBERS)
TWO-CAM EIGHT-VALVE RACER
TWO-CAM F-HEAD RACER

• NEW FEATURES
FRONT BRAKE

• COLOURS
OLIVE GREEN. A RANGE OF EIGHT
COLOURS AVAILABLE AT EXTRA COST
ON TWINS.

1929

New model C single features a bigger
engine. Also first year of model D
45cu. in. side-valve V-twin. Last year
of AA and BA singles, models J, JD, F,
and FD, as well as eight-valve racers.

MODEL A

• ENGINE FLATHEAD SINGLE

• CAPACITY 21CU. IN.

MODEL VARIATIONS

A; AA (OHV ENGINE)

MODEL B

• ENGINE FLATHEAD SINGLE

• CAPACITY 21CU. IN.

MODEL VARIATIONS

B/BA; BAF (OHV ENGINE)

MODEL C

• ENGINE FLATHEAD SINGLE

• CAPACITY 30.5CU. IN.

MODEL D

• ENGINE FLATHEAD V-TWIN

• CAPACITY 45CU. IN.

MODEL VARIATIONS

D/DL

MODEL J

• ENGINE F-HEAD V-TWIN

• CAPACITY 61CU. IN.

MODEL VARIATIONS

J/JS/JXL/JH

MODEL F

• ENGINE F-HEAD V-TWIN

• CAPACITY 61CU. IN.

MODEL VARIATIONS

F/FL/FS

MODEL JD

• ENGINE F-HEAD V-TWIN

• CAPACITY 74CU. IN.

MODEL VARIATIONS

JD/JDH(TWO-CAM)//JDF/JDXL/JDS

MODEL FD

• ENGINE F-HEAD V-TWIN

• CAPACITY 74CU. IN.

MODEL VARIATIONS

FD/FDH/FDL/FDS

RACING MODELS

SA/SMA (21CU. IN. OHV SINGLES)
MODEL T (V-TWIN)
FHAC (61CU. IN. RACER)
FHAD (61CU. IN. HILL-CLIMBER)
TWO-CAM EIGHT-VALVE RACER
TWO-CAM F-HEAD RACER

• NEW FEATURES
DUAL BULLET HEADLIGHTS
FOUR-TUBE "PIPE O' PAN" SILENCERS

• COLOURS
OLIVE GREEN. A RANGE OF EIGHT
COLOURS AVAILABLE AT EXTRA COST
ON TWINS.

1930

New flathead model V replaces F-head big-twins, boasting magnesium-alloy pistons and Ricardo heads.

MODEL A

• ENGINE FLATHEAD SINGLE

• CAPACITY 21CU. IN.

MODEL B

• ENGINE FLATHEAD SINGLE

• CAPACITY 21CU. IN.

MODEL VARIATIONS

B/BR; BAF (OHV ENGINE)

MODEL C

• ENGINE FLATHEAD SINGLE

• CAPACITY 30.5CU. IN.

MODEL VARIATIONS

C/CM

MODEL D

• ENGINE FLATHEAD V-TWIN

• CAPACITY 45CU. IN.

• MODEL VARIATIONS

D/DL/DLD/DS

MODEL V

• ENGINE FLATHEAD V-TWIN

• CAPACITY 74CU. IN.

MODEL VARIATIONS

V/VS/VL/VLM/VC/VCM/VM/
VMS/VMG

RACING MODELS

HILL-CLIMBER AND OTHER RACERS
WERE MADE AS ONE-OFF BIKES
THROUGHOUT THE 1930s

1930 HILL-CLIMBER

• NEW FEATURES
DROP-CENTRE WHEEL RIMS
FORGED "I" BEAM FORKS

• COLOURS
OLIVE GREEN. A RANGE OF SIX
COLOURS AVAILABLE AT EXTRA COST
ON TWINS.

1931

Model B produced for export only this year. Last year of model D. Low production levels in post-crash slump.

MODEL B

• ENGINE FLATHEAD SINGLE

• CAPACITY 21CU. IN.

MODEL C

• ENGINE FLATHEAD SINGLE

• CAPACITY 30.5CU. IN.

MODEL VARIATIONS

C/CH/CMG/CC

MODEL D

• ENGINE FLATHEAD V-TWIN

• CAPACITY 45CU. IN.

MODEL VARIATIONS

D/DL/DLD/DC/DS

MODEL V

• ENGINE FLATHEAD V-TWIN

• CAPACITY 74CU. IN.

MODEL VARIATIONS

VVS/VL/VLM/VC/VSR/VMG/VMS

• NEW FEATURES
"SUNBURST" HORN (ALL MODELS
EXCEPT B)
SCHEBLER DELUXE CARBURETTOR
ON TWINS

• COLOURS
OLIVE GREEN. A RANGE OF FIVE
COLOURS AVAILABLE AT EXTRA COST.

1932

New model R replaces model D. First year of three-wheeled model G Servi-Car. Model B produced for domestic market again.

MODEL B

• ENGINE FLATHEAD SINGLE

• CAPACITY 21CU. IN.

MODEL C

• ENGINE FLATHEAD SINGLE

• CAPACITY 30.5CU. IN.

MODEL VARIATIONS

C/CC/CR/CS

MODEL R

• ENGINE FLATHEAD V-TWIN

• CAPACITY 45CU. IN.

MODEL VARIATIONS

R/RL/RLD/RS

MODEL G SERVI-CAR

• ENGINE FLATHEAD V-TWIN

• CAPACITY 45CU. IN.

MODEL VARIATIONS

G/GA/GD/GE

MODEL V

• ENGINE FLATHEAD V-TWIN

• CAPACITY 74CU. IN.

MODEL VARIATIONS

V/VS/VL/VC

• COLOURS
OLIVE GREEN. A RANGE OF SEVEN
COLOURS AVAILABLE AT EXTRA COST.

1933

Lay-offs and reduced production in 1932 mean little change in 1933. Joe Petrali adds a note of optimism to the gloom by winning the second of four consecutive national hill-climbing championships on a Harley. He won six in total.

MODEL B

• ENGINE FLATHEAD SINGLE

• CAPACITY 21CU. IN.

MODEL C

• ENGINE FLATHEAD SINGLE

• CAPACITY 30.5CU. IN.

MODEL VARIATIONS

C/CB/CS

MODEL R

• ENGINE FLATHEAD V-TWIN

• CAPACITY 45CU. IN.

MODEL VARIATIONS

R/RL/RLD/RS/RE/RLE/RLDE

MODEL G SERVI-CAR

• ENGINE FLATHEAD V-TWIN

• CAPACITY 45CU. IN.

MODEL VARIATIONS

G/GA/GD/GDT/GE

MODEL V

• ENGINE FLATHEAD V-TWIN

• CAPACITY 74CU. IN.

MODEL VARIATIONS

V/VS/VL/VLD/VC/VE/VF/VFS/
VLE/VSE

1933 VLE

• NEW FEATURES
ART DECO-STYLE BIRD MOTIF ON
TANK (THIS YEAR ONLY)
REVERSE GEAR OPTIONAL ON
R MODELS
BUDDY SEAT DEBUTS AS ACCESSORY

• COLOURS OLIVE GREEN NO
LONGER STANDARD COLOUR.
SINGLES AND MODEL G IN SILVER
AND TURQUOISE. TWINS IN A RANGE
OF FIVE STANDARD COLOURS.

1934

Last year of model B and C singles. New Art Deco styling touches added to the bikes, including stylized handlebars and motif and streamlined tail lights. Production rises to around 10,000 bikes, almost trebling previous year's output.

MODEL B

• ENGINE FLATHEAD SINGLE

• CAPACITY 21CU. IN.

MODEL C

• ENGINE FLATHEAD SINGLE

• CAPACITY 30.5CU. IN.

MODEL VARIATIONS

C/CB

MODEL R

• ENGINE FLATHEAD V-TWIN

• CAPACITY 45CU. IN.

MODEL VARIATIONS

R/RL/RLD/RLDX/RLX/RS/RSX/RX

MODEL G SERVI-CAR

• ENGINE FLATHEAD V-TWIN

• CAPACITY 45CU. IN.

MODEL VARIATIONS

G/GA/GD/GDT/GE

MODEL V

• ENGINE FLATHEAD V-TWIN

• CAPACITY 74CU. IN.

MODEL VARIATIONS

V/VD/VLD/VDS/VFD/VFDS

• NEW FEATURES
AIRFLOW TAIL LIGHT
DIAMOND-SHAPED LOGO ON TANK

• COLOURS
SINGLES IN SILVER AND RED OR
OLIVE GREEN AND BLACK. TWINS IN
A RANGE OF SIX STANDARD COLOURS.

1935

New 80cu. in. unit available for model V, using same chassis as on 74cu. in. model. Joe Petrali wins every round of dirt-track championship.

MODEL R

• ENGINE FLATHEAD V-TWIN

• CAPACITY 45CU. IN.

MODEL VARIATIONS

R/RL/RLD/RLDR/RS/RSR

1935 RL

MODEL G SERVI-CAR

• ENGINE Flathead V-twin

• CAPACITY 45CU. IN.

MODEL VARIATIONS

G/GA/GD/GDT/GE

MODEL V

• ENGINE Flathead V-twins

• CAPACITY 74CU. IN. & 80CU. IN.

MODEL VARIATIONS

VD/VLD/VLDJ/VDS/VFD/VFDS
(74CU. IN.)
VLDD/VDDS (80CU. IN.)

• NEW FEATURES
Constant-mesh three-speed
transmission on model R
New gearbox for models R and G
Beehive tail light

• COLOURS
A range of six two-tone
colours as standard. Two
optional colours available at
extra cost.

1936

New 61cu. in. OHV "Knucklehead"
V-twin engine on new model E. Last
year of model V flathead big-twins.

MODEL R

• ENGINE Flathead V-twin

• CAPACITY 45CU. IN.

MODEL VARIATIONS

R/RL/RLD/RLDR/RS/RSR

MODEL G SERVI-CAR

• ENGINE Flathead V-twin

• CAPACITY 45CU. IN.

MODEL VARIATIONS

G/GA/GD/GDT/GE

MODEL E

• ENGINE OHV V-twin

• CAPACITY 61CU. IN.

MODEL VARIATIONS

E/EL/ES

1936 61EL

MODEL V

• ENGINE Flathead V-twins

• CAPACITY 74CU. IN. & 80CU. IN.

MODEL VARIATIONS

VD/VLD/VMG/VDS/VFD/VFDS
(74CU. IN.)
VLH/VHS/VFH/VFHS (80CU. IN.)

• NEW FEATURES
Dry sump lubrication (model E)
Four-speed gearbox

(MODEL E & option on MODEL V)
Bullet and circle logo
(all models)

• COLOURS
A range of five two-tone
colours as standard.

1937

Revised flathead engines for new
models W and U. All models restyled
to follow the look of the model E.
Dry sump recirculating oil system
now on all models.

MODEL W

• ENGINE Flathead V-twin

• CAPACITY 45CU. IN.

MODEL VARIATIONS

W/WL/WLD/WLDR/WS/WSR

MODEL G SERVI-CAR

• ENGINE Flathead V-twin

• CAPACITY 45CU. IN.

MODEL VARIATIONS

G/GA/GD/GDT/GE

MODEL E

• ENGINE OHV V-twin

• CAPACITY 61CU. IN.

• MODEL VARIATIONS

E/EL/ES

MODEL U

• ENGINE Flathead V-twin

• CAPACITY 74CU. IN. & 80CU. IN.

MODEL VARIATIONS

U/UL/US/UMG (74CU. IN.)
UH/ULH/UHS (80CU. IN.)

• NEW FEATURES
Dry sump lubrication (now on
all models)
Instrument panel on fuel tank
(as per 1936 model E)

• COLOURS
A range of colours became
available as standard.

1938

Revisions to all models. All bikes
ordered with an option package.
Joe Petrali retires from racing.

MODEL W

• ENGINE Flathead V-twin

• CAPACITY 45CU. IN.

MODEL VARIATIONS

W/WL/WLD/WLDR/WS

MODEL G SERVI-CAR

• ENGINE Flathead V-twin

• CAPACITY 45CU. IN.

MODEL VARIATIONS

G/GA/GD/GDT/GE

MODEL E

• ENGINE OHV V-twin

• CAPACITY 61CU. IN.

MODEL VARIATIONS

EL/ES

MODEL U

• ENGINE Flathead V-twins

• CAPACITY 74CU. IN. & 80CU. IN.

MODEL VARIATIONS

U/UL/US/UMG (74CU. IN.)
UH/ULH/UHS (80CU. IN.)

• COLOURS
A range of six colours as
standard.

1939

Another year of modifications across
the ranges. Body of the Servi-Car is
enlarged. First WLA Army model
shipped to Fort Knox.

MODEL W

• ENGINE Flathead V-twin

• CAPACITY 45CU. IN.

MODEL VARIATIONS

W/WL/WLD/WLDR/WS

MODEL G SERVI-CAR

• ENGINE Flathead V-twin

• CAPACITY 45CU. IN.

MODEL VARIATIONS

G/GA/GD/GDT/GE

MODEL E

• ENGINE OHV V-twin

• CAPACITY 61CU. IN.

• MODEL VARIATIONS

EL/ES

MODEL U

• ENGINE Flathead V-twins

• CAPACITY 74CU. IN. & 80CU. IN.

• MODEL VARIATIONS

U/UL/US/UMG (74CU. IN.)
UH/ULH/UHS (80CU. IN.)

• NEW FEATURES
"Boat-tail" tail light
"Cats eye" instrument console

• COLOURS
A range of four colours as
standard.

1940

First full production year of WLA,
military version of model W. Tank
badges chrome-plated across the range.

MODEL W

• ENGINE Flathead V-twin

• CAPACITY 45CU. IN.

MODEL VARIATIONS

W/WL/WLD/WLDR/WS/WLA

MODEL G SERVI-CAR

• ENGINE Flathead V-twin

• CAPACITY 45CU. IN.

MODEL VARIATIONS

G/GA/GD/GDT

MODEL E

• ENGINE OHV V-twin

• CAPACITY 61CU. IN.

MODEL VARIATIONS

EL/ES

MODEL U

• ENGINE Flathead V-twins

• CAPACITY 74CU. IN. & 80CU. IN.

MODEL VARIATIONS

U/UL/US/UMG (74CU. IN.)
UH/ULH/UHS (80CU. IN.)

• NEW FEATURES
Chrome-plated tank nameplate

• COLOURS A range of five
colours as standard.

1941

First year of new OHV 74cu. in. model
F. New model UA is army version of
model U flathead. Civilian bike
production suspended during the year.
Last year of 80cu. in. big-twins.

MODEL W

• ENGINE Flathead V-twin

• CAPACITY 45CU. IN.

MODEL VARIATIONS

WL/WLS/WLD/WLDR/
WR/WLA/WLC

1941 WLD

MODEL G SERVI-CAR

• ENGINE Flathead V-twin

• CAPACITY 45CU. IN.

MODEL VARIATIONS

G/GA/GD/GDT

MODEL E

• ENGINE OHV V-twin

• CAPACITY 61CU. IN.

MODEL VARIATIONS

E/EL/ES

MODEL F

• ENGINE OHV V-twin

• CAPACITY 74CU. IN.

MODEL VARIATIONS
F/FL/FS

MODEL U

- ENGINE FLATHEAD V-TWINS
- CAPACITY 74CU. IN. & 80CU. IN.

MODEL VARIATIONS
U/UL/US/UA (74CU. IN.)
UH/ULH/UHS (80CU. IN.)

- NEW FEATURES
REVISED "AIRCRAFT-STYLE"
SPEEDOMETER

- COLOURS
A RANGE OF FIVE COLOURS AS
STANDARD.

1942

First year of new shaft-drive model XA twin for military use only. Blackout lights and other military modifications feature on WLA. Death of Walter Davidson, one the founding brothers and President of the company.

MODEL W

- ENGINE FLATHEAD V-TWIN
- CAPACITY 45CU. IN.

MODEL VARIATIONS
WL/WLS/WLD/WLA/WLC

1942 WLA

MODEL G SERVI-CAR

- ENGINE FLATHEAD V-TWIN
- CAPACITY 45CU. IN.

MODEL VARIATIONS
G/GA

MODEL XA

- ENGINE FLATHEAD
SHAFT-DRIVE OPPOSED TWIN
- CAPACITY 45CU. IN.

1942 XA

MODEL E

- ENGINE OHV V-TWIN
- CAPACITY 61CU. IN.

MODEL VARIATIONS
E/EL/ES/ELC

MODEL F

- ENGINE OHV V-TWIN
- CAPACITY 74CU. IN.

MODEL VARIATIONS
F/FL/FS

MODEL U

- ENGINE FLATHEAD V-TWIN
- CAPACITY 74CU. IN.

MODEL VARIATIONS
U/UL/US

- COLOURS A RANGE OF FIVE
COLOURS AS STANDARD.

1943

Model WLA accounts for virtually all Harley production, with most sent abroad. Last year of XA.

MODEL W

- ENGINE FLATHEAD V-TWIN
- CAPACITY 45CU. IN.

MODEL VARIATIONS
WLA/WLC

MODEL G SERVI-CAR

- ENGINE FLATHEAD V-TWIN
- CAPACITY 45CU. IN.

MODEL VARIATIONS
G/GA

MODEL XA

- ENGINE FLATHEAD SHAFT-DRIVE
OPPOSED TWIN
- CAPACITY 45CU. IN.

MODEL E

- ENGINE OHV V-TWIN
- CAPACITY 61CU. IN.

MODEL VARIATIONS
E/EL/ES

MODEL F

- ENGINE OHV V-TWIN
- CAPACITY 74CU. IN.

MODEL VARIATIONS
F/FL/FS

MODEL U

- ENGINE FLATHEAD V-TWIN
- CAPACITY 74CU. IN.

MODEL VARIATIONS
U/UL/US

- NEW FEATURES
"WINGED-FACE" HORN

- COLOURS
GREY OR SILVER.

1944

Bulk of production again for the military, with only a very few bikes manufactured for civilians or the police.

MODEL W

- ENGINE FLATHEAD V-TWIN
- CAPACITY 45CU. IN.

MODEL VARIATIONS
WL/WLA/WLC/WSR

MODEL G SERVI-CAR

- ENGINE FLATHEAD V-TWIN
- CAPACITY 45CU. IN.

MODEL VARIATIONS
G/GA

MODEL E

- ENGINE OHV V-TWIN
- CAPACITY 61CU. IN.

MODEL VARIATIONS
E/EL/ES

MODEL F

- ENGINE OHV V-TWIN
- CAPACITY 74CU. IN.

MODEL VARIATIONS
F/FL/FS

MODEL U

- ENGINE FLATHEAD V-TWIN
- CAPACITY 74CU. IN.

MODEL VARIATIONS
U/UL/US

- COLOURS
GREY OR SILVER.

1944 U

1945

Civilian production resumes in November, with options packages now available once more. No chrome finishes on any models.

MODEL W

- ENGINE FLATHEAD V-TWIN
- CAPACITY 45CU. IN.

MODEL VARIATIONS
WL/WLA/WSR

MODEL G SERVI-CAR

- ENGINE FLATHEAD V-TWIN
- CAPACITY 45CU. IN.

MODEL VARIATIONS
G/GA

MODEL E

- ENGINE OHV V-TWIN
- CAPACITY 61CU. IN.

MODEL VARIATIONS
E/EL/ES

MODEL F

- ENGINE OHV V-TWIN
- CAPACITY 74CU. IN.

MODEL VARIATIONS
F/FL/FS

MODEL U

- ENGINE FLATHEAD V-TWIN
- CAPACITY 74CU. IN.

MODEL VARIATIONS
U/UL/US

- COLOURS GREY.

1946

US Government sells off thousands of surplus WLAs, but WL model remains the most popular bike.

MODEL W

- ENGINE FLATHEAD V-TWIN
- CAPACITY 45CU. IN.

MODEL VARIATIONS
WL/WL-SP

MODEL G SERVI-CAR

- ENGINE FLATHEAD V-TWIN
- CAPACITY 45CU. IN.

MODEL VARIATIONS
G/GA

MODEL E

- ENGINE OHV V-TWIN
- CAPACITY 61CU. IN.

MODEL VARIATIONS
E/EL/ES

MODEL F

- ENGINE OHV V-TWIN
- CAPACITY 74CU. IN.

MODEL VARIATIONS
F/FL/FS

MODEL U

- ENGINE FLATHEAD V-TWIN
- CAPACITY 74CU. IN.

MODEL VARIATIONS
U/UL/US

- COLOURS
GREY OR FLIGHT RED.

1947

Harley acquires rights to produce German DKW 125cc machine. First year of Harley's model S lightweight. Last year of "Knucklehead" V-twin. New manufacturing plant opens at Capitol Drive, Milwaukee.

MODEL S

• ENGINE AIR-COOLED TWO-STROKE SINGLE

• CAPACITY 125cc

MODEL W

• ENGINE FLATHEAD V-TWIN

• CAPACITY 45CU. IN.

MODEL VARIATIONS
WL/WL-SP

MODEL G SERVI-CAR

• ENGINE FLATHEAD V-TWIN

• CAPACITY 45CU. IN.

MODEL VARIATIONS
G/GA

MODEL E

• ENGINE OHV V-TWIN

• CAPACITY 61CU. IN.

MODEL VARIATIONS
E/EL/ES

MODEL F

• ENGINE OHV V-TWIN

• CAPACITY 74CU. IN.

MODEL VARIATIONS
F/FL/FS

MODEL U

• ENGINE FLATHEAD V-TWIN

• CAPACITY 74CU. IN.

MODEL VARIATIONS
U/UL/US

• NEW FEATURES
"TOMBSTONE" TAIL LIGHT
NEW RED BALL HARLEY EMBLEM

• COLOURS
RANGE OF FIVE COLOURS NOW AVAILABLE AGAIN AS STANDARD.

1948

New OHV "Panhead" engine with hydraulic valve lifters for models E and F big-twins. Last year of model U flathead V-twin.

MODEL S

• ENGINE AIR-COOLED TWO-STROKE SINGLE

• CAPACITY 125cc

MODEL W

• ENGINE FLATHEAD V-TWIN

• CAPACITY 45CU. IN.

MODEL VARIATIONS
WL/WLS/WR/WL-SP

MODEL G SERVI-CAR

• ENGINE FLATHEAD V-TWIN

• CAPACITY 45CU. IN.

MODEL VARIATIONS
G/GA

MODEL E

• ENGINE OHV V-TWIN

• CAPACITY 61CU. IN.

MODEL VARIATIONS
E/EL/ES

MODEL F

• ENGINE OHV V-TWIN

• CAPACITY 74CU. IN.

MODEL VARIATIONS
F/FL/FS

MODEL U

• ENGINE FLATHEAD V-TWIN

• CAPACITY 74CU. IN.

MODEL VARIATIONS
U/UL/US

• NEW FEATURES
"PANHEAD" ENGINE

• COLOURS
RANGE OF FOUR COLOURS AVAILABLE AS STANDARD.

1949

Hydraulic front forks on models E and F big-twins give birth to the Hydra-Glide name. Leading-link forks still available as an option.

MODEL S

• ENGINE AIR-COOLED TWO-STROKE SINGLE

• CAPACITY 125cc

MODEL W

• ENGINE FLATHEAD V-TWIN

• CAPACITY 45CU. IN.

MODEL VARIATIONS
WL/WLS/WR/WL-SP

1949 WR DIRT TRACK

MODEL G SERVI-CAR

• ENGINE FLATHEAD V-TWIN

• CAPACITY 45CU. IN.

MODEL VARIATIONS
G/GA

MODEL E

• ENGINE OHV V-TWIN

• CAPACITY 61CU. IN.

MODEL VARIATIONS
E/ES/EL/ELP/EP

MODEL F

• ENGINE OHV V-TWIN

• CAPACITY 74CU. IN.

MODEL VARIATIONS
F/FL/FS/FP/FLP

• NEW FEATURES
HYDRAULIC FORKS ON MODELS E & F

• COLOURS
BLACK ONLY FOR SINGLE. RANGE OF FOUR STANDARD COLOURS FOR TWINS, WITH ONE OPTIONAL COLOUR.

1950

Models FL, S, and EL are manufactured in largest quantities. Death of Arthur Davidson, last of the original four founders. Safety bars optional on Hydra-Glides.

MODEL S

• ENGINE AIR-COOLED TWO-STROKE SINGLE

• CAPACITY 125cc

MODEL W

• ENGINE FLATHEAD V-TWIN

• CAPACITY 45CU. IN.

MODEL VARIATIONS
WL/WLA/WLS/WR/WL-SP

MODEL G SERVI-CAR

• ENGINE FLATHEAD V-TWIN

• CAPACITY 45CU. IN.

MODEL VARIATIONS
G/GA

MODEL E

• ENGINE OHV V-TWIN

• CAPACITY 61CU. IN.

MODEL VARIATIONS
E/ES/EL

MODEL F

• ENGINE OHV V-TWIN

• CAPACITY 74CU. IN.

MODEL VARIATIONS
F/FL/FS/

• NEW FEATURES
REDESIGNED CYLINDER HEADS ON "PANHEAD" ENGINE

• COLOURS
RANGE OF FOUR STANDARD COLOURS, WITH FOUR EXTRAS AVAILABLE FOR TWINS.

1951

Last year of model WL. Model S gets telescopic forks and is known as the Tele-Glide S.

MODEL S

• ENGINE AIR-COOLED TWO-STROKE SINGLE

• CAPACITY 125cc

MODEL W

• ENGINE FLATHEAD V-TWIN

• CAPACITY 45CU. IN.

MODEL VARIATIONS
WL/WLA/WLS/WR/WRTT/WL-SP

MODEL G SERVI-CAR

• ENGINE FLATHEAD V-TWIN

• CAPACITY 45CU. IN.

MODEL VARIATIONS
G/GA

MODEL E

• ENGINE OHV V-TWIN

• CAPACITY 61CU. IN.

MODEL VARIATIONS
EL/ELS

MODEL F

• ENGINE OHV V-TWIN

• CAPACITY 74CU. IN.

MODEL VARIATIONS
FL/FLS

1951 74FL

• NEW FEATURES
REDESIGNED HARLEY SCRIPT ON TANK

• COLOURS
RANGE OF THREE COLOURS AND TWO EXTRAS FOR SINGLES. THREE STANDARD AND THREE EXTRAS FOR TWINS.

1952

First year of new 45cu. in. flathead model K Sport. Last year of 61cu. in. model E, model S 125, and the few remaining model Ws. Last year that special sidecar models are listed.

MODEL S

• ENGINE AIR-COOLED TWO-STROKE SINGLE

• CAPACITY 125cc

MODEL W

- ENGINE Flathead V-twin
- CAPACITY 45CU. IN.

MODEL VARIATIONS

WR/WLS

MODEL G SERVI-CAR

- ENGINE Flathead V-twin
- CAPACITY 45CU. IN.

MODEL VARIATIONS

G/GA

MODEL K

- ENGINE Flathead V-twin
- CAPACITY 45CU. IN.

MODEL VARIATIONS

K

1952 K

RACING MODELS

KR/KRTT

MODEL E

- ENGINE OHV V-twin
- CAPACITY 61CU. IN.

MODEL VARIATIONS

EL/ELS/ELF

MODEL F

- ENGINE OHV V-twin
- CAPACITY 74CU. IN.

MODEL VARIATIONS

FL/FLS/FLF

- NEW FEATURES
45CU. IN. UNIT CONSTRUCTION
ENGINE ON MODEL K
Optional foot shift on models E
AND F (ELF AND FLF)

- COLOURS
RANGE OF THREE COLOURS WITH
ONE OPTIONAL FOR SINGLES, FIVE
COLOURS WITH THREE OPTIONAL
FOR TWINS, AND THREE COLOURS
WITH ONE OPTIONAL FOR MODEL K.

1953

First year of ST, Harley's single now
uprated to 165cc. Last year of
model K. The Indian Motorcycle
Company ceases trading, leaving
Harley-Davidson as the only major
US manufacturer.

MODEL ST

- ENGINE Air-cooled two-
stroke single
- CAPACITY 165CC

MODEL G SERVI-CAR

- ENGINE Flathead V-twin
- CAPACITY 45CU. IN.

MODEL VARIATIONS

G/GA

MODEL K

- ENGINE Flathead V-twin
- CAPACITY 45CU. IN.

MODEL VARIATIONS

K

RACING MODELS

KK/KR/KRTT (RACERS)

MODEL F

- ENGINE OHV V-twin
- CAPACITY 74CU. IN.

MODEL VARIATIONS

FL/FLE/FLEF/FLF

- NEW FEATURES
New Stewart-Warner "edge-
lighted" speedometer on twins

- COLOURS
RANGE OF THREE COLOURS WITH ONE
EXTRA FOR SINGLE, FIVE COLOURS
WITH THREE EXTRA FOR TWINS.

1954

In an attempt to improve
performance, new 55cu. in. flathead
V-twin model KH replaces model K.
Model S returns with two-strokes now
called Hummers. Old 45cu. in. unit
retained in racers.

MODEL S

- ENGINE Air-cooled two-
stroke single
- CAPACITY 125CC

MODEL ST

- ENGINE Air-cooled two-
stroke single
- CAPACITY 165CC

MODEL VARIATIONS

ST/STU

MODEL G SERVI-CAR

- ENGINE Flathead V-twin
- CAPACITY 45CU. IN.

MODEL VARIATIONS

G/GA

MODEL KH

- ENGINE Flathead V-twin
- CAPACITY 55CU. IN.

MODEL VARIATIONS

KH

RACING MODELS

KHRM (RACER)
KR/KRTT (45CU. IN. RACERS)

MODEL F

- ENGINE OHV V-twin
- CAPACITY 74CU. IN.

MODEL VARIATIONS

FL/FLE/FLEF/FLF

- NEW FEATURES
55CU. IN. ENGINE ON MODEL KH
Dual exhaust system an option
on model F Hydra-Glides

- COLOURS
RANGE OF 15 SOLID AND TWO-TONE
COLOURS AS STANDARD.

1955

First year of Super Sport FLH and
FLHF models added to the Hydra-
Glide range.

MODEL S

- ENGINE Air-cooled two-
stroke single
- CAPACITY 125CC

MODEL ST

- ENGINE Air-cooled two-
stroke single
- CAPACITY 165CC

MODEL VARIATIONS

ST/STU

1955 ST

MODEL G SERVI-CAR

- ENGINE Flathead V-twin
- CAPACITY 45CU. IN.

MODEL VARIATIONS

G/GA

MODEL KH

- ENGINE Flathead V-twin
- CAPACITY 55CU. IN.

MODEL VARIATIONS

KH/KHK

RACING MODELS

KHRM/KHRM/KHRTT
KR/KRTT (45CU. IN.)

MODEL F

- ENGINE OHV V-twin
- CAPACITY 74CU. IN.

MODEL VARIATIONS

FL/FLE/FLEF/FLF/FLH/FLHF

- NEW FEATURES
Tank emblem with letter "V" and
HARLEY-DAVIDSON in script behind

- COLOURS
RANGE OF SEVEN SOLID COLOURS AS
STANDARD. TWO-TONE
COMBINATIONS AT EXTRA COST.

1956

Last year of KH production bikes.
Elvis Presley appears on the cover of
The Enthusiast magazine sitting on a
Harley-Davidson.

MODEL S

- ENGINE Air-cooled two-
stroke single
- CAPACITY 125CC

MODEL ST

- ENGINE Air-cooled two-
stroke single
- CAPACITY 165CC

MODEL VARIATIONS

ST/STU

MODEL G SERVI-CAR

- ENGINE Flathead V-twin
- CAPACITY 45CU. IN.

MODEL VARIATIONS

G/GA

MODEL KH

- ENGINE Flathead V-twin
- CAPACITY 55CU. IN.

MODEL VARIATIONS

KH/KHK

RACING MODELS

KHRTT (RACER)
KR/KRTT (45CU. IN. RACERS)

MODEL F

- ENGINE OHV V-twin
- CAPACITY 74CU. IN.

MODEL VARIATIONS

FL/FLE/FLEF/FLF/FLH/FLHF

- NEW FEATURES
Round tail light on Hummer
"Victory" camshaft on FLH

- COLOURS
RANGE OF SIX SOLID COLOURS
AS STANDARD. METALLIC GREEN
AVAILABLE AT EXTRA COST
ON TWINS.

1957

First year of XL Sportster, based on
model KH. It will go on to become the
longest-running model in motorcycle
history. The model K series now
consists of racing bikes only.

MODEL S

- ENGINE Air-cooled two-
stroke single
- CAPACITY 125CC

MODEL ST

- **ENGINE** AIR-COOLED TWO-STROKE SINGLE
- **CAPACITY** 165cc

MODEL VARIATIONS

ST/STU

MODEL G SERVI-CAR

- **ENGINE** FLATHEAD V-TWIN
- **CAPACITY** 45CU. IN.

MODEL VARIATIONS

G/GA

MODEL XL

- **ENGINE** OHV V-TWIN
- **CAPACITY** 55CU. IN.

1957 XL SPORTSTER

MODEL F

- **ENGINE** OHV V-TWIN
- **CAPACITY** 74CU. IN.

MODEL VARIATIONS

FL/FLF/FLH/FLHF

MODEL K RACERS

- **ENGINE** FLATHEAD V-TWINS
- **CAPACITY** 45CU. IN & 55CU. IN.

MODEL VARIATIONS

Models KR/KRTT (45CU. IN. Flathead V-twins)
Model KHRTT (55CU. IN. Flathead V-twin)

- **NEW FEATURES**
OHV V-TWIN UNIT CONSTRUCTION ENGINE ON XL
NEW TANK LOGO (DESIGNED BY WILLIE G. DAVIDSON) HAS RED HARLEY-DAVIDSON SCRIPT OVER SILVER AND RED QUADRANTS

- **COLOURS**
RANGE OF SEVEN COLOURS AS STANDARD.

1958

Expanded XL range. Rear suspension on model F big-twins sees Harley's first Duo-Glides.

MODEL S

- **ENGINE** AIR-COOLED TWO-STROKE SINGLE
- **CAPACITY** 125cc

MODEL ST

- **ENGINE** AIR-COOLED TWO-STROKE SINGLE
- **CAPACITY** 165cc

MODEL VARIATIONS

ST/STU

MODEL G SERVI-CAR

- **ENGINE** FLATHEAD V-TWIN
- **CAPACITY** 45CU. IN.

MODEL VARIATIONS

G/GA

MODEL XL

- **ENGINE** OHV V-TWIN
- **CAPACITY** 55CU. IN.

MODEL VARIATIONS

XL/XLH/XLC/XLCH

RACING MODELS

XLRTT

MODEL F

- **ENGINE** OHV V-TWIN
- **CAPACITY** 74CU. IN.

MODEL VARIATIONS

FL/FLF/FLH/FLHF

- **NEW FEATURES**
REAR SHOCK ABSORBERS ON MODEL F, NOW DUBBED THE DUO-GLIDE

MODEL KR RACERS

- **ENGINE** FLATHEAD V-TWIN
- **CAPACITY** 45CU. IN.

MODEL VARIATIONS

KR/KRTT

- **COLOURS**
WIDE RANGE OF COLOURS, ALL AS STANDARD.

1959

Last year of models S and ST. Also last year of XL in standard Sportster form.

MODEL S

- **ENGINE** AIR-COOLED TWO-STROKE SINGLE
- **CAPACITY** 125cc

MODEL ST

- **ENGINE** AIR-COOLED TWO-STROKE SINGLE
- **CAPACITY** 165cc

MODEL VARIATIONS

ST/STU

MODEL G SERVI-CAR

- **ENGINE** FLATHEAD V-TWIN
- **CAPACITY** 45CU. IN.

MODEL VARIATIONS

G/GA

MODEL XL

- **ENGINE** OHV V-TWIN
- **CAPACITY** 55CU. IN.

MODEL VARIATIONS

XL/XLH/XLC/XLCH

RACING MODELS

XLRTT

MODEL F

- **ENGINE** OHV V-TWIN
- **CAPACITY** 74CU. IN.

MODEL VARIATIONS

FL/FLF/FLH/FLHF

MODEL KR RACERS

- **ENGINE** FLATHEAD V-TWIN
- **CAPACITY** 45CU. IN.

MODEL VARIATIONS

KR/KRTT

- **NEW FEATURES**
"Arrow-flight" TANK BADGE

- **COLOURS**
RANGE OF SEVEN COLOURS AS STANDARD.

1960

Harley-Davidson tries to entice scooter buyers with its new Topper scooter. Model BT replaces ST with upgraded 165cc engine. Harley buys a controlling stake in Italian small-bike manufacturer, Aermacchi.

MODEL A TOPPER

- **ENGINE** AIR-COOLED TWO-STROKE SINGLE
- **CAPACITY** 165cc

MODEL VARIATIONS

A/AU

MODEL BT SUPER 10

- **ENGINE** AIR-COOLED TWO-STROKE SINGLE
- **CAPACITY** 165cc

MODEL VARIATIONS

BT/BTU

MODEL G SERVI-CAR

- **ENGINE** FLATHEAD V-TWIN
- **CAPACITY** 45CU. IN.

MODEL VARIATIONS

G/GA

MODEL XL

- **ENGINE** OHV V-TWIN
- **CAPACITY** 55CU. IN.

MODEL VARIATIONS

XLH/XLCH

RACING MODELS

XLRTT

MODEL F

- **ENGINE** OHV V-TWIN
- **CAPACITY** 74CU. IN.

MODEL VARIATIONS

FL/FLF/FLH/FLHF

1960 FLH DUO-GLIDE

MODEL KR RACERS

- **ENGINE** FLATHEAD V-TWIN
- **CAPACITY** 45CU. IN.

MODEL VARIATIONS

KR/KRTT

- **NEW FEATURES**
165CC ENGINE ON MODELS A AND BT

- **COLOURS**
RANGE OF COLOURS AS STANDARD. SPECIAL PAINT FINISHES AT EXTRA COST.

1961

First year for Aermacchi-derived Sprint, last year for BT Super 10. Dual exhaust optional on Duo-Glides.

MODEL AH TOPPER

- **ENGINE** AIR-COOLED TWO-STROKE SINGLE
- **CAPACITY** 165cc

MODEL VARIATIONS

AH/AH

MODEL BT SUPER 10

- **ENGINE** AIR-COOLED TWO-STROKE SINGLE
- **CAPACITY** 165cc

MODEL VARIATIONS

BT/BTU

SPRINT

- **ENGINE** HORIZONTAL OHV FOUR-STROKE SINGLE
- **CAPACITY** 250cc

MODEL VARIATIONS

C

RACING MODELS

CRTT

MODEL G SERVI-CAR

- **ENGINE** FLATHEAD V-TWIN
- **CAPACITY** 45CU. IN.

MODEL VARIATIONS

G/GA

MODEL XL

- **ENGINE** OHV V-TWIN
- **CAPACITY** 55CU. IN.

MODEL VARIATIONS

XLH/XLCH

RACING MODELS

XLRTT

MODEL F

- **ENGINE** OHV V-TWIN
- **CAPACITY** 74CU. IN.

MODEL VARIATIONS

FL/FLF/FLH/FLHF

MODEL KR RACERS

- **ENGINE** FLATHEAD V-TWIN
- **CAPACITY** 45CU. IN.

MODEL VARIATIONS

KR/KRTT

- **NEW FEATURES** NEW CIRCLE AND STAR TANK EMBLEM
- **COLOURS** RANGE OF COLOURS AS STANDARD. SPECIAL PAINT FINISHES AT EXTRA COST.

1962

Single range expanded to include 175cc models. Last year of 165cc in BT range. Harley-Davidson buys 60 per cent stake in Tomahawk Boat Company for fibreglass components.

MODEL AH TOPPER

- **ENGINE** AIR-COOLED TWO-STROKE SINGLE
- **CAPACITY** 165cc

MODEL VARIATIONS

AH/AU

MODEL B SINGLES

- **ENGINE** AIR-COOLED TWO-STROKE SINGLES
- **CAPACITY** 165cc & 175cc

MODEL VARIATIONS

BTU PACER/BTF RANGER (165CC)
BT PACER/BTH SCAT(175CC)

SPRINT

- **ENGINE** HORIZONTAL OHV FOUR-STROKE SINGLE
- **CAPACITY** 250cc

MODEL VARIATIONS

C/H

RACING MODELS

CRTT

MODEL G SERVI-CAR

- **ENGINE** FLATHEAD V-TWIN
- **CAPACITY** 45CU. IN.

MODEL VARIATIONS

G/GA

MODEL XL

- **ENGINE** OHV V-TWIN
- **CAPACITY** 55CU. IN.

MODEL VARIATIONS

XLH/XLCH

RACING MODELS

XLRTT

MODEL F

- **ENGINE** OHV V-TWIN
- **CAPACITY** 74CU. IN.

MODEL VARIATIONS

FL/FLF/FLH/FLHF

MODEL KR RACERS

- **ENGINE** FLATHEAD V-TWIN
- **CAPACITY** 45CU. IN.

MODEL VARIATIONS

KR/KRTT

- **NEW FEATURES** NEW 175CC SINGLE ENGINE "TOMBSTONE" SPEEDOMETER FEATURED ON TWINS
- **COLOURS** RANGE OF COLOURS AS STANDARD. SPECIAL PAINT FINISHES AVAILABLE AT EXTRA COST.

1963

F models are biggest sellers this year. Willie G. Davidson joins the Harley-Davidson board.

MODEL AH TOPPER

- **ENGINE** AIR-COOLED TWO-STROKE SINGLE
- **CAPACITY** 165cc

MODEL VARIATIONS

AH/AU

MODEL B SINGLES

- **ENGINE** AIR-COOLED TWO-STROKE SINGLE
- **CAPACITY** 175cc

MODEL VARIATIONS

BT PACER/BTU PACER/BTH SCAT

SPRINT

- **ENGINE** HORIZONTAL OHV FOUR-STROKE SINGLE
- **CAPACITY** 250cc

MODEL VARIATIONS

C/H

RACING MODELS

CRTT

MODEL G SERVI-CAR

- **ENGINE** FLATHEAD V-TWIN
- **CAPACITY** 45CU. IN.

MODEL VARIATIONS

G/GA

MODEL XL

- **ENGINE** OHV V-TWIN
- **CAPACITY** 55CU. IN.

MODEL VARIATIONS

XLH/XLCH

RACING MODELS

XLRTT

MODEL F

- **ENGINE** OHV V-TWIN
- **CAPACITY** 74CU. IN.

MODEL VARIATIONS

FL/FLF/FLH/FLHF

MODEL KR RACERS

- **ENGINE** FLATHEAD V-TWIN
- **CAPACITY** 45CU. IN.

MODEL VARIATIONS

KR/KRTT

- **NEW FEATURES** REVISED TANK EMBLEM
- **COLOURS** RANGE OF COLOURS AS STANDARD. SPECIAL PAINT FINISHES AVAILABLE AT EXTRA COST.

1964

Last year of AU, restricted version of Topper. Last year of Duo-Glide. Servi-Car gets Harley's first electric starter.

MODEL AH TOPPER

- **ENGINE** AIR-COOLED TWO-STROKE SINGLE
- **CAPACITY** 165cc

MODEL VARIATIONS

AH/AU

1964 AH TOPPER

MODEL B SINGLES

- **ENGINE** AIR-COOLED TWO-STROKE SINGLE
- **CAPACITY** 175cc

MODEL VARIATIONS

BT PACER/BTU PACER/BTH SCAT

SPRINT

- **ENGINE** HORIZONTAL OHV FOUR-STROKE SINGLE
- **CAPACITY** 250cc

MODEL VARIATIONS

C/H

RACING MODELS

CRTT

MODEL GE SERVI-CAR

- **ENGINE** FLATHEAD V-TWIN
- **CAPACITY** 45CU. IN.

MODEL XL

- **ENGINE** OHV V-TWIN
- **CAPACITY** 55CU. IN.

MODEL VARIATIONS

XLH/XLCH

RACING MODELS

XLRTT

MODEL F

- **ENGINE** OHV V-TWIN
- **CAPACITY** 74CU. IN.

MODEL VARIATIONS

FL/FLF/FLH/FLHF

MODEL KR RACERS

- **ENGINE** FLATHEAD V-TWIN
- **CAPACITY** 45CU. IN.

MODEL VARIATIONS

KR/KRTT

- **NEW FEATURES** ELECTRIC STARTER ON MODEL GE SERVI-CAR
- **COLOURS** RANGE OF FOUR COLOURS AS STANDARD. SPECIAL PAINT FINISHES AT EXTRA COST.

1965

Electric starter on model F gives birth to the Electra Glide name. New model M 50cc Italian bikes. Last year of "Panhead" engine, Topper scooter, and Scat and Pacer singles.

MODEL M LEGGERO

- **ENGINE** AIR-COOLED TWO-STROKE SINGLE
- **CAPACITY** 50cc

MODEL AH TOPPER

- **ENGINE** AIR-COOLED SINGLE
- **CAPACITY** 165cc

MODEL B SINGLE

- **ENGINE** AIR-COOLED TWO-STROKE SINGLE
- **CAPACITY** 175cc

MODEL VARIATIONS

BT PACER/BTH SCAT

SPRINT

- **ENGINE** HORIZONTAL OHV FOUR-STROKE SINGLE
- **CAPACITY** 250cc

MODEL VARIATIONS

C/H

RACING MODELS

CRTT

MODEL GE SERVI-CAR

- **ENGINE** FLATHEAD V-TWIN
- **CAPACITY** 45CU. IN.

MODEL XL

- ENGINE OHV V-TWIN
- CAPACITY 55CU. IN.

MODEL VARIATIONS

XLH/XLCH

RACING MODELS

XLRTT

MODEL F

- ENGINE OHV V-TWIN
- CAPACITY 74CU. IN.

MODEL VARIATIONS

FLHB/FLHFB/FLB/FLFB

MODEL KR RACERS

- ENGINE Flathead V-TWIN
- CAPACITY 45CU. IN.

MODEL VARIATIONS

KR/KRTT

- NEW FEATURES
ELECTRIC STARTER ON MODEL F
- COLOURS
RANGE OF COLOURS AS STANDARD.
SPECIAL PAINT FINISHES AVAILABLE
AT EXTRA COST.

1966

First year of new "Shovelhead" OHV engine, a revision of the "Panhead" unit. Only year of Bobcat. Last year of 50cc in M series and US-made singles.

MODEL M LEGGERO

- ENGINE AIR-COOLED TWO-STROKE SINGLE
- CAPACITY 50cc

MODEL VARIATIONS

M-50/M-50 SPORT

1966 M-50 SPORT

MODEL BTH BOBCAT

- ENGINE AIR-COOLED TWO-STROKE SINGLE
- CAPACITY 175cc

SPRINT

- ENGINE HORIZONTAL OHV FOUR-STROKE SINGLE
- CAPACITY 250cc

MODEL VARIATIONS

C/H

RACING MODELS

CRTT

MODEL GE SERVI-CAR

- ENGINE Flathead V-TWIN
- CAPACITY 45CU. IN.

MODEL XL

- ENGINE OHV V-TWIN
- CAPACITY 55CU. IN.

MODEL VARIATIONS

XLH/XLCH

RACING MODELS

XLRTT

MODEL F

- ENGINE OHV V-TWIN
- CAPACITY 74CU. IN.

MODEL VARIATIONS

FLHB/FLHFB/FLB/FLFB

MODEL KR RACERS

- ENGINE Flathead V-TWIN
- CAPACITY 45CU. IN.

MODEL VARIATIONS

KR/KRTT

- NEW FEATURES
"SHOVELHEAD" ENGINE FOR MODEL F
HEXAGONAL TANK BADGE
- COLOURS
RANGE OF FOUR COLOURS AS
STANDARD. SPECIAL PAINT FINISHES
AT EXTRA COST.

1967

New version of model M added with larger-capacity engine. XLH model gets an electric starter.

MODEL M LEGGERO

- ENGINE AIR-COOLED TWO-STROKE SINGLE
- CAPACITY 65cc

MODEL VARIATIONS

M-65/M-65 SPORT

SPRINT

- ENGINE HORIZONTAL OHV FOUR-STROKE SINGLE
- CAPACITY 250cc

MODEL VARIATIONS

SS/H

RACING MODELS

CRTT

1967 CRTT

MODEL GE SERVI-CAR

- ENGINE Flathead V-TWIN
- CAPACITY 45CU. IN.

MODEL XL

- ENGINE OHV V-TWIN
- CAPACITY 55CU. IN.

MODEL VARIATIONS

XLH/XLCH

MODEL F

- ENGINE OHV V-TWIN
- CAPACITY 74CU. IN.

MODEL VARIATIONS

FLHB/FLHFB/FLB/FLFB

- COLOURS
BLACK OR BLUE ON TWINS.
OTHER COLOURS AVAILABLE
AT EXTRA COST.

1968

M model has 125cc version added. Last year for 250cc Sprint. Cal Raybourn rides a KRTT to victory at Daytona 200. First year of no kick-starter on Sportsters.

MODEL M

- ENGINE AIR-COOLED TWO-STROKE SINGLES
- CAPACITY 65cc & 125cc

MODEL VARIATIONS

M-65/M-65 SPORT,
M-125 RAPIDO

SPRINT

- ENGINE HORIZONTAL OHV FOUR-STROKE SINGLE
- CAPACITY 250cc

MODEL VARIATIONS

SS/H

MODEL GE SERVI-CAR

- ENGINE Flathead V-TWIN
- CAPACITY 45CU. IN.

MODEL XL

- ENGINE OHV V-TWIN
- CAPACITY 55CU. IN.

MODEL VARIATIONS

XLH/XLCH

MODEL F

- ENGINE OHV V-TWIN
- CAPACITY 74CU. IN.

MODEL VARIATIONS

FLHB/FLHFB/FLB/FLFB

- NEW FEATURES
125cc ENGINE IN M-RAPIDO
ELECTRIC STARTER AND RESTYLED
INSTRUMENT CONSOLE ON
SPORTSTERS
- COLOURS
BLACK OR ORANGE ON TWINS.
OTHER COLOURS AVAILABLE AT
EXTRA COST.

1969

American Machine and Foundry Company (AMF) buys controlling stake in Harley-Davidson. First year of 350cc Sprint.

MODEL M

- ENGINE AIR-COOLED TWO-STROKE SINGLES
- CAPACITY 65cc & 125cc

MODEL VARIATIONS

M-65/M-65 SPORT, M-125 RAPIDO

SPRINT

- ENGINE HORIZONTAL OHV FOUR-STROKE SINGLE
- CAPACITY 350cc

MODEL VARIATIONS

SS/ERS

MODEL GE SERVI-CAR

- ENGINE Flathead V-TWIN
- CAPACITY 45CU. IN.

1969 GE SERVI-CAR

MODEL XL

- ENGINE OHV V-TWIN
- CAPACITY 55CU. IN.

MODEL VARIATIONS

XLH/XLCH

MODEL F

- ENGINE OHV V-TWIN
- CAPACITY 74CU. IN.

MODEL VARIATIONS

FLHB/FLHFB/FLB/FLFB

- NEW FEATURES
350cc ENGINE IN SPRINT
- COLOURS
BLACK, ORANGE, OR WHITE ON
TWINS. OTHER COLOURS AVAILABLE
AT EXTRA COST.

1970

First year of new 45cu. in. racer, the XR750, which goes on to be Harley's most successful racing bike. Also first year of "Shovelhead" with alternator rather than generator and the 100cc Aermacchi Baja.

MODEL M

- ENGINE AIR-COOLED TWO-STROKE SINGLES
- CAPACITY 65cc, 100cc & 125cc

MODEL VARIATIONS

M-65 LEGERRO (65cc), MSR BAJA (100cc), MLS RAPIDO (125cc)

SPRINT

- ENGINE HORIZONTAL OHV FOUR-STROKE SINGLE

- CAPACITY 350cc

MODEL VARIATIONS

SS/ERS

MODEL GE SERV-CAR

- ENGINE FLATHEAD V-TWIN

- CAPACITY 45cu. IN.

MODEL XR

- ENGINE OHV V-TWIN

- CAPACITY 45cu. IN.

MODEL XL

- ENGINE OHV V-TWIN

- CAPACITY 55cu. IN.

MODEL VARIATIONS

XLH/XLCH

MODEL F

- ENGINE OHV V-TWIN

- CAPACITY 74cu. IN.

MODEL VARIATIONS

FLH/FLHF/FLP/FLPF

- NEW FEATURES "SHOVELHEAD" UNIT NOW HAS ALTERNATOR INSTEAD OF GENERATOR
NEW RACING V-TWIN FOR XR750

- COLOURS
WHITE OR BLUE.

1971

First year of new FX Super Glide, brainchild of Willie G. Davidson and Harley's first official custom bike. Last year of 55cu. in. Sportster and M-65. XLCH is the most popular model this year.

MODEL M

- ENGINE AIR-COOLED TWO-STROKE SINGLES

- CAPACITY 65cc, 100cc, & 125cc

MODEL VARIATIONS

M-65 LEGERRO (65cc), MSR BAJA (100cc), MLS RAPIDO (125cc)

SPRINT

- ENGINE HORIZONTAL OHV FOUR-STROKE SINGLE

- CAPACITY 350cc

MODEL VARIATIONS

SS/SX/ERS

MODEL GE SERV-CAR

- ENGINE FLATHEAD V-TWIN

- CAPACITY 45cu. IN.

MODEL XR

- ENGINE OHV V-TWIN

- CAPACITY 45cu. IN.

MODEL XL

- ENGINE OHV V-TWIN

- CAPACITY 55cu. IN.

MODEL VARIATIONS

XLH/XLCH

MODEL F

- ENGINE OHV V-TWIN

- CAPACITY 74cu. IN.

MODEL VARIATIONS

FLH/FLHF/FLP/FLPF

MODEL FX

- ENGINE OHV V-TWIN

- CAPACITY 74cu. IN.

1971 FX

- NEW FEATURES
AMF LOGO NOW ADDED TO TANK

- COLOURS
WHITE OR BLUE.

1972

First year for 61cu. in. Sportster and last year for Baja and Rapido singles. AMF adds its name to tank logos across the range. Harley enters into production of snowmobiles.

MODEL M

- ENGINE AIR-COOLED TWO-STROKE SINGLES

- CAPACITY 65cc, 100cc, & 125cc

MODEL VARIATIONS

M-65 LEGERRO/MC-65 SPORTSTER (65cc), MSR BAJA (100cc)
MLS RAPIDO (125cc)

SPRINT

- ENGINE HORIZONTAL OHV FOUR-STROKE SINGLE

- CAPACITY 350cc

MODEL VARIATIONS

SS/SX/ERS

MODEL GE SERV-CAR

- ENGINE FLATHEAD V-TWIN

- CAPACITY 45cu. IN.

MODEL XR RACER

- ENGINE OHV V-TWIN

- CAPACITY 45cu. IN.

MODEL XRTT RACER

- ENGINE OHV V-TWIN

- CAPACITY 45cu. IN.

1972 XRTT

MODEL XL

- ENGINE OHV V-TWIN

- CAPACITY 61cu. IN.

MODEL VARIATIONS

XLH/XLCH

MODEL F

- ENGINE OHV V-TWIN

- CAPACITY 74cu. IN.

MODEL VARIATIONS

FLH/FLHF/FLP/FLPF

MODEL FX

- ENGINE OHV V-TWIN

- CAPACITY 74cu. IN.

- NEW FEATURES
RECTANGULAR AMF/HD BADGE

- COLOURS
WHITE OR BLUES.

1973

Last year of model GE Servi-Car, with disc brakes added. New range of 90cc and 125cc singles introduced.

TWO-STROKE SINGLES

- ENGINE AIR-COOLED TWO-STROKE SINGLES

- CAPACITY 90cc & 125cc

MODEL VARIATIONS

X-90/Z-90 (90cc)
125SS/125SX (125cc)

SPRINT

- ENGINE HORIZONTAL OHV FOUR-STROKE SINGLE

- CAPACITY 350cc

MODEL VARIATIONS

SS/SX

MODEL GE SERV-CAR

- ENGINE FLATHEAD V-TWIN

- CAPACITY 45cu. IN.

MODEL XR

- ENGINE OHV V-TWIN

- CAPACITY 45cu. IN.

MODEL XL

- ENGINE OHV V-TWIN

- CAPACITY 61cu. IN.

MODEL VARIATIONS

XLH/XLCH

MODEL F

- ENGINE OHV V-TWIN

- CAPACITY 74cu. IN.

MODEL VARIATIONS

FLH/FLHF/FLP/FLPF

MODEL FX

- ENGINE OHV V-TWIN

- CAPACITY 74cu. IN.

MODEL VARIATIONS

XLH/XLCH

MODEL F

- ENGINE OHV V-TWIN

- CAPACITY 74cu. IN.

MODEL VARIATIONS

FLH/FLHF/FLP/FLPF

MODEL FX

- ENGINE OHV V-TWIN

- CAPACITY 74cu. IN.

- NEW FEATURES
90cc SINGLE ENGINE
125cc SINGLE ENGINE

- COLOURS
WHITE OR BLUE.

1974

First year for 175cc singles and electric start Super Glide. Harley wins 250cc World Championship with Aermacchi machine. Last year for Sprint and 90cc bikes.

TWO-STROKE SINGLES

- ENGINE AIR-COOLED TWO-STROKE SINGLES

- CAPACITY 90cc, 125cc, AND 175cc

MODEL VARIATIONS

X-90/Z-90 (90cc)
125SS/125SX (125cc)
175SS/175SX (175cc)

SPRINT

- ENGINE HORIZONTAL OHV FOUR-STROKE SINGLE

- CAPACITY 350cc

MODEL VARIATIONS

SS/SX

MODEL XR

- ENGINE OHV V-TWIN

- CAPACITY 45cu. IN.

MODEL XL

- ENGINE OHV V-TWIN

- CAPACITY 61cu. IN.

MODEL VARIATIONS

XLH/XLCH

MODEL F

- ENGINE OHV V-TWIN

- CAPACITY 74cu. IN.

MODEL VARIATIONS

FL/FLH/FLHF

MODEL FX

- ENGINE OHV V-TWIN

- CAPACITY 74cu. IN.

MODEL VARIATIONS

FX/FXE

- **New Features**
Electric starter now available on Super Glide (FXE)

- **Colours**
White, burgundy, black, or blue.

1975

First year for new 250cc two-stroke singles. Chassis manufacture and final bike assembly moved to larger premises in York, Pennsylvania, with engine manufacture kept in Milwaukee.

TWO-STROKE SINGLES

- **Engine** Air-cooled two-stroke singles
- **Capacity** 125cc, 175cc, & 250cc

MODEL VARIATIONS
125SS/125SX (125cc)
175SS/175SX (175cc)
250SS/250SX (250cc)

MODEL XR
- **Engine** OHV V-twin
- **Capacity** 45cu. in.

MODEL XL
- **Engine** OHV V-twin
- **Capacity** 61cu. in.

MODEL VARIATIONS
XLH/XLCH

MODEL F
- **Engine** OHV V-twin
- **Capacity** 74cu. in.

MODEL VARIATIONS
FL/FLH/FLHF

MODEL FX
- **Engine** OHV V-twin
- **Capacity** 74cu. in.

MODEL VARIATIONS
FX/FXE

- **Colours**
White, burgundy, black, or blue.

1976

Only year that the World Championship-winning RR250 is catalogued. Production rises to almost 50,000 bikes this year.

TWO-STROKE SINGLES
- **Engine** Air-cooled two-stroke singles
- **Capacity** 125cc, 175cc, & 250cc

MODEL VARIATIONS
125SS/125SX (125cc)
175SS/175SX (175cc)
250SS/250SX (250cc)

MODEL RR250
- **Engine** Two-stroke twin
- **Capacity** 250cc

1976 RR250

MODEL XRTT
- **Engine** OHV V-twin
- **Capacity** 45cu. in.

MODEL XL
- **Engine** OHV V-twin
- **Capacity** 61cu. in.

MODEL VARIATIONS
XLH/XLCH (plus special "Liberty" editions)

MODEL F
- **Engine** OHV V-twin
- **Capacity** 74cu. in.

MODEL VARIATIONS
FLH/FLH "Liberty" edition

MODEL FX
- **Engine** OHV V-twin
- **Capacity** 74cu. in.

MODEL VARIATIONS
FX/FXE (plus "Liberty" editions)

- **Colours**
White, burgundy, black, orange, silver, brown, or blue.

1977

First year of XLCR Café Racer, FXS Low Rider, and FLT. Only year of FLHS Electra Glide. Last year of Harley's singles.

TWO-STROKE SINGLES
- **Engine** Air-cooled two-stroke singles
- **Capacity** 125cc, 175cc, & 250cc

MODEL VARIATIONS
125SS/125SX (125cc)
175SS/175SX (175cc)
250SS/250SX (250cc)

MODEL MX RACER
- **Engine** Two-stroke single
- **Capacity** 250cc

MODEL XR
- **Engine** OHV V-twin
- **Capacity** 45cu. in.

MODEL XL
- **Engine** OHV V-twin
- **Capacity** 61cu. in.

MODEL VARIATIONS
XLH/XLCH/XLT/XLCR

MODEL F
- **Engine** OHV V-twin
- **Capacity** 74cu. in.

MODEL VARIATIONS
FLH/FLHS

MODEL FX
- **Engine** OHV V-twin
- **Capacity** 74cu. in.

MODEL VARIATIONS
FX/FXE/FXS

- **New Features**
Redesigned frame for new XLCR

- **Colours**
Choice of eight standard colours.

1978

First year of new 80cu. in. "Shovelhead" unit. Last year of XLCR, XLT, and FX Super Glide. Harley ends its association with the Aermacchi company.

MODEL MX RACER
- **Engine** Two-stroke single
- **Capacity** 250cc

MODEL XR
- **Engine** OHV V-twin
- **Capacity** 45cu. in.

MODEL XL
- **Engine** OHV V-twin
- **Capacity** 61cu. in.

MODEL VARIATIONS
XLH/XLH/XLCH/XLT/XLCR
XLH (Anniversary edition)

1978 XLCR

MODEL F
- **Engine** OHV V-twins
- **Capacity** 74cu. in. & 80cu. in.

MODEL VARIATIONS
FLH/FLH (Anniversary edition)
FLH (80cu. in.)

MODEL FX
- **Engine** OHV V-twin
- **Capacity** 74cu. in.

MODEL VARIATIONS
FX/FXE/FXS

- **New Features**
80cu. in. big-twin engine
Dual disc front brakes on Sportsters

- **Colours**
Choice of nine standard colours.

1979

First year of new XLS "roadster" model, FXEF Fat Bobs, FLHC Electra Glide Classic, and FXS Low Rider with larger 80cu. in. engine. Last year of XLCH.

MODEL XR
- **Engine** OHV V-twin
- **Capacity** 45cu. in.

MODEL XL
- **Engine** OHV V-twin
- **Capacity** 61cu. in.

MODEL VARIATIONS
XLH/XLCH/XLS

MODEL F
- **Engine** OHV V-twins
- **Capacity** 74cu. in. & 80cu. in.

MODEL VARIATIONS
FLH/FLH(police)(74cu. in.)
FLH/FLH(police)/FLHC (80cu. in.)

MODEL FX
- **Engine** OHV V-twins
- **Capacity** 74cu. in. & 80cu. in.

MODEL VARIATIONS
FX/FXE/FXS/FXEF (74cu. in.)
FX/FXS/FXEF (80cu. in.)

- **Colours**
Choice of nine standard colours.

1980

Last year of 74cu. in. "Shovelhead" unit. New models FLT Tour Glide, FXB Sturgis, FXWG Wide Glide, and XLH Hugger.

MODEL XR
- **Engine** OHV V-twin
- **Capacity** 45cu. in.

MODEL XL
- **Engine** OHV V-twin
- **Capacity** 61cu. in.

MODEL VARIATIONS
XLH/XLS

MODEL FLH
- **Engine** OHV V-twins
- **Capacity** 74cu. in. & 80cu. in.

MODEL VARIATIONS
FLH (74cu. in.)
FLH/FLHS/FLHC (80cu. in.)

MODEL FLT

- ENGINE OHV V-twin
- CAPACITY 80cu. in.

MODEL FX

- ENGINE OHV V-twins
- CAPACITY 74cu. in. & 80cu. in.

MODEL VARIATIONS

FXE/FXS (74cu. in.)
FXB/FXS/FXEF/FXWG
(80cu. in.)

- NEW FEATURES
RUBBER-MOUNTED ENGINE TO
REDUCE VIBRATION ON FLT
FIVE-SPEED GEARBOX ON FLT
BELT FINAL-DRIVE ON FXB

- COLOURS
CHOICE OF EIGHT STANDARD
COLOURS.

1981

Harley-Davidson management buys company back from AMF. Advertising slogan is "The Eagle Soars Alone". First year for 80cu. in. FXE Super Glide, replacing 74cu. in model.

MODEL XR

- ENGINE OHV V-twin
- CAPACITY 45cu. in.

MODEL XL

- ENGINE OHV V-twin
- CAPACITY 61cu. in.

MODEL VARIATIONS

XLH/XLS

MODEL FLH

- ENGINE OHV V-twin
- CAPACITY 80cu. in.

MODEL VARIATIONS

FLH/FLH (Heritage)/
FLHS/FLHC

MODEL FLT

- ENGINE OHV V-twin
- CAPACITY 80cu. in.

MODEL VARIATIONS

FLT/FLTC

MODEL FX

- ENGINE OHV V-twin
- CAPACITY 80cu. in.

MODEL VARIATIONS

FXE/FXS/FXB/FXEF/FXWG

- NEW FEATURES
FLH HERITAGE IS RETURNED
TO ORIGINAL STYLING WITH
FEATURES SUCH AS LEATHER
SADDLEBAGS

- COLOURS
CHOICE OF 12 STANDARD COLOURS.

1982

Despite streamlining of the company resulting in a number of lay-offs, new FXR and FXRS Super Glides launched in exciting new era for the company. Last year for Fat Bob, Low Rider, and Sturgis. The Sportster celebrates its 25th anniversary, with special editions released.

MODEL XR

- ENGINE OHV V-twin
- CAPACITY 45cu. in.

MODEL XL

- ENGINE OHV V-twin
- CAPACITY 61cu. in.

MODEL VARIATIONS

XLH/XLS, XLHA/XLSA
(ANNIVERSARY EDITIONS)

MODEL FLH

- ENGINE OHV V-twin
- CAPACITY 80cu. in.

MODEL VARIATIONS

FLH/FLHS/FLHF

MODEL FLT

- ENGINE OHV V-twin
- CAPACITY 80cu. in.

MODEL VARIATIONS

FLT/FLTC

MODEL FX

- ENGINE OHV V-twin
- CAPACITY 80cu. in.

MODEL VARIATIONS

FXE/FXS/FXB/FXWG

MODEL FXR

- ENGINE OHV V-twin
- CAPACITY 80cu. in.

MODEL VARIATIONS

FXR/FXRS

- NEW FEATURES New frame on
XL MODELS WITH REPOSITIONED OIL
TANK AND BATTERY

- COLOURS
CHOICE OF 13 STANDARD COLOURS.

1983

New model XR1000 sports bike based on Sportster engine and XLH chassis. Various new styles and models released based on 80cu. in. engine, including FXSB Low Rider and FXDG with rear disc wheel. Harley Owners' Group (H.O.G.) formed.

MODEL XL/XR

- ENGINE OHV V-twin
- CAPACITY 61cu. in.

MODEL VARIATIONS

XLH/XLS/XLX-61/XR1000

MODEL FLH

- ENGINE OHV V-twin
- CAPACITY 80cu. in.

MODEL VARIATIONS

FLH/FLHS

MODEL FLT

- ENGINE OHV V-twin
- CAPACITY 80cu. in.

MODEL VARIATIONS

FLT/FLTC/FLHT/FLHTC

MODEL FX

- ENGINE OHV V-twin
- CAPACITY 80cu. in.

MODEL VARIATIONS

FXE/FXSB/FXDG/FXWG

MODEL FXR

- ENGINE OHV V-twin
- CAPACITY 80cu. in.

MODEL VARIATIONS

FXR/FXRS/FXRT

- NEW FEATURES
ALUMINIUM DISC REAR WHEEL ON
FXDG
BELT FINAL-DRIVE ON MOST MODELS

- COLOURS
CHOICE OF NINE STANDARD
COLOURS.

1984

Last year of "Shovelhead" and first year of all-new V2 "Evolution" engine. New FXST Softail is an update of "hardtail" bikes, with rear suspension incorporated behind frame. Only year of limited-edition FXRDG, based on FXRS, with rear disc wheel. Last year of XR1000. Sportsters switch to single front disc brake.

MODEL XL/XR

- ENGINE OHV V-twin
- CAPACITY 61cu. in.

MODEL VARIATIONS

XLH/XLS/XLX-61/XR1000

1984 XR1000

MODEL FLH

- ENGINE OHV V-twin
(SHOVELHEAD)
- CAPACITY 80cu. in.

MODEL VARIATIONS

FLH/FLHS/FLHX

1984 FLHX

MODEL FLT

- ENGINE OHV V-twin
(EVOLUTION)
- CAPACITY 80cu. in.

MODEL VARIATIONS

FLTC/FLHTC

MODEL FX

- ENGINE OHV V-twin
(SHOVELHEAD)
- CAPACITY 80cu. in.

MODEL VARIATIONS

FXE/FXSB/FXWG

MODEL FXR

- ENGINE OHV V-twin
(EVOLUTION)
- CAPACITY 80cu. in.

MODEL VARIATIONS

FXRS/FXRT/FXRP/FXRDG

MODEL FXST

- ENGINE OHV V-twin
(EVOLUTION)
- CAPACITY 80cu. in.

- NEW FEATURES
FXST SOFTAIL FEATURES REAR
SUSPENSION HIDDEN UNDER FRAME

- COLOURS
CHOICE OF NINE STANDARD
COLOURS.
[SOME EARLIER BIKES MARKED AS
HAVING THE EVOLUTION ENGINE
MAY WELL HAVE USED THE
SHOVELHEAD UNIT.]

1985

First and only year for FXRC Low Glide Custom as well as FXEF and FXSB Fat Bobs. Evolution engine now used right across the big-twin range. Belt drive on most models.

MODEL XL

- ENGINE OHV V-twin
- CAPACITY 61cu. in.

MODEL VARIATIONS

XLH/XLS/XLX-61

MODEL FLT

- ENGINE OHV V-twin
- CAPACITY 80cu. in.

MODEL VARIATIONS

FLTC/FLHTC

MODEL FXWG

- **ENGINE** OHV V-twin
- **CAPACITY** 80cu. in.

MODEL FXR

- **ENGINE** OHV V-twin
- **CAPACITY** 80cu. in.

MODEL VARIATIONS

FXRS/FXRT/FXRC

MODEL FXS

- **ENGINE** OHV V-twin
- **CAPACITY** 80cu. in.

MODEL VARIATIONS

FXST/FXSB/FXEF

- **COLOURS**
CHOICE OF SIX STANDARD COLOURS.

1986

Revamp of the Sportster range, with new 883cc and 1100cc Evolution engines. Special "Liberty" editions of some models introduced, with special graphics. New FLST Heritage Softail in style of old Hydra-Glide, with wire-spoked wheels and shrouds on front forks. FXR reintroduces the Super Glide name, with chain drive for this year only.

MODEL XLH

- **ENGINE** OHV V-twins
- **CAPACITY** 883cc & 1100cc

MODEL VARIATIONS

XLH-883 (3 styles)/XLH-1100
XLH-1100 (Liberty edition)

MODEL FLH

- **ENGINE** OHV V-twin
- **CAPACITY** 80cu. in.

MODEL VARIATIONS

FLHTC

MODEL FLT

- **ENGINE** OHV V-twin
- **CAPACITY** 80cu. in.

MODEL VARIATIONS

FLTC

MODEL FXR

- **ENGINE** OHV V-twin
- **CAPACITY** 80cu. in.

MODEL VARIATIONS

FXR/FXRS/FXRT/FXRD

MODEL FXS

- **ENGINE** OHV V-twin
- **CAPACITY** 80cu. in.

MODEL VARIATIONS

FXST/FXSTC/FXWG/FLST

- **NEW FEATURES**
883cc AND 1100cc EVOLUTION ENGINES FOR SPORTSTER RANGE

- **COLOURS**
CHOICE OF SEVEN STANDARD COLOURS. SPECIAL ANNIVERSARY EDITIONS OF SOME MODELS.

1987

Harley-Davidson floats on the stock market. First year of FLHS Electra Glide Sport and FLSTC, with special touring accessories. Super Glides get belt final drive. Harley celebrates 30th anniversary of Sportster and renews contracts with police departments.

MODEL XLH

- **ENGINE** OHV V-twins
- **CAPACITY** 883cc & 1100cc

MODEL VARIATIONS

XLH-883 (3 styles)/XLH-1100
XLH-1100 (Anniversary edition)

1987 XLH-883

MODEL FLH

- **ENGINE** OHV V-twin
- **CAPACITY** 80cu. in.

MODEL VARIATIONS

FLHS/FLHTC

MODEL FLT

- **ENGINE** OHV V-twin
- **CAPACITY** 80cu. in.

MODEL VARIATIONS

FLTC

MODEL FXR

- **ENGINE** OHV V-twin
- **CAPACITY** 80cu. in.

MODEL VARIATIONS

FXR/FXRS/FXRT/FXRD

SOFTAILS

- **ENGINE** OHV V-twin
- **CAPACITY** 80cu. in.

MODEL VARIATIONS

FXST/FXSTC/FLST/FLSTC

- **NEW FEATURES**
DETACHABLE WINDSCREEN ON FLHS

- **COLOURS**
CHOICE OF SEVEN STANDARD COLOURS. ANNIVERSARY EDITIONS OF SOME MODELS.

1988

Larger 1200cc unit replaces 1100cc engine in Sportster range. First year of Springer Softail, deploying leading-link forks.

MODEL XLH

- **ENGINE** OHV V-twins
- **CAPACITY** 883cc & 1200cc

MODEL VARIATIONS

XLH-883 (3 styles)/XLH-1200

MODEL FLH

- **ENGINE** OHV V-twin
- **CAPACITY** 80cu. in.

MODEL VARIATIONS

FLHS/FLHTC

MODEL FLT

- **ENGINE** OHV V-twin
- **CAPACITY** 80cu. in.

MODEL VARIATIONS

FLTC

MODEL FXR

- **ENGINE** OHV V-twin
- **CAPACITY** 80cu. in.

MODEL VARIATIONS

FXR/FXRS/FXRT/FXLR

SOFTAILS

- **ENGINE** OHV V-twin
- **CAPACITY** 80cu. in.

MODEL VARIATIONS

FXST/FXSTC/FXSTS/FLST/FLSTC

- **NEW FEATURES**
1200cc SPORTSTER ENGINE
SPRINGER LEADING-LINK FORKS RETURN ON THE FXST

- **COLOURS**
CHOICE OF 12 STANDARD COLOURS. SOME 85TH ANNIVERSARY MODELS ALSO PRODUCED.

1989

New racing series begins based solely on the 883 Sportster. Ultra package available for Electra Glide.

MODEL XLH

- **ENGINE** OHV V-twins
- **CAPACITY** 883cc & 1200cc

MODEL VARIATIONS

XLH-883 (3 styles)/XLH-1200

MODEL FLH

- **ENGINE** OHV V-twin
- **CAPACITY** 80cu. in.

MODEL VARIATIONS

FLHS/FLHTC/FLHTCU

MODEL FLT

- **ENGINE** OHV V-twin
- **CAPACITY** 80cu. in.

MODEL VARIATIONS

FLTC/FLTCU

1989 FLTC

MODEL FXR

- **ENGINE** OHV V-twin
- **CAPACITY** 80cu. in.

MODEL VARIATIONS

FXR/FXRS/FXRT/FXLR

SOFTAILS

- **ENGINE** OHV V-twin
- **CAPACITY** 80cu. in.

MODEL VARIATIONS

FXST/FXSTC/FXSTS/FLST/FLSTC

- **NEW FEATURES**
"Ultra" ACCESSORY PACKAGE (WITH U DESIGNATION) OFFERS CRUISE CONTROL AND MUSIC SYSTEM

- **COLOURS**
CHOICE OF 11 STANDARD COLOURS.

1990

First year of FLSTF "Fat Boy", with disc wheels, dual exhaust system, and unique Harley styling. Self-cancelling indicators now on all models.

MODEL XLH

- **ENGINE** OHV V-twins
- **CAPACITY** 883cc & 1200cc

MODEL VARIATIONS

XLH-883 (3 styles)/XLH-1200

MODEL FLH

- **ENGINE** OHV V-twin
- **CAPACITY** 80cu. in.

MODEL VARIATIONS

FLHS/FLHTC/FLHTCU

MODEL FLT

- **ENGINE** OHV V-twin
- **CAPACITY** 80cu. in.

MODEL VARIATIONS

FLTC/FLTCU/

MODEL FXR

- **ENGINE** OHV V-twin
- **CAPACITY** 80cu. in.

MODEL VARIATIONS
FXR/FXRS/FXRT/FXLR

SOFTAILS
- ENGINE OHV V-twin
- CAPACITY 80cu. in.

MODEL VARIATIONS
FXST/FXSTC/FXSTS/FLST/
FLSTC/FLSTF
- NEW FEATURES
Disc wheels on FLSTF
- COLOURS
Choice of 12 standard colours.

1991

First and only year of FXDB Dyna-Glide Sturgis, using new Dyna-Glide frame with rubber engine mountings.

MODEL XLH
- ENGINE OHV V-twins
- CAPACITY 883cc & 1200cc

MODEL VARIATIONS
XLH-883 (3 styles)/XLH-1200

MODEL FLH
- ENGINE OHV V-twin
- CAPACITY 80cu. in.

MODEL VARIATIONS
FLHS/FLHTC/FLHTCU

MODEL FLT
- ENGINE OHV V-twin
- CAPACITY 80cu. in.

MODEL VARIATIONS
FLTC/FLTCU

MODEL FXR
- ENGINE OHV V-twin
- CAPACITY 80cu. in.

MODEL VARIATIONS
FXR/FXRS/FXRT/FXLR

MODEL FXD
- ENGINE OHV V-twin
- CAPACITY 80cu. in.

SOFTAILS
- ENGINE OHV V-twin
- CAPACITY 80cu. in.

MODEL VARIATIONS
FXSTC/FXSTS/FLSTC/FLSTF
- NEW FEATURES
DYNA CHASSIS WITH LARGE SECTION SPINE AND VIBRATION-ISOLATING RUBBER MOUNTING SYSTEM
Five-speed gearbox on SPORTSTERS, SOME WITH BELT DRIVE
- COLOURS
Choice of 11 standard colours.

1992

First (and only) year of FXDB Dyna-Glide Daytona and FXDC Super Dyna-Glide Custom.

MODEL XLH
- ENGINE OHV V-twins
- CAPACITY 883cc & 1200cc

MODEL VARIATIONS
XLH-883 (3 styles)/XLH-1200

MODEL FLH
- ENGINE OHV V-twin
- CAPACITY 80cu. in.

MODEL VARIATIONS
FLHS/FLHTC/FLHTCU

MODEL FLT
- ENGINE OHV V-twin
- CAPACITY 80cu. in.

MODEL VARIATIONS
FLTC/FLTCU

MODEL FXR
- ENGINE OHV V-twin
- CAPACITY 80cu. in.

MODEL VARIATIONS
FXR/FXRS/FXRT/FXLR

MODEL FXD
- ENGINE OHV V-twin
- CAPACITY 80cu. in.

MODEL VARIATIONS
FXDB/FXDC

SOFTAILS
- ENGINE OHV V-twin
- CAPACITY 80cu. in.

MODEL VARIATIONS
FXSTC/FXSTS/FLSTC/FLSTF
- NEW FEATURES Gold wheels and rear sprocket on FXDB
- COLOURS
Wide choice of standard colours available.

1993

Harley buys a stake in Buell sports bike company. Return of the Wide Glide in the form of the new FXDWG. New FXDL Low Rider, also based on Dyna-Glide chassis. FLSTN is limited-edition Nostalgia version of Heritage Softail.

MODEL XLH
- ENGINE OHV V-twin
- CAPACITY 883cc & 1200cc

MODEL VARIATIONS
XLH-883 (3 styles)/XLH-1200/
XLH-1200(anniversary model)

MODEL FLH
- ENGINE OHV V-twin
- CAPACITY 80cu. in.

MODEL VARIATIONS
FLHS/FLHTC/FLHTCU

MODEL FLT
- ENGINE OHV V-twin
- CAPACITY 80cu. in.

MODEL VARIATIONS
FLTC/FLTCU

MODEL FXR
- ENGINE OHV V-twin
- CAPACITY 80cu. in.

MODEL VARIATIONS
FXR/FXRS/FXLR

MODEL FXD
- ENGINE OHV V-twin
- CAPACITY 80cu. in.

MODEL VARIATIONS
FXDL/FXDWG

SOFTAILS
- ENGINE OHV V-twin
- CAPACITY 80cu. in.

MODEL VARIATIONS
FXSTC/FXSTS/FLSTC/FLSTF/
FLSTN
- COLOURS
CHOICE OF 10 STANDARD COLOURS.
SPECIAL ANNIVERSARY EDITIONS OF SOME MODELS.

1994

Last year of FXR models. First year of FLHR Road King and FXDS Convertible, with detachable panniers allowing it to convert from a tourer to a custom bike and back again.

MODEL XLH
- ENGINE OHV V-twins
- CAPACITY 883cc & 1200cc

MODEL VARIATIONS
XLH-883 (3 styles)/XLH-1200

MODEL FLH
- ENGINE OHV V-twin
- CAPACITY 80cu. in.

MODEL VARIATIONS
FLHR/FLHTC/FLHTCU

MODEL FLT
- ENGINE OHV V-twin
- CAPACITY 80cu. in.

MODEL VARIATIONS
FLTC/FLTCU

MODEL FXR
- ENGINE OHV V-twin
- CAPACITY 80cu. in.

MODEL VARIATIONS
FXR/FXLR

MODEL FXD
- ENGINE OHV V-twin
- CAPACITY 80cu. in.

MODEL VARIATIONS
FXDL/FXDWG/FXDS

SOFTAILS
- ENGINE OHV V-twin
- CAPACITY 80cu. in.

MODEL VARIATIONS
FXSTC/FXSTS/FLSTC/FLSTF/
FLSTN
- COLOURS
CHOICE OF FIVE STANDARD COLOURS.

1995

Harley-Davidson's first fuel-injected model, the FLHTCUI. Electra Glide celebrates its 30th anniversary, with some special editions produced. New base models for both the Electra Glide and the Super Glide, plus a new Bad Boy with Springer forks.

MODEL XLH
- ENGINE OHV V-twins
- CAPACITY 883cc & 1200cc

MODEL VARIATIONS
XLH-883 (3 styles)/XLH-1200

MODEL FLH
- ENGINE OHV V-twin
- CAPACITY 80cu. in.

MODEL VARIATIONS
FLHR/FLHT/FLHTC/FLHTCU/
FLHTCUI (ANNIVERSARY EDITION)

MODEL FLT
- ENGINE OHV V-twin
- CAPACITY 80cu. in.

MODEL VARIATIONS
FLTC/FLTCU

MODEL FXD
- ENGINE OHV V-twin
- CAPACITY 80cu. in.

MODEL VARIATIONS
FXD/FXDL/FXDWG/FXDS

SOFTAILS
- ENGINE OHV V-twin
- CAPACITY 80cu. in.

MODEL VARIATIONS
FXSTC/FXSTS/FXSTSB/FLSTC/
FLSTF/FLSTN

• NEW FEATURES
SEQUENTIAL PORT FUEL-INJECTION ON FLHTCUI
ADJUSTABLE SUSPENSION ON FLHT MODELS

• COLOURS
CHOICE OF 11 STANDARD COLOURS.

1996

Revised Sportster range sees expanded 1200cc models including Custom and Sport bikes. Custom has laced front wheel and disc rear wheel. Fuel injection now on a number of Electra Glide models.

MODEL XLH

• ENGINE OHV V-TWINS

• CAPACITY 883cc & 1200cc

MODEL VARIATIONS
XLH-883 (2 styles)
XLH-1200/XLH-1200C/XLH-1200S

MODEL FLH

• ENGINE OHV V-TWIN

• CAPACITY 80CU. IN.

MODEL VARIATIONS
FLHR/FLHRI

MODEL FLHT

• ENGINE OHV V-TWIN

• CAPACITY 80CU. IN.

MODEL VARIATIONS
FLHT/FLHTC/FLHTCU/FLHTCUI

MODEL FXD

• ENGINE OHV V-TWIN

• CAPACITY 80CU. IN.

MODEL VARIATIONS
FXD/FXDL/FXDWG/FXDS

SOFTAILS

• ENGINE OHV V-TWIN

• CAPACITY 80CU. IN.

MODEL VARIATIONS
FXSTC/FXSTS/FXSTSB/FLSTC/FLSTF/FLSTN

• COLOURS
CHOICE OF TEN STANDARD COLOURS.

1997

Very little change in model range, but new FLSTS Heritage Springer Softail revisits late-1940s styling.

MODEL XLH

• ENGINE OHV V-TWINS

• CAPACITY 883cc & 1200cc

MODEL VARIATIONS
XLH-883 (2 styles)
XLH-1200/XLH-1200C/XLH-1200S

MODEL FLH

• ENGINE OHV V-TWIN

• CAPACITY 80CU. IN.

MODEL VARIATIONS
FLHR/FLHRI

1997 FLHRI

MODEL FLHT

• ENGINE OHV V-TWIN

• CAPACITY 80CU. IN.

MODEL VARIATIONS
FLHT/FLHTC/FLHTCU/FLHTCUI

MODEL FXD

• ENGINE OHV V-TWIN

• CAPACITY 80CU. IN.

MODEL VARIATIONS
FXD/FXDL/FXDWG/FXDS

SOFTAILS

• ENGINE OHV V-TWIN

• CAPACITY 80CU. IN.

MODEL VARIATIONS
FXSTC/FXSTS/FLSTC/FLSTF/FLSTS

• COLOURS
WIDE CHOICE OF STANDARD COLOURS.

1998

New Sportster Sport released with chrome and silver finish and digital single-fire ignition system. Rumours of the release of Harley's new big-twin engine after five years in development.

MODEL XLH

• ENGINE OHV V-TWINS

• CAPACITY 883cc & 1200cc

MODEL VARIATIONS
XLH-883 (2 STYLES)
XLH-1200/XLH-1200C/XLH-1200S

MODEL FLH

• ENGINE OHV V-TWIN

• CAPACITY 80CU. IN.

MODEL VARIATIONS
FLHR/FLHRCI

MODEL FLHT

• ENGINE OHV V-TWIN

• CAPACITY 80CU. IN.

MODEL VARIATIONS
FLHT/FLHTCI/FLHTCUI

MODEL FXD

• ENGINE OHV V-TWIN

• CAPACITY 80CU. IN.

MODEL VARIATIONS
FXD/FXDL/FXDWG/FXDS

SOFTAILS

• ENGINE OHV V-TWIN

• CAPACITY 80CU. IN.

MODEL VARIATIONS
FXSTC/FXSTS/FLSTS/FLSTC/FLSTF

• COLOURS
WIDE RANGE OF STANDARD COLOURS.

1999

Introduction of Harley's largest ever engine, the Twin Cam 88 on Dyna and FLH/T models. Increased engine displacement with increased bore and shorter stroke create an estimated 10 per cent power increase over the Evolution.

MODEL XL/XLH

• ENGINE OHV V-TWINS

• CAPACITY 883cc & 1200cc

MODEL VARIATIONS
XL53C (883cc)
XLH-883/XLH-883 HUGGER/
XLH-883C
XLH-1200/XLH-1200C/XLH-1200S

MODEL FLH

• ENGINE OHV V-TWIN

• CAPACITY 88CU. IN.

MODEL VARIATIONS
FLHR/FLHRCI

MODEL FLHT

• ENGINE OHV V-TWIN

• CAPACITY 88CU. IN.

MODEL VARIATIONS
FLHT/FLHTCI/FLHTCUI

MODEL FXD

• ENGINE OHV V-TWIN

• CAPACITY 88CU. IN.

MODEL VARIATIONS
FXD/FXDS/FXDWG/FXDL

1999 FXDS

SOFTAILS

• ENGINE OHV V-TWIN

• CAPACITY 80CU. IN.

MODEL VARIATIONS
FXST/FXSTS/FXSTC/FLSTS/
FLSTF/FLSTC

1999 FLSTF FAT BOY

• COLOURS
WIDE RANGE OF STANDARD COLOURS.

2000

Revised Softail range, with Twin Cam engine introduced across the range in a revised chassis. FXSTD is new Softail model.

MODEL XL/XLH

• ENGINE OHV V-TWINS

• CAPACITY 883cc & 1200cc

MODEL VARIATIONS
XL53C (883cc)
XLH-883/XLH-883 HUGGER/
XLH-883C
XLH-1200/XLH-1200C/XLH-1200S

MODEL FLH

• ENGINE OHV V-TWIN

• CAPACITY 88CU. IN.

MODEL VARIATIONS
FLHR/FLHRCI

MODEL FLHT

• ENGINE OHV V-TWIN

• CAPACITY 88CU. IN.

MODEL VARIATIONS
FLHT/FLHTCUI/FLTRI/

MODEL FXD

• ENGINE OHV V-TWIN

• CAPACITY 88CU. IN.

MODEL VARIATIONS
FXD/FXDX/FXDWG/FXDL

SOFTAILS

• ENGINE OHV V-TWIN

• CAPACITY 88CU. IN.

MODEL VARIATIONS
FXST/FXSTB/FXSTD/FXSTS/
FLSTC/FLSTF

• NEW FEATURES FOUR-PISTON CALLIPER BRAKES ON ALL MODELS
FULLY ADJUSTABLE FRONT AND REAR SUSPENSION ON FXDX

• COLOURS
WIDE RANGE OF STANDARD COLOURS.

2001

Introduction of Super Glide T-Sport variant, effectively a Super Glide wih handlebar fairing and panniers.

MODEL XL/XLH

- ENGINE OHV V-TWIN
- CAPACITY 883cc & 1200cc

MODEL VARIATIONS

XL53C (883cc)
XLH-883/XLH-883 HUGGER/ XLH-883C
XLH-1200/XLH-1200C/XLH-1200S

2001 XLH-883

MODEL FLH

- ENGINE OHV V-TWIN
- CAPACITY 88cu. in.

MODEL VARIATIONS

FLHR/FLHRCI

MODEL FLHT

- ENGINE OHV V-TWIN
- CAPACITY 88cu. in.

MODEL VARIATIONS

FLHT/FLHTCUI/FLTRI/

MODEL FXD

- ENGINE OHV V-TWIN
- CAPACITY 88cu. in.

MODEL VARIATIONS

FXD/FXDX/FXDWG/FXDL

2001 FXDX

SOFTAILS

- ENGINE OHV V-TWIN
- CAPACITY 88cu. in.

MODEL VARIATIONS

FXST/FXSTB/FXSTD/FXSTS/ FLSTC/FLSTF

- NEW FEATURES Four-piston calliper brakes on all models. Fully adjustable front and rear suspension on FXDX

- COLOURS
Wide range of standard colours.

2002

Introduction of flat-track inspired 883R. Introduction of all-new 1130cc VRSCA V-Rod, one of the most radical machines ever built by Harley-Davidson. Features a completely new, liquid-cooled, 60° V-twin engine in a cruiser-style chassis. Smaller "bullet" indicators used across the range.

MODEL XL/XLH

- ENGINE OHV V-TWIN
- CAPACITY 883cc & 1200cc

MODEL VARIATIONS

XL53C (883cc)
XLH-883/XLH-883 HUGGER/ XL-883R
XL-1200C/XL-1200S

MODEL FLH

- ENGINE OHV V-TWIN
- CAPACITY 88cu. in.

MODEL VARIATIONS

FLHT/FLHTCUI/FLTRI

FLHTCUI

MODEL FXD (DYNAS)

- ENGINE OHV V-TWIN
- CAPACITY 88cu. in.

MODEL VARIATIONS

FXD/FXDX/FXDWG/FXDL

2002 FXDL

SOFTAILS

- ENGINE OHV V-TWIN
- CAPACITY 88cu. in.

MODEL VARIATIONS

FXST/FXSTB/FXSTE/FXSTD/ FLSTF/FLSTC/FLSTS

2002 FSXTB

2003

Centennial colour schemes with special paint and anniversary badges across the range.

MODEL XL/XLH

- ENGINE OHV V-TWIN
- CAPACITY 883cc & 1200cc

MODEL VARIATIONS

XL53C (883cc)
XLH-883/XLH-883 HUGGER/ XL-883R
XL-1200C/XL-1200S

2003 XLH883R

MODEL FLH

- ENGINE OHV V-TWIN
- CAPACITY 88cu. in.

MODEL VARIATIONS

FLHR/FLHRCI

MODEL FLHT

- ENGINE OHV V-TWINS
- CAPACITY 88cu. in.

MODEL VARIATIONS

FLHTCUI

MODEL FXD (DYNAS)

- ENGINE OHV V-TWIN
- CAPACITY 88cu. in.

MODEL VARIATIONS

FXD/FXDX/FXDWG/FXDL/ FXDXT

SOFTAILS

- ENGINE OHV V-TWIN
- CAPACITY 88cu. in.

MODEL VARIATIONS

FXST/FXSTB/FXSTDI/FXSTS/ FLSTFI/FLSTCI/FLSTS

V-ROD

- ENGINE DOHC V-TWIN
- CAPACITY 1130cc

MODEL VARIATIONS

VRSCA

2003 VRSCA V-ROD

2004

New chassis and uprated engines for the Sportster range. CVO models use bigger 1550cc (95cu in) and 1690cc (103cu in) engines.

SPORTSTERS (XL)

- ENGINE OHV V-TWIN
- CAPACITY 883cc & 1200cc

MODEL VARIATIONS

XL883/XL883C/XL1200C/ XL1200R

TOURERS (FL)

- ENGINE OHV V-TWIN
- CAPACITY 88cu. in. (1450cc)

MODEL VARIATIONS

FLHR/FLHRC/FLHRS/FLHT/ FLHTC/FLHTC/FLHTCU

DYNAS (FXD)

- ENGINE OHV V-TWIN
- CAPACITY 88cu. in. (1450cc)

MODEL VARIATIONS

FXD/FXDL/FXDWG/FXDX

SOFTAILS (ST)

- ENGINE OHV V-TWIN
- CAPACITY 88cu. in. (1450cc)

MODEL VARIATIONS

FLSTC/FLSTF/FXST/FXSTB/ FXSTD/FXSTS

V-ROD

- ENGINE DOHC V-TWIN
- CAPACITY 1130cc

MODEL VARIATIONS

VRSCDX/VRSCF

2005

New Softail models and CVO versions of V-Rod, Fat Boy, and Electra Glide.

SPORTSTERS (XL)

- ENGINE OHV V-TWIN
- CAPACITY 883cc & 1200cc

MODEL VARIATIONS

XL883/XL883C/883L/883R
XL1200C /XL1200R

TOURERS (FL)

- ENGINE OHV V-TWIN
- CAPACITY 88cu. in. (1450cc)

MODEL VARIATIONS

FLHR/FLHRC/FLHRS/FLHT/ FLHTC/ FLHTCU/FLTR

DYNAS (FXD)

- **ENGINE** OHV V-TWIN
- **CAPACITY** 88CU. IN. (1450CC)

MODEL VARIATIONS

FXD/FXDL/FXDW G/FXDX/FXDC

SOFTAILS (ST)

- **ENGINE** OHV V-TWIN
- **CAPACITY** 88CU. IN. (1450CC)

MODEL VARIATIONS

FLSTC/FLSTSC/FLSTN/FLSTF/
FXST/FXSTB/FXSTD/FXSTS

V-ROD

- **ENGINE** DOHC V-TWIN
- **CAPACITY** 1130CC

MODEL VARIATIONS

VRSCB/VRSCA

2006

Dyna range re-engineered with new frame and a six-speed gearbox, includes a 35th anniversary Super Glide.

SPORTSTERS (XL)

- **ENGINE** OHV V-TWIN
- **CAPACITY** 883CC & 1200CC

MODEL VARIATIONS

XL883/XL883L/XL883C/XL883R/
XL1200C/XL1200R/XL1200L

TOURERS (FL)

- **ENGINE** OHV V-TWIN
- **CAPACITY** 88CU. IN. (1450CC)

MODEL VARIATIONS

FLHR/FLHRS/FLHRC/FLTR/
FLHX/FLHT/FLHTC/FLHTCU

DYNAS (FXD)

- **ENGINE** OHV V-TWIN
- **CAPACITY** 88CU. IN. (1450CC)

MODEL VARIATIONS

FXD/FXDC/FXD35/FXDB/FXDL/
FXDWG

SOFTAILS (ST)

- **ENGINE** OHV V-TWIN
- **CAPACITY** 88CU. IN. (1450CC)

MODEL VARIATIONS

FXST/FXSTB/FXSTS/FXSTS/
FXSTD/FLST/FLSTF/FLSTN/
FLSTSC/FLSTC

V-ROD

- **ENGINE** DOHC V-TWIN
- **CAPACITY** 1130CC

MODEL VARIATIONS

VRSCA/VRSCD/VRSCR

2007

New 96 cu. in. (1584cc) engine for Dyna, Softail and Touring models, now all with 6-speed gearbox. V-Rod capacity increases to 1250cc. 50th anniversary Sportster.

SPORTSTERS (XL)

- **ENGINE** OHV V-TWIN
- **CAPACITY** 883CC & 1200CC

MODEL VARIATIONS

XL883/XL883L/XL883R/XL883C/
XL50/XL1200L/XL1200R/XL1200C

TOURERS (FL)

- **ENGINE** OHV V-TWIN
- **CAPACITY** 96CU. IN. (1584CC)

MODEL VARIATIONS

FLHX/FLHR/FLHRS/FLHRC/
FLHT/FLHTC/FLHTCU/FLHR

DYNAS (FXD)

- **ENGINE** OHV V-TWIN
- **CAPACITY** 96CU. IN. (1584CC)

MODEL VARIATIONS

FXD/FXDB/FXDL/FXDC/FXDWG

SOFTAILS (ST)

- **ENGINE** OHV V-TWIN
- **CAPACITY** 96CU. IN. (1584CC)

MODEL VARIATIONS

FXSTC/FLSTN/FLSTSC/FLSTC/
FXST/FXSTB/FXSTD

V-ROD

- **ENGINE** DOHC V-TWIN
- **CAPACITY** 1250CC

MODEL VARIATIONS

VRSCAW/VRSCX/VRSCDX/
VRSCD/VRSCDX

2008

105th anniversary models, include the new, custom-look Rocker and Rocker C Softail models. And Europe gets the XR1200.

SPORTSTERS (XL)

- **ENGINE** OHV V-TWIN
- **CAPACITY** 883CC & 1200CC

MODEL VARIATIONS

XL883/XL883L/XL883C/XL1200L/
XL1200R/XL1200C

TOURERS (FL)

- **ENGINE** OHV V-TWIN
- **CAPACITY** 96CU. IN. (1584CC)

MODEL VARIATIONS

FLHR/FLHRC/FLHX/FLHTR/
FLHT/FLHTC/FLHTCU

DYNAS (FXD)

- **ENGINE** OHV V-TWIN
- **CAPACITY** 96CU. IN. (1584CC)

MODEL VARIATIONS

FXD/FXDB/FXDL/FXDC/FXDWG/
FXDL/FXDWC

SOFTAILS (ST)

- **ENGINE** OHV V-TWIN
- **CAPACITY** 96CU. IN. (1584CC)

MODEL VARIATIONS

FXSTB/FXSRC/FLSTF/FLSTN/
FLSTC/FLSTSB/FXCW/FXCWC

V-ROD

- **ENGINE** DOHC V-TWIN
- **CAPACITY** 1250CC

MODEL VARIATIONS

VRSCAW/VRSCD/VRSCDX

2009

Tourers get a new frame, and there is also a trike.

SPORTSTERS (XL)

- **ENGINE** OHV V-TWIN
- **CAPACITY** 883CC & 1200CC

MODEL VARIATIONS

XL883L/XL883N/XL883C/
XL1200L/XL1200N/XL1200C/
XR1200

TOURERS (FL)

- **ENGINE** OHV V-TWIN
- **CAPACITY** 96CU. IN. (1584CC)

MODEL VARIATIONS

FLHR/FLHRC/FLHT/FLHTC/
FLHTCU/FLHX/FLTR

DYNAS (FXD)

- **ENGINE** OHV V-TWIN
- **CAPACITY** 96CU. IN. (1584CC)

MODEL VARIATIONS

FXD/FXDB/FXDC/FXDF/FXDL

SOFTAILS (ST)

- **ENGINE** OHV V-TWIN
- **CAPACITY** 96CU. IN. (1584CC)

MODEL VARIATIONS

FXSTC/FXSTB/FXCWC/
FXCWFLSTB/FLSTN/FLSTF/
FLSTC

V-ROD

- **ENGINE** DOHC V-TWIN
- **CAPACITY** 1250CC

MODEL VARIATIONS

VRSCAW/ VRSCDX/VRSCF

TRI-GLIDE

- **ENGINE** OHV V-TWIN
- **CAPACITY** 103CU. IN.

MODEL VARIATIONS

FLHTCUTG

MODEL CVO

- **ENGINE** OHV V-TWIN
- **CAPACITY** 110CU. IN.

MODEL VARIATIONS

FXSTS/FXDF/FLTR/FLHTCU

2010

Detail changes across the range. Police, Firefighter and Shrine special editions available.

SPORTSTERS (XL)

- **ENGINE** OHV V-TWIN
- **CAPACITY** 883CC & 1200CC

MODEL VARIATIONS

XL883L/XL883N/Forty-Eight/
XL1200L/XL1200N/XL1200C/
XR1200

2010 XR1200X

TOURERS (FL)

- **ENGINE** OHV V-TWIN
- **CAPACITY** 96CU. IN.(1584CC)

MODEL VARIATIONS

FLHR/FLHRC/FLHTC/FLHTK/
FLHTCU/FLHX/FLTRX

DYNAS (FXD)

- **ENGINE** OHV V-TWIN
- **CAPACITY** 96CU. IN.(1584CC)

MODEL VARIATIONS

FXD/FXDB/FXDC/FXDF/FXDWG

SOFTAILS (ST)

- ENGINE OHV V-TWIN
- CAPACITY 96cu. in. (1584cc)

MODEL VARIATIONS

FXSTC/FXCWC/FLSTB/FLSTN/
FLSTSB/FLSTN/FLSTFB/FLSTF/
FLSTC

V-ROD

- ENGINE DOHC V-TWIN
- CAPACITY 1250cc

MODEL VARIATIONS

VRSCAW/ VRSCDX/VRSCF

2010 VRSCDX

TRI-GLIDE

- ENGINE OHV V-TWIN
- CAPACITY 103cu. in.

MODEL VARIATIONS

FLHTCUTG/FLHXXX

MODEL CVO

- ENGINE OHV V-TWIN
- CAPACITY 110cu. in.

MODEL VARIATIONS

FLST/FLHX/FLHTCU/FXDF

2011

The 2011 range included the new "Super Low" Sportster 883 and the Road Glide Ultra featuring the 130 cu. in. engine.

SPORTSTERS (XL)

- ENGINE OHV V-TWIN
- CAPACITY 883cc & 1200cc

MODEL VARIATIONS

XL883L/XL883N/Forty-Eight/
XL1200L/XL1200N/XL1200C/
XR1200X

TOURERS (FL)

- ENGINE OHV V-TWIN
- CAPACITY 96cu. in. (1584cc)

MODEL VARIATIONS

FLHR/FLHRC/FLHTC/FLHTCU/
FLHTK/FLHX/FLTRU/FLTRX

DYNAS (FXD)

- ENGINE OHV V-TWIN
- CAPACITY 96cu. in. (1584cc)

MODEL VARIATIONS

FXDB/FXDC/FXDF/FXDWG

SOFTAILS (ST)

- ENGINE OHV V-TWIN
- CAPACITY 96cu. in. (1584cc)

MODEL VARIATIONS

FXS/FXCWC/FLSTFB/FLSTF/
FLSTC/FLSTN/FLSTSB

V-ROD

- ENGINE DOHC V-TWIN
- CAPACITY 1250cc

MODEL VARIATIONS

VRSCDX/VRSCF

TRI-GLIDE

- ENGINE OHV V-TWIN
- CAPACITY 103cu. in.

MODEL VARIATIONS

FLHTCUTG/FLHXXX

MODEL CVO

- ENGINE OHV V-TWIN
- CAPACITY 110cu. in.

MODEL VARIATIONS

FLTRU/FLHTCU/FLHX/FLST

2012

New 103cu. in. (1690cc) engine on Softail and Touring models, and most Dynas. New Seventy Two Sportster.

SPORTSTERS (XL)

- ENGINE OHV V-TWIN
- CAPACITY 883cc & 1200cc

MODEL VARIATIONS

XL883L/XL883N/XL1200V
Seventy Two/XL1200X Forty-Eight/XL1200C/XL1200N/
XR1200X

TOURERS (FL)

- ENGINE OHV V-TWIN
- CAPACITY 96cu. in. (1584cc)

MODEL VARIATIONS

FLHR/FLHRC/FLHTC/FLHTCU/
FLHTK/FLHX/FLTRX/FLHTRU

DYNAS (FXD)

- ENGINE OHV V-TWIN
- CAPACITY 96cu. in. (1584cc)

MODEL VARIATIONS

FXD/FXDB/FXDL/FXDC/FXDWG

SOFTAILS (ST)

- ENGINE OHV V-TWIN
- CAPACITY 96cu. in. (1584cc)

MODEL VARIATIONS

FLS/FLSTN/FLSTFB/FLSTF/
FLSTC/FLSTN/FXS

V-ROD

- ENGINE DOHC V-TWIN
- CAPACITY 1250cc

MODEL VARIATIONS

VRSCDX/VRSCF

TRIKE

- ENGINE OHV V-TWIN
- CAPACITY 103cu. in.

MODEL VARIATIONS

FLHTCUTG

MODEL CVO

- ENGINE OHV V-TWIN
- CAPACITY 110cu. in.

MODEL VARIATIONS

FLTRX/FLHX/FLST/FLHT

2013

The company celebrate their 110th anniversary with special detailing and graphics. The only significant new model is the FXBSE Breakout, a custom-style Softail with CVO finishes and an 1802cc engine.

SPORTSTERS (XL)

- ENGINE OHV V-TWIN
- CAPACITY 883cc & 1200cc

MODEL VARIATIONS

XL883L/XL883N/XL1200C/
XL1200X/XR1200V

TOURERS (FL)

- ENGINE OHV V-TWIN
- CAPACITY 103cu. in. (1690cc) & 110cu. in. (1802cc)

MODEL VARIATIONS

FLHR/FLHRC/FLHX/FLTRX/
FLTRU/FLHTC/FLHTCU/FLHTK

DYNAS (FXD)

- ENGINE OHV V-TWIN
- CAPACITY 96cu. in. (1584cc) & 103cu. in. (1690cc)

MODEL VARIATIONS

FXDB/FXDC/FXDWG/FXDF/FLD

SOFTAILS (ST)

- ENGINE OHV V-TWIN
- CAPACITY 103cu. in. (1690cc) & 110 cu. in (1802cc)

MODEL VARIATIONS

FLSTF/FLSTFB/FXS/FLSTN/
FLSTC/FLS/FXSBSE

V-ROD

- ENGINE DOHC V-TWIN
- CAPACITY 76.25cu. in. (1250cc)

MODEL VARIATIONS

VRSCDX/VRSCF

TRIKE

- ENGINE OHV V-TWIN
- CAPACITY 103cu. in. (1690cc)

MODEL VARIATIONS

FLHTCUTG

Harley-Davidson Model Designations

Harley-Davidson introduced its lettering system in 1909 to differentiate between models. No numbers are included, but up until 1916 the prefix number was four fewer than the actual year (so 1912 models were prefixed by the number 8) and from 1916 the year was used as the prefix (so 1922 models were prefixed by 22). Some letters are placed first in the designation to describe engine type, some are suffixes that add extra information about the engine, and others are purely descriptive. The system doesn't really start to make sense until the 1920s, so no designations from before this date are included in this rough guide.

KEY TO ENGINE TYPE:
sv = side-valve ohv = overhead-valve
ts = two-stroke ioe = inlet-over-exhaust

MODEL A PEASHOOTER

A: DESIGNATIONS

A: (1926–30) sv 21cu. in. "Peashooter" single with magneto

A: (1960–65) ts 165cc A Topper scooter

A: Army version (i.e. 1942 WLA)

A: Ohv version of the A and B singles (i.e. 1926 AA and BA)

B: DESIGNATIONS

B: (1926–28) sv 21cu. in. "Peashooter" single with battery ignition and lights

B: (1955–59) 125cc ts single "Hummer"

BT: (1960–66) 165cc ts single

C: DESIGNATIONS

C: (1929–34) sv/ohv 30.5cu. in. single

C: Custom/classic/cafe

CH: Magneto ignition Sportster

C: Canadian army version (i.e. 1942 WLC)

D: DESIGNATIONS

D: (1929–31) sv 45cu. in. twin

D 74cu. in. version of J series (i.e. 1921 JD)

D: "Dyna" frame (i.e. FXDWG)

D: High-compression version (i.e. 1932 RLD)

DG: Disc Glide (i.e. FXDG)

E: DESIGNATIONS

E: (1936–52) 61cu. in. ohv twin "Knucklehead" or "Panhead"

E: Electric starting (i.e. 1974 FXE)

E: Police/Traffic Combination engine (i.e. 1954 FLE)

F: DESIGNATIONS

F: (1914–25) ioe 61cu. in. magneto ignition twin

F: (1941–78) ohv 74cu. in. twin (note: since 1978 the F initial has also been used on 80cu. in. and 88cu. in. engines)

F: Battery ignition flat twin (i.e. 1922 WF)

F: Footshift

G: DESIGNATIONS

G: (1933–73) Servi-Car

H: DESIGNATIONS

H: Larger engine version of existing model (i.e. 1936 VH, 1955 KH)

H: More powerful engine (i.e. 1959 XLH)

I: DESIGNATIONS

I: Fuel injection (i.e. 1995 FLHTCUI)

J: DESIGNATIONS

J: (1915–29) 61cu. in. ioe twin

J: Magneto ignition flat-twin (i.e. 1922 WJ)

K: DESIGNATIONS

K: More powerful KH model (i.e. 1956 KHK)

K: (1952_53) 45cu. in. sv twin

L: DESIGNATIONS

L: Higher compression engine (i.e. 1936 EL)

M: DESIGNATIONS

M: (1965–72) 50cc/65cc ts single

N: DESIGNATIONS

N: Nostalgia (i.e. 1993 FLSTN)

P: DESIGNATIONS

P: Police model

R: DESIGNATIONS

R: (1932–36) 45cu. in. sv twin

R: Rubber-mounted engine on FX model (i.e. 1983 FXR)

R: Racing model (i.e. 1957 KR)

R: Race-derived model (i.e. 1984 XR1000)

S: DESIGNATIONS

S: (1926–30) 21cu. in. ohv racer

S: (1948–52) 125cc ts single

ST: (1953–59) 165cc ts single

S: Sport (i.e. FXS)

S: Sidecar model (i.e. 1926 JDS)

S: Softail

T: DESIGNATIONS

T: (1921) twin-cylinder racer

T: Touring version (i.e. 1978 XLT)

TT: Road-race version of competition bike (i.e. XRTT)

U: DESIGNATIONS

U: (1937–48) sv 74cu. in. twin

U: Restricted version (i.e. STU and AU Topper)

U: Ultra accessory package

V: DESIGNATIONS

V: (1930–36) sv 74cu. in. twin

V: (1994–) dual overhead cam 61cu. in. twin for Superbike racing (i.e. 1994 VR1000)

W: DESIGNATIONS

W: (1919–23) sv 36cu. in. flat-twin

W: (1937-51) sv 45cu. in. twin

WG: Wide-Glide (i.e. 1980 FXWG)

X: DESIGNATIONS

XL: (1957–) 55/61/74cu. in. ohv twin Sportster

XA: (1944) 45cu. in. sv flat-twin for the US army

X: Super Glide (i.e. 1971 FX)

Z: DESIGNATIONS

Z: (1973) 90cc ts single

XR1000 SPORTSTER

Index

Note: Models are listed both under their designation and under their name. So, for example, the AH Topper comes under "A" as well as under "T". No models from the catalogue are included except for those included in the text that summarizes each year.

1915 KT BOARD RACER

E

Knucklehead Engine

F

G

H

I

1941 WLD

1941 WLD

T

U-V

W

1941 W<small>LD</small>

X-Y

Acknowledgments

The author's acknowledgments
Harley-Davidson is a legend. And that legend is
built on the passion of the people involved in
making, riding, racing, and fixing Harleys. Lots of
them offered advice, opinion, and encouragement in the
making of this book. These are just a few of them.
Everyone at the extraordinary Barber Vintage Motorsports
Museum in Birmingham, Alabama. Especially George Barber,
Jeff Ray, Brian Slark, Joe Bruton, and the super hospitable
Lee Clark. (I'll get the grits next time.) Patrick Delli of the
Harley-Davidson Rider's Club UK, Steve Slocombe of VL
Heaven, and John Warr and Martin Szlagowski of Warr's
Harley-Davidson all provided advice and support. Richard
Rosenthal and Alan Seeley gave invaluable last-minute
assistance and were recipients of bizarre late-night telephone
calls. Jeremy Pick of Harley-Davidson UK and Doug Strange of
the Antique Motorcycle Club of America both helped out.
As did Gary Inman.
Dave King once again took superb photographs and was
great company.

Thanks to everyone at Dorling Kindersley. Special
gratitude to Mark Johnson Davies and most
especially to Phil Hunt. You were very patient.
I'll get the drinks in.
Also everyone at *Bike* magazine who covered for me,
especially Richard Fincher who is a believer. Thank you.
This book is intended as an introduction to Harley-
Davidson and its motorcycles. If you want more detailed
information, the work of Allan Girdler, Jerry Hatfield,
and Rick Conner pointed me in the right direction.
*This book is dedicated to the residents of Thornley Village,
County Durham, in memory of the walks in the Wild Woods.*

Dorling Kindersley would like to thank the following:
The Barber Vintage Motorsports Museum for being
accommodating beyond belief; Simon Murrell for additional
design assistance; Mariana Sonnenberg for additional picture
research; Roy Bacon for casting an experienced eye over the
details; Rachael Parfitt for being queen courier; the
knowledgeable folks on the Harley e-mail digest; and
Margaret McCormack for compiling the index.

Picture Credits

**Dorling Kindersley would like to thank the following for allowing their bikes
to be photographed:**

The Barber Vintage Motorsports Museum: pp.32–33; 34–35; 46–47; 49; 56–57;
62–63; 70–71; 72–73; 81; 96–97; 108–09; 110–11; 112–13; 114–15; 128–29;
174–75; 176–77
Steve Slocombe: pp.60–61
Rick Sasnett: pp.90–91
Stanley M. Brock: p.94
Jeremy Pick at Harley-Davidson UK: pp.134–35; 136–37; 152–53; 158–59;
160–61; 166–67; 182–83; 184–85
Dave Griffiths: pp.92–93
Tony Dowden: pp.74–75; 96–97
Warr's Harley-Davidson: pp.102–03; 126–27; 154–55; 180–81
Harley-Davidson Motor Company India Pvt. Ltd.: 138-39; 186-87; 209; 210

All photography by Dave King.

**The publisher would like to thank the following for their kind permission to
reproduce their photographs:**

Key: a-above; b-below/bottom; c-centre; f-far; l-left; r-right; t-top

Alamy Images: Chuck Eckert 22ca; **Allsport:** Tony Duffy 19cra; **American
Motorcycle Heritage Foundation:** Motorcycle Hall of Fame Museum 44–45, 45tr,
100–101, 129tr, 191bc; **Bike magazine:** 164–65; **Corbis UK Ltd:** Everett
Collection 21tl; Rick Friedman 22cb; UPI 42–43, 55tc, 58–59, 188–189; **Dorling
Kindersley:** Alan Purvis 170-71; Michael Watson 162-63; **Ronald Grant
Archive:** Columbia Pictures Corporation 95tr; © The Solomon R. Guggenheim

Foundation, New York: David Heald 71tr; **Harley-Davidson Archives:** 2–3, 3c,
12bc, 12cb, 13tr, 14–15, 15cr, 17tr, 24-25, 25ca, 26–27, 30tr, 31br, 49tr, 81br, 116–
17, 156tl, 156cl, 156–57, 157br, 169tc, 169bc, 189c, 190bl; **Hulton Getty:** 13cb,
15crb, 98–99; MacGregor 14cb; **Imperial War Museum:** 16clb; **Kobal Collection:**
American International Pictures 76–77; **Randy Leffingwell:** © The Solomon R.
Guggenheim Foundation, New York 6, 7, 13br, 191tr, 211bl; **Andrew Morland:**
20ca; **Don Morley:** 145tr; **Mortons Motorcycle Media Ltd:** 12–13, 39tc, 64tl;
Moviestore Collection: Columbia Pictures Corporation 18–19; **National Motor
Museum, Beaulieu:** 4, 33tr, 73tr; **Motoring Picture Library / National Motor
Museum:** 16-17c; **Rex Features:** Simon Webster 23; **Frank Spooner Pictures:**
Liaison/R. Rotolo 20cb; **Tony Stone Images:** Ralf Schultheiss 10–11; Oli Tennent
172–73; Nicholas De Vore 140–41; **Garry Stuart:** 5c, 64–65, 80–81, 86–87,
94–95, 144–45; **Vin Mag Archive:** 17c, 18cl; Columbia Pictures Corporation
18tc; **Yamaha UK:** 169bc.

HARLEY-DAVIDSON IS A TRADEMARK OWNED BY H-D USA, LLC. THE HARLEY-DAVIDSON
NAME AND MODEL NAMES FEATURED IN THIS BOOK ARE USED FOR DESCRIPTIVE
PURPOSES ONLY AND REMAIN THE PROPERTY OF H-D USA, LLC.

All other images © Dorling Kindersley
For further information see:
www.dkimages.com